41.50

EUROPEAN RESEARCH IN
INTERNATIONAL BUSINESS

EUROPEAN RESEARCH IN INTERNATIONAL BUSINESS

Edited by
MICHEL GHERTMAN
Associate Professor
C.E.S.A.
Jouy-en-Josas, France

and

JAMES LEONTIADES
Senior Lecturer in
International Management
Manchester Business School

1978

NORTH-HOLLAND PUBLISHING COMPANY
AMSTERDAM • NEW YORK • OXFORD

Published by:

NORTH-HOLLAND PUBLISHING COMPANY – AMSTERDAM • NEW YORK • OXFORD

Distributors for the U.S.A. and Canada:
Elsevier North-Holland, Inc.
52 Vanderbilt Avenue
New York, N.Y. 10017

Library of Congress Cataloging in Publication Data
Main entry under title:

European research in international business.

   Papers selected from four conferenees held during
the period 1973-1976.
   1. International business enterprises--Management--
Addresses, essays, lectures.   I. Ghertman, Michel.
II. Leontiades, James.
HD69.I7E82   658.1'8   77-16087
ISBN 0-444-85089-9

Printed in The Netherlands by Krips Repro Meppel

INTRODUCTION

In recent years the study of multinational companies and other
aspects of international business has become firmly established
in a number of European institutions of higher learning. Histori-
cally, international business has been a major concern of European
firms. Exports and foreign investment have constituted a very
high proportion of total business operations, much more so than
in the U.S. Inevitably, the rapidly growing centres of business
education in Europe reflected this involvement. Concentrations
of faculty in the area of international business took on major
importance within these institutions. This produced a growing
volume of research in this area, frequently carried out by
researchers insulated one from the other by national boundaries.

An initiative to create a communications network was taken jointly in 1973 by the European Institute for Advanced Studies in
Management (Brussels) and the Centre d'Enseignement Supérieur des
Affaires (Jouy-en-Josas, France). The practical result of this
was the first of two conferences entitled "Recent Research on
the Multinational Corporation". These brought together a broad
spectrum of European scholars in international business. To further expand and institutionalise this communications network
the European International Business Association (E.I.B.A.) was
founded in December 1974 at Jouy-en-Josas, France. Since then,
the association had held two meetings featuring research presen-
tations in this field.

The 17 papers in this volume are an outstanding selection from
the more than 60 presented at these four conferences during the
period 1973 - 1976. As such they are indicative of the development and progress of international business research in Europe.
Many of the contributions are those of authors who have already
established strong reputations by their various publications in
both Europe and the United States. Other represent those by promising new scholars.

Most papers included in this volume have not been published elsewhere. They address a broad number of key issues, including the
theory of international business and multinational corporations,
strategy and planning in the multinational corporation, ownership
patterns and organization of the multinational corporation,

international finance and control, international marketing and
international management of human resources.

This volume will be of major interest to scholars in international
business, as well as researchers in other areas of business administration interested in international aspects of their discipline. It can also be used as a book of readings for advanced semi-
nars on European operations of multinational firms.

We are indebted to the European Institute for Advanced Studies in
Management for typing the final manuscript, and particularly to
Christiane Merckaert for her invaluable assistance in this task.

CONTENTS

A THEORY OF INTERNATIONAL OPERATIONS

Peter J. Buckley & Mark Casson
University of Bradford

This paper provides a theoretical framework for the explanation and prediction of the methods of market servicing (or "sourcing policies") of multinational enterprises (MNEs).

1. *The Division of National Markets*

A national market for a final product can be served in four main ways : by indigenous firms, by subsidiaries of MNEs located in the market, by exports to the market from foreign locally owned firms and by exports from foreign plants owned by MNEs. The first two methods are distinguished from the second two by the "location effect" : the market is served by local production rather than export. The first method is distinguished from the second and the third method from the fourth by the "ownership effect" : production is owned and controlled by domestic nationals rather than by a foreign-owned international corporation.

Final goods markets cannot, however, be considered in isolation from the markets for the intermediate goods involved in the production process. Intermediate goods too are subject to ownership and location effects. In order to service a final product market it may be advantageous to locate different stages of production in different locations. Also the ownership of "the good" may change as we move through the process – an example of this is licensing where essential proprietary knowledge to produce the final good is licensed from one producer to another.

In order to examine these factors in detail the following sections deal firstly with location effects and then with ownership effects.

2. *The location of production facilities*

Production in a multi stage process can be characterised as a sequence of distinct activities linked by the transport of semi-processed materials. The orthodox theory of location assumes

constant returns to scale, freely available and therefore standardised technology and that firms are price takers in all factor
markets. Given such assumptions, a firm chooses its optimal location for each stage of production by evaluating regional production costs and choosing the set of locations for which the overall
average cost of production is minimised. Regional production
costs vary only according to regional differentials in non tra-
deable goods (the price of tradeables is standardised by trade),
the relative prices of tradeables and non tradeables and elasticities of substitution between pairs of non tradeables and between
tradeables and non tradeables. Overall average production costs
are minimised by the correct choice of the least cost "route" from
the location of raw materials through to the final destination[1].

This location strategy is complicated in practice by a number of
factors.

First, there are increasing returns to scale in many activities.
Where only one destination is to be serviced, increasing returns
means that location strategy may change in response to a change in
the size of market. Where more than one destination is to be
serviced, increasing returns in either production or transportation create an incentive to concentrate each stage of production
at just a few locations. Increasing returns at any one stage of
production or in the transport of any one semi-processed material
may be diffused through the entire process, leading to the relo-
cation of plants involved in quite remote stages of production,
and to the reorganisation of the entire network of trade.

The second major factor is that modern businesses perform many
activities other than routine production. Such activities require
different inputs from production, but need to be integrated with
the production process. They have a twofold influence on location: their own least cost location will differ from that of routine production because of their differing input requirements and
secondly they will exercise a locational "pull" on routine production. Two important non-production activities are marketing
and research and development (R&D).[2]   Both these functions represent an integral set of activities. Marketing has three main constituents : stockholding, distribution and advertising. The
location of stockholding depends on the interplay between the
better quality of service provided by decentralised stockholding
and the declining costs of large, centralised warehouses. Only
above a certain market size is local stockholding efficient.
Routine advertising and distribution are generally located in the
final market. The location of R&D will depend largely on the
regional differentials in the price of the most important non
traded input - skilled labour. However, this will be modified by
information costs which play the same role as transport costs in
routine production. Where a firm relies on the creation and

internal use of productive knowledge from its own R&D department,
there are strong reasons for centralising this creative function
and integrating it closely with the more creative aspects of marketing and production[3]. Constant reworking of ideas through teamwork is necessary for least cost innovation and the importance of
information flows will encourage the centralisation of these activities. However the more routine "development" work may be much
more diffused : the communications problem is not so great and
local knowledge and inputs are more important. We conclude that
the location strategy of a firm which integrates production marketing and R&D is highly complex. The activities are normally
interdependent and information flows as well as transport costs
must be considered. Information costs which increase with distance encourage the centralisation of activities where exchanges of
knowledge through teamwork are of the essence. Such activities
are the "high level" ones of basic research, innovative production
and the development marketing strategy ; they require large inputs
of skilled labour, and the availability of skilled labour will
therefore exert a significant influence on the location strategy
of such firms.[4]

The third factor which complicates the location strategies of
firms is that in practice they operate largely in imperfectly competitive markets. This means that, in many cases, MNEs cannot be
considered as price takers in intermediate and factor markets.
Consequently, a firm which can force down input or factor prices
in a particular region will tend to concentrate the production
processes which are intensive in these inputs in that region. It
has been argued that the explanation of monopsony power may also
exert a significant influence on firm's choice of production technique in a particular region[5].

The fourth factor is government intervention. The influence of
taxes and tariffs and other regulations such as preferential duties
has been shown by many analysts to affect location[6] and it is
unnecessary to elaborate on this here.

Finally, location decisions will be influenced by the ownership
effect, or the extent to which the internalisation of markets in
the firm modify the above considerations. This is examined in
detail in the following section.

To sum up, the location decisions of firms in the international
economy will in practice differ considerably from the predictions
of the theory of the location of production under ideal competitive conditions where transport costs are the only barrier to trade.
The possibilities of economies of scale in certain activities,the
complexities of the activities, the extent of their integration,
the type of market structure and the extent of Government inter-
vention will all influence location strategy. We now examine

ownership effects and the extent to which location strategy is
dependent on the replacement of external markets by internal markets within the firm.

3. *The ownership of production*

Having considered location effects in some detail, we can now turn
our attention to the ownership of production, considering production locations unchanged. A strong case can be made for the contention that the major dynamic of the world economy is changing
<u>ownership</u> effects which influence the pattern of distribution of
production between MNEs and national firms. Resource endowments
are to a large extent geographically fixed : copper, bauxite and
oil reserves for instance. The question at issue is why US owned
copper companies, US and Canadian aluminium producers and US and
UK oil companies should dominate their markets. We argue here
that the essence of the ownership effect can be explained in terms
of the internalisation of key intermediate goods markets within
firms of particular nationalities.

In a situation where firms are attempting to maximise profits in
a world of imperfect markets, there will often exist an incentive
to bypass imperfect markets in intermediate products. Their activities which were previously linked by the market mechanism are
brought under common ownership and control in a "market" internal
to the firm. Where markets are internalised across national
boundaries, MNEs are created.[7]

Benefits of internalisation arise from the avoidance of imperfec-
tions in the external market, but there are also costs. The optimum size of firm is set where the costs and benefits of further
internalisation are equalised at the margin. We now go on to
examine these costs and benefits and to consider how they apply
in practice.

Benefits from "internalisation" arise from five main types of
market imperfection. Firstly, production takes time. Often activities linked by the market involve significant time lags and the
relevant futures markets required for their coordination are inadequate or completely lacking. This creates a strong incentive
for the creation of an internal future market. Secondly, the
efficient explanation of market power may require discriminating
pricing of a type not feasible in an external market — this will
encourage the monopolist to integrate forward and the monopsonist
to integrate backwards. Thirdly, internal markets remove — or
prevent the growth of — bilateral concentrations of market power,
and thus reduce the likelihood of unstable bargaining situations.
The fourth type of imperfection occurs where there is inequality
between buyer and seller with respect to the evaluation of a

product. "Buyer uncertainty" is prevalent where the product in
question is a type of knowledge, which cannot be properly valued
unless the valuer is in full possession of it. Buyer uncertainty
is eliminated when buyer and seller are part of the same organisation. Fifth, internalisation may be a way of avoiding Government
intervention. Prices reported in an organisation are much more
difficult to monitor than those in an external market. Consequently government evaluation of tax and tariff payments and its enfor-
cement of exchange control regulations becomes difficult, and the
firm is able to exploit this through transfer pricing.

There are also costs of internalisation which may offset the benefits. Firstly some of the costs of operating a market — whether
internal or external — are fixed independently of the volume of
transactions, so that if a single external market is split up and
internalised within a number of distinct firms the costs of market
organisation for each firm will tend to rise. Secondly when a
single external market is replaced by several internal ones it may
be necessary for firms to adjust the scales of the activities
linked by the markets to make them compatible ; this may mean that
some activities have to be operated on a less efficient scale
than would be possible with a larger external market. Thirdly there
may be increased communication costs. In an external market only
Price and quantity information is exchanged, but the demands of
an internal market are normally greater because of the additional
flows of accounting and control information. Finally internalisation costs have an international dimension arising from problems
associated with foreign ownership and control. It should be noted
that such problems can in varying degrees, be reduced or eliminated by partially internalising a market ; for instance disposing
of excess output on the open market or subcontracting outside the
firm.

Having set out the general theory of the costs and benefits of
internalising markets, we now turn to the application of the
theory. It can be argued that the benefits of internalisation
are particularly large in two cases. Firstly in industries where
firms need to receive future supplies of vital raw materials and
secondly in industries where flows of technical and marketing
knowledge are important. The first phase of the growth of MNEs
(up to the end of World War I) was concerned with maintaining and
developing raw material supplies through vertical integration.
However the major force in the world economy at the present time
arises from the special advantages of internalising flows of knowledge. It is this factor to which we look to account for the
continued strength of the ownership effect.

The production of knowledge (through R & D) is a lengthy process
which requires careful synchronisation with other activities within
the firm. Knowledge is a (temporary) "natural monopoly" which is

best exploited through discriminatory pricing. The buyers of
knowledge are in many cases monopsonists, by virtue of control of
regional distribution outlets, and so bilateral monopoly is likely
if knowledge is licensed through an external market. Buyer uncertainty applies with particular force, for knowledge cannot be
valued until it is in full possession of the valuer. Finally,
because of difficulties of evaluation, knowledge flows provide an
excellent basis for transfer pricing.

Internalisation across national boundaries of markets in
knowledge-based products is clearly of great importance in accounting for overseas production by MNEs. Subsidiaries of MNEs are
likely to be successful in taking a large share of foreign markets
because of the "branch plant effect" arising from subsidiary unit's
access to the internal markets of MNEs. This access gives it a
great advantage over those firms which have access only to (often
inadequate) external markets. The greater the market imperfec-
tions, the more disadvantaged are "national" firms in competing
with MNEs.

Branch plant effect – the fact that subsidiaries of MNEs can out-
perform national firms arise not from multinationality but from
access to internal markets . This has two main aspects. Firstly,
subsidiaries can obtain inputs which are simply not available in
external markets. Most important among such inputs are proprietary knowledge (the output of past R & D), marketing know-how
(arising from a worldwide intelligence system) and production
experience. Secondly, branch plants can often obtain inputs more
cheaply within the firm than their competitors can on the open
market. This price differential arises, not from plant economies,
but from access to the firm's internal futures markets, and from
tax savings arising from transfer pricing.

Ownership effects may impinge on the location policies of MNEs.
Firstly efficient transfer pricing normally involves giving the
highest mark-up to operations in the lowest tax area. This policy
may imply a complete change of location strategy within the scheme
of section 2. Secondly, internalisation involves increased communication costs in the form of accounting and control information.
As communication costs increase with geographical, social and linguistic "distance", this will bias the location of internally
coordinated activities towards a central region.

4. *The Division of National Markets Explained*

Combining both ownership and location effects allows us to give
the reasons for the division of particular markets between domestic producers, local subsidiaries of MNEs, exports from foreign-
owned plants and exports from MNEs. The division between exports

and local servicing is largely the result of the economics of location. Least cost location, influenced by regional price differentials and by barriers to trade largely governs the proportion of a market serviced by exports. This however is modified by the economics of internalising a market, for not only can this affect the least cost location of any stage of production but the strategy of a MNE after having internalised a market may differ from that which external market forces would dictate. Consequently, the question of servicing a final market is inextricably bound up with the nature and ownership of internal markets - which will be dictated by the costs of benefits of internalisation.

In order to predict the division of national markets between the above groups we must have information relating to the following variables.

(1) <u>Industry specific factors</u> : the nature of the product, the structure of the external market and the relation between the optimal scales of the activities linked by the market ;

(2) <u>Region specific factors</u> : factor costs in different regions, intermediate and raw material availability, the geographical and social distance between the regions involved ;

(3) <u>Nation specific factors</u> : the political and fiscal structures particularly of the nations involved.

(4) <u>Firm specific-factors</u> : in particular the ability of management to communicate internally across national boundaries, and to cope with the legal and accounting complexities of international ownership.

From the above, the strategy of MNEs can be explained by combining our knowledge of locational influences with the opportunities of internalising markets profitably. Location and ownership effects are interdependent for the least cost location of an activity is at least partly determined by the ownership of the activities integrated with it.

References

1. For a full exposition see Peter J. Buckley and Mark Casson
   The Future of the Multinational Enterprise, Macmillan London
   1976.   Chapter II Section 3

2. R & D includes the innovative aspects of advertising.

3. Note the similarity of this argument with Raymond Vernon "International Investment and International Trade in the Product
   Cycle", Journal of Economics, Vol. 80 (1966),pp. 190-207.

4. This agrees with Hymer's "Law of Uneven Development" : the
   centralisation of "higher order activities" in the parent.
   See S. Hymer "The Multinational Corporation and the Law of
   Uneven Development" in J.N. Bhagwati (Ed.), Economics and World
   Order, Macmillan, 1972.

5. See e.g. D.E. de Meza, Multinationals' Choice of Technique,
   mimeo, Reading 1975.

6. Notably T. Horst, "The Theory of the Multinational Firm : Optimal Behaviour under Different Tariff and Tax Rates", Journal
   of Political Economy, Vol. 79, (1971), pp. 1059-1072.

7. Note the similarity of this argument with Stephen H. Hymer,
   The international operations of national firms, M.I.T. Press,
   Cambridge, Mass., 1976.

A MODEL FOR THE DECISION MAKING PROCESS AFFECTING THE PATTERN AND PACE OF THE INTERNATIONALIZATION OF THE FIRM

Jan Johanson
Center for International Business Studies
University of Uppsala

Jan-Erik Vahlne
Institute of International Business
Stockholm School of Economics

Introduction

Several studies of international business have indicated that internationalization of the firm is a process in which companies gradually increase their international involvement. It seems reasonable to assume that, within the frame of economic and business factors, the characteristics of this process influence the pattern and pace of internationalization. In this paper we develop a model of the internationalization process of the firm. The model focuses on the development of the individual firm, and particularly on its gradual acquisition, integration and use of knowledge about foreign markets and operations, and on its successively increasing commitment to foreign markets. The basic assumptions of the model are that a lack of such knowledge is an important obstacle to the development of international operations and that the necessary knowledge can be acquired through operations abroad. This holds for the two directions of internationalization identified here : increasing involvement of the firm in the individual foreign country, and successive establishment of operations in new countries. In this paper we will, however, concentrate on the extension of operations in individual markets.

We have incorporated in our model some results of previous empirical studies of the development of international operations, seeking theoretical explanation through the behavioral theory of the firm (Cyert and March, 1963). Specifically, we believe that internationalization is the product of a series of incremental decisions. Our aim is to identify elements shared in common by the

Reprinted by permission of the publisher from the Journal of International Business Studies.

successive decision situations and to thereby develop a model of
the internationalization process which will have explanatory
value. Because we, for the time being, disregard the decision-
style of the decision-maker himself, and, to a certain extent,
the specific properties of the various decision situations, our
model has only limited predictive value. We believe, however, that
all the decisions that, taken together, constitute the internationalization process - decisions to start exporting to a country,
to establish export channels, to start a selling subsidiary and
so forth - have some common characteristics which are also very
important to the subsequent internationalization. Our model
focuses on these common traits.

We hope that the model will contribute to conceptualization in
the field of internationalization of the firm and thus increase
understanding of the development of international operations as
described in the empirical studies. We also hope that it can
serve as a frame of reference for future studies in the problem
area. It can also, hopefully, be useful as a tool in the analysis
of the effects of various factors on the pattern and pace of
internationalization of the firm.

In the first section we describe the empirical background of our
study. Next we outline the model of the internationalization
process, defining the main variables and the interaction among
them. We then sum up by discussing some implications of the model
and suggesting some problems for future research.

Empirical Background

The model is based on empirical observations from our studies in
international business at the University of Uppsala, showing that
Swedish firms often develop their international operations in
small steps, rather than making large foreign production investments at single points in time. Typically, firms start exporting
to a country via an agent, later establish a sales subsidiary
and eventually, in some cases, begin production in the host country.

We have also observed a similar successive establishment of operations in new countries. Of particular interest in the present
context is that the time order of such establishments seems to be
related to the psychic distance between the home and the import/
host countries (Hörnell, Vahlne & Widersheim-Paul, 1972, Johanson
& Wiedersheim-Paul, 1974). The psychic distance is defined as
the sum of factors preventing the flows of information from and
to the market. Examples are differences in language, education,
business practices, culture, industrial development, etc.

Studies of the export organization of Swedish special steel works
(Johanson, 1966) and of Swedish pulp and paper industry (Forsgren
& Kinch, 1970) have shown that almost all sales subsidiaries of
Swedish steel companies and pulp and paper companies have been
established through acquisition of the former agent or have been
organized around some person employed by the agent. Most of the
establishments were occasioned by various kinds of economic crises in the agent firms. Sales to a market by an agent had preceded
establishment of a sales subsidiary in each of nine cases investigated by Hörnell and Vahlne (1972). Further case studies of the
development of international activities by Swedish firms have
allowed us to generalize our observations : sales subsidiaries
are preceded in virtually all cases by selling via agent ; local
production is similarly generally proceded by sales subsidiaries.

Below we give a summary of the results we reached in two studies.
They are by no means meant to be statistically representative, but
the results are typical of studies we know. The first is a case
study of the internationalization process of the second largest
Swedish pharmaceutical firm, Pharmacia. At the time of the case
study (1972) Pharmacia had organizations of its own in nine countries, of which three were performing manufacturing activities.
In eight of these cases the development pattern was as follows.
The firm received orders from the foreign market and after some
time made an agreement with an agent (or sold licenses regarding
some parts of the product line). After a few years Pharmacia established sales subsidiaries in seven of those countries (and in
the eighth they bought a manufacturing company bearing the same
name, Pharmacia, that had previously served as an agent). Two of
the seven sales subsidiaries further increased their involvement
by starting manufacturing activities. It is interesting to note
that even this production decision was incremental ; the new
production units began with the least complicated manufacturing
activities and later successively added more complicated ones.

In the ninth country Pharmacia started a sales subsidiary almost
immediately when demand from the market was discovered. But in
fact the company did not totally lack experience even in this case.
The decision-maker had received parts of his education in the
country in question, and before the decision he had become acquain-
ted with the representative of another pharmaceutical firm who was
later made the head of the subsidiary (Hörnell, Vahlne & Wiedersheim-Paul, 1973).

In another study we investigated the internationalization of four
Swedish engineering firms. Below we quote some of the conclusions
of the study (Johanson & Wiedersheim-Paul, 1975).

"The establishment chain - no regular export, independent representative (agent), sales subsidiary, production - seems to be a

correct description of the order of the development operations of
the firms in individual countries. This is illustrated in table
I. Of sixty-three sales subsidiaries fifty-six were preceded by
agents ; this pattern holds for all the firms. With regard to the
production establishments there is a difference between Sandvik
and Atlas Copco on one hand, where twenty-two out of twenty-seven
establishments were preceded by sales subsidiaries and Facit and
Volvo on the other, where five out of seven occurred without the
firm having any sales subsidiary in the country. However, in no
case has a firm started production in a country without having
sold in the country via an agent or a sales subsidiary before.

Regarding the first establishments of sales subsidiaries, they do
not seem to have been a step in a conscious and goal directed
internationalization - at least not in Sandvik, Atlas Copco and
Volvo. For various reasons they had to take over representatives
or start subsidiaries. As they gradually have gained experience
in starting and managing subsidiaries, they have developed policies of marketing through subsidiaries in some of the firms. It
should be noted that the firm, Atlas Copco, which most consistently used subsidiaries for export marketing did so when it got a
new general manager, a former manager of a department store.

The producing subsidiaries almost all produce for local or in
some cases regional markets. Their activity embraces finishing,
assembly or component works which could be called marketing production. The only exception is Atlas Copco's factory in Belgium
making stationary pneumatic equipment.

Generally the development of the firm seems to be in accordance
with the incremental internationalization view discussed".

This gradual internationalization is not exclusively a Swedish
phenomenon, as the following quotations demonstrate :

"On its part exporting is a means also of reducing costs of market
development. Even if investment is necessary in the future, exporting helps to determine the nature and size of the market. As
the market develops, warehouse facilities are established : later
sales branches and subsidiaries (Singer, National Cash Register,
United Show Machinery). The record of company development indicates that the use of selling subsidiaries at an early stage reduced the later risks of manufacturing abroad. These selling affiliates permitted the slow development of manufacturing - from
repairing, to packaging, to mixing, to finishing, to processing or
assembling operations, and finally to full manufacture".
(Behrman, 1969, p 3).

Table 1. Establishment patterns for the investigated firms.

Firm	Pattern	Sales subsidiary		Production subsidiary		
		n↓s	a↓s	n↓p	a↓p	s↓p
Sandvik		2	18	0	2	13
Atlas Copco		3	14	0	3	9
Facit		0	14	0	2	3
Volvo		2	10	0	2	3
		7	56	0	9	28

Note : n = no regular export, a = agent, s = sales subsidiary,
       p = production subsidiary.

"Within countries, there is often a pattern of exports from the
United States, followed by the establishment of an assembly or
packaging plant, followed by progressively more integrated manufacturing activities".
(Vaupel, 1971, p 42).

Without reference to any specific empirical observations Gruber,
Mehta and Vernon (1967) mention that "one way of looking at the
overseas direct investments of US producers of manufacturers is
that they are the final step in a process which begins with the
involvement of such producers in export trade". Knickerbocker
(1972) also refers to this process and explicitly distinguishes
agents and sales subsidiaries as separate steps in the process.
Lipsey and Weiss (1969 ; 1972) refer to a "market cycle" model
with similar characteristics. However, in none of those cases
have the dynamics of this process been investigated. It has only
been used as an argument in the discussion of related problems.

Specification of the Problem

If internationalization indeed follows the pattern described above,
how can we explain it ? We do not believe that it is the result
of a strategy for optimum allocation of resources to different
countries, where alternative ways of exploiting foreign markets
are compared and evaluated. We see it rather as the consequence
of a process of incremental adjustments to changing conditions
of the firm and its environment (cf. Aharoni, 1966).

Changes in the firm and its environment expose new problems and
opportunities. Lacking routines for the solution of such sporadic
problems, the concern's management "searches in the area of the
problem" (Cyert and March, 1963). Each new discontinuity is
regarded as an essentially unprecedented and unparalleled case ;
the problems and opportunities presented are handled in their
contexts. Thus commitments to other markets are not explicitly
taken into consideration ; resource allocations do not compete
with each other.

Another constraint on the problem solution is the lack of, and
difficulty in obtaining, market knowledge in international operations. That internationalization decisions have an incremental
character is, we feel, largely due to this lack of market information and the uncertainty thereby occasioned (Hörnell, Vahlne
and Wiedersheim-Paul, 1972 ; Johanson, 1970). We believe that
lack of knowledge due to differences between countries with regard
to, for example, language and culture, is an important obstacle
to decision making connected with the development of international
operations. We would even say that these differences constitute
the main characteristic of international, as distinct from

domestic operations. By market knowledge we mean information
about markets, and operations in those markets which is somehow
stored and reasonably retrievable - in the mind of individuals, in
computer memories, and in written reports. In our model we consider knowledge to be vested in the decision-making system : we
do not deal explicitly with the individual decision-maker.

The Internationalization Model

As indicated in the introduction a model in which the same basic
mechanism can be used to explain all steps in the internationalization would be useful. We also think that a dynamic model would
be suitable. In such a model the outcome of one decision - or
more generally one cycle of events - constitutes the input of the
next. To clarify, we can say that the present state of internationalization is one important factor explaining the course of
following internationalization.

The state aspects we consider are the present resource commitment
to foreign markets - market commitment - and knowledge about
foreign markets and operations. The change aspects are decisions
to commit resources and the performance of current business activities. The basic mechanism is illustrated schematically in
figure 1.

Present market knowledge and market commitment are assumed to
affect both commitment decisions and the way current activities
are performed. These in turn change knowledge and commitment
(cf. Aharoni, 1966).

In the model, it is assumed that the firm strives to increase its
long term profit, which is assumed to be equivalent to growth
(Willianson, 1966). The firm is also striving to keep risk-taking
at a low level. These strivings are assumed to characterize
decision-making on all levels.   Given this, and state of the
economic and business factors which constitute the frame in which
a decision is taken, the model assumes that the state of internationalization affects perceived opportunities and risks which
in turn influence commitment decisions and current activities. We
will discuss the mechanism in detail below.

State Aspects

The two state aspects are resources committed to foreign markets
- market commitment - and knowledge about foreign markets possessed by the firm at a given point of time. We assume that commitment to a market affects the firm's perceived opportunities and
risk.

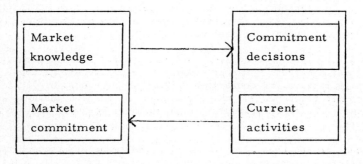

Figure 1. The basic mechanism of internationalization – state
          and change aspects.

Market Commitment

Let us first take a look at the market commitment concept.   To
begin with, we assume that it is composed of two factors - the
amount of resources committed and the degree of commitment, that
is, the difficulty in finding an alternative use for the resources
and transferring them to it.   Resources located in a particular
market area can often be considered a commitment to that market.
However, in some cases such resources can be sold and the financial resources can easily be used for other purposes.   The degree
of commitment is higher the more the resources in question are
integrated with other parts of the firm and their value is derived
from these integrated activities.   Thus, as a rule, vertical
integration means a higher degree of commitment than a conglomera-
tive foreign investment.   An example of resources which cannot
easily be directed to another market or used for other purposes
is a marketing organization that is specialized around the products of the firm and has established integrated customer relations.   However, resources located in the home country and employed in development and production of products for a separate market
also constitute a commitment to that market.   The more specialized
the resources are to the specific market the greater is the
degree of commitment.   And even if such resources can easily be
directed to development and production for other markets, as for
example engineers in a central engineering department, they cannot
always be profitably used there.   Consider Volvo - the Swedish
car manufacturer - with a large part of its production capacity
employed in production of cars for the US market. Even if that
capacity is not highly committed to the US production, it is not
easy, at least in the short run, to use it for production for
other markets.   The engineers employed in adapting the car to the
US requirements can probably be used for another purpose, but it
is not certain that they can be profitably employed there. On the
whole, it seems reasonable to assume that the resources that are
located in the particular market are most committed to that
market.   But we shall not disregard the commitment that follows
from employing parts of the domestic capacity for a particular
market.

The other part of market commitment - the amount of resources
committed - is easy to grasp.   It is close to the size of the
investment in the market, using this concept in its broader sense,
including investment in marketing, organization, personnel, etc.

Market knowledge

In our model, knowledge is of interest because commitment decisions
are based on some kinds of knowledge.   First, knowledge of opportunities or problems are assumed to initiate decisions.   Second,

evaluation of alternatives is based on some knowledge about relevant parts of the market environment and about performance of various activities. Very generally the knowledge "relates to present and future demand and supply, to competition and to channels for distribution, to payment conditions and the transferability of money, and those things vary from country, and from time to time" (Carlson, 1974).

A classification of knowledge which is useful for us is based on the way in which knowledge is acquired (Penrose, 1966, p 53). One type, objective knowledge, can be taught : the other experience or experiental knowledge can only be learned through personal experience. "With experiential knowledge, emphasis is placed on the change in the services the human resources can supply which arises from their activity" (ibid, p 53). And ".... experience itself can never be transmitted ; it produces a change - frequently a subtle change - in individuals and cannot be separated from them" (ibid, p 53). "Much of the experience of businessmen is frequently so closely associated with a particular set of circumstances that a large part of a man's most valuable services may be available only under these circumstances" (ibid, p 53).

We believe that this experiental knowledge is the critical kind of knowledge in the present context. It is critical because it cannot be so easily acquired as objective knowledge. In domestic operations, we can to a large extent rely on life-long basic experiences to which we can add specific experience in individuals, organizations and markets. In foreign operations, however, we have no such basic experiential knowledge to start with. It must be gained successively during the operations in the country.

We believe that the less structured and well-defined the activities and the required knowledge, the more important is experiential knowledge. In particular we think it is important in connection with activities that are based on relations to other individuals. Managerial work and marketing are examples of such activities. Especially in marketing of complex and soft-ware-intensive products experiential knowledge is crucial.

An important aspect of experiential knowledge is that it provides the framework for perceiving and formulating opportunities. On the basis of objective market knowledge it is possible to formulate only theoretical opportunities ; experiential knowledge makes it possible to perceive "concrete" opportunities - to have a "feeling" about how they fit into the present and future activities.

We can also distinguish between general knowledge and market-specific knowledge. General knowledge concerns, in the present context, marketing methods and common characteristics of certain types of customers, irrespective of their geographical location, depending, for example, in the case of industrial customers, on similarities in the production process. The market-specific knowledge is knowledge about characteristics of the specific national market - its business climate, cultural patterns, struc- ture of the market system and, most importantly, characteristics of the individual customer firms and their personnel.

Establishment and performance of a certain kind of operation or activity in a country requires both general knowledge and market- specific knowledge. Market-specific knowledge can mainly be gain- ed through experience in the market, whereas knowledge of the operation often can be transferred from one country to another country. It is the diffusion of this general knowledge which facilitates lateral growth ; that is, the establishment of tech- nically similar activities in dissimilar business environments.

There is a direct relation between market knowledge and market commitment. Knowledge can be considered a resource (or, perhaps preferably, a dimension of the human resources), and consequently the better the knowledge about a market the more valuable are the resources and the stronger is the commitment to the market. This is especially the case with experiential knowledge, which usually is associated with the particular conditions in the market in question and thus cannot be transferred to other individuals or other markets.

Change Aspects

The change aspects we have considered are current activities, and decisions to commit resources to foreign operation.

Current business activities

There is, to begin with, a lag between most current activities and their consequences. Those consequences may, in fact, not be rea- lized unless the activities are repeated more or less continuous- ly. Consider, for example, marketing activities, which generally do not result in sales unless they are repeated for some time. In many cases the time lag is considerable, and the marketing invest- ment represents an important and ever-increasing commitment to the market. The longer the lag the higher the commitment of the firm mounts up. It seems reasonable to assume that the more complicated and the more differentiated the product is, the larger the total commitment as a consequence of current activities will come to be.

Current activities are also the prime source of experience. It could be argued that experience could alternatively be gained through hiring of personnel with experience, or through advice from persons with experience. To clarify the roles of these alternative ways of integrating experience into the firm in the internationalization process, we distinguish between firm experience and market experience, both of which are essential. Persons working on the boundary between the firm and its market must be able to interpret information from inside the firm and from the market. The interpretation of one kind of information is possible only for one who has experience from the other part. We conclude that, for performance of marketing activities, both kinds of experience are required, and in this area it is difficult to substitute personnel or advice from outside for current activities. The more the activities are production-oriented, or the less required interaction between the firm and its market environment, the easier it will be to substitute hired personnel or advice for current activities, and consequently the easier it will be to start new operations which are not incremental additions to the former operations. It should be remembered, however, that even production activities are dependent on the general business climate, which cannot easily be assessed in other ways than by performance of business activities.

To some extent it may be possible to hire personnel with market experience and to use this profitably after some time in marketing activities. The delay is occasioned by the need for the new personnel to gain the necessary experience in the firm. But if the new personnel have already worked as representatives for the exporter the delay may approach zero. Thus, the best way to quickly get hold of and use market experience is to hire a sales manager or salesman of a representative or to buy the whole or part of the firm. In many cases this kind of experience is not for sale ; at the time of entry to a market the experience may not even exist. It has to be acquired through the long learning process in connection with current activities. This is an important reason why the internationalization process often proceeds slowly.

Commitment decisions

Decisions to commit resources to foreign operations provide a second change aspect. We assume that such decisions are dependent on what decision alternatives are raised and how they are chosen. Regarding the first part we assume that decisions are made in response to perceived problems and/or opportunities in the market. Problems and opportunities, that is awareness of need and possibilities for business actions, are assumed to be dependent on experience. Like Penrose we might even say that opportunities - and problems - are part of that experience. Firm experience, as well as market experience, is relevant. Problems are mainly

discovered by those parts of the organization that are responsible
for operations in the market and primarily by those who are working there. For them, the natural solution to problems will be
extension of the operations on the market to complementing operations. In any case we assume solutions to market operations problems are searched for in the neighbourhood of the problem symptom,
that is in the market activities (Cyert & March, 1963). In the
same way opportunities will mainly be perceived by those who are
working in the market, and such opportunities will also lead to
extension of the operations in the market. They will be related
to those parts of the environment that the firm is interacting
with (Pfeffer, 1974). Thus whether decision alternatives are raised in response to problems or in response to opportunities, they
will be related to the operations currently performed in the
market. Alternative solutions will generally consist of activities
that mean an extension of the boundaries of the organization and
an increase in commitment to the market. We could speak of an
opportunity horizon that- given the operations performed -
describes the kind of activities that are likely to be suggested
by those responsible for operations.

But opportunities are also seen by individuals in organizations
with which the firm is interacting ; these individuals may propose alternative solutions to the firm in the form of offers or
demands. The probability that the firm is offered opportunities
from outside is dependent on the scale and type of operations it
is performing ; that is, on its commitment to the market.

We distinguish between an economic effect and an uncertainty effect
of each additional commitment. We assume that the economic effect
primarily is associated with increases in scale of operations in
the market and that the uncertainty effect concerns the market
uncertainty, that is the decision-makers' perceived lack of ability to estimate the present and future market and market-influen-
cing factors. We mean that this market uncertainty is reduced
through increases in interaction and integration with the market
environment - steps such as increases in communication with
customers, establishment of new service activities or, in the
extreme case, the taking over of customers.

Our thinking on this point is further illustrated by the system
of relationships below :

R_i^+ = maximum tolerable market (market i) risk = f (firm's
resource position, firm's risk approach)

R_i = existing market risk situation = C_i . U_i
where C_i = existing market commitment
U_i = existing market uncertainty

ΔR_i = incremental risk implied by an incremental addition to operations in market i.

Scale increasing decisions are assumed to affect the size of C_i but not the size of U_i so that

$$\Delta R_i = U_i \cdot \Delta C_i > 0$$

Uncertainty reducing decisions are assumed to affect U_i primarily so that

$$\Delta R_i = \Delta U_i (C_i + \Delta C_i) + \Delta C_i \cdot U_i < 0$$

Using this framework we say that scale increasing decisions will be taken when $R_i < R_i^+$. The firm will incrementally extend its scale of existing operations in the market - in expectation of large returns - until its tolerable risk frontier (R_i^+) is met. Scale-increasing commitments may, for example, be occasioned by a decline in uncertainty about the market (U_i) incident to gaining market knowledge acquired with experience. Such a decline in market uncertainty can be expected when the market conditions are fairly stable and heterogenous. If market conditions are very unstable, experience cannot be expected to lead to decreased uncertainty. And if market conditions are very homogenous experience is probably not a necessary requirement for market knowledge. Under such market conditions an "optimal" scale of operations can be chosen from the beginning. Market uncertainty can also decline as a consequence of a competitive - or political - stabilization of market conditions. Scale increasing commitments may also follow on a rise of the maximum tolerable risk level due to an increase in the total resources of the firm or a more aggressive approach toward risk. We can, in any event, say that large increases in the scale of operations in the market will only take place in firms with large total resources or in firms which feel little uncertainty about the market.

Uncertainty reducing commitments on the other hand will be made when $R_i > R_i^+$. The firm will respond to this imbalance by steps to increase interaction and integration with the market environment. Such an imbalance may be the result of a decrease in the maximum tolerable market risk (R_i^+) or an increase in the existing risk situation in the market (R_i). The latter case may, in its turn, be occasioned by an increase in market commitment (C_i) or market uncertainty (U_i). Market commitments that increase risk are according to our assumptions those that increase the scale of existing operations in the market. Such increases are likely to be associated with current activities in an expanding market but can also be a consequence of the scale increasing decisions discussed above. Note that increases in scale of operations in the market can be expected to lead to uncertainty reducing commitments, that is increased interaction and integration with the market environment. Market uncertainty (U_i) can be expected to rise as a consequence of experience in a dynamic market environment showing that the original perception of the market was too simple. It may also rise because of a structural change in market conditions, for example, in connection with the entrance of new competitors in the market or introduction of new techniques. A typical example of the former is the change of the market situation of Swedish pulp and paper firms due to the entrance of North American producers on the European market (Kinch, 1974). However, increases in market uncertainty due to political changes cannot be expected to lead to the uncertainty reducing commitments discussed here as such commitments cannot be expected to affect the political situation.

This discussion requires some further comments. Firstly, it is very partial as we do not take into account how various factors other than scale may affect the economy of the market operations. The technology of the firm has probably a great impact on the economy of different types of market operations. Secondly, the variable "firm's approach to market risk" is a very complicated factor. We can, for example, distinguish between three different strategies with respect to this factor. One may be that a high risk level in one market is compensated by a low risk level on other markets. Another is that the tolerable risk level is the same in all markets. A third is that risk taking on the market is delegated to those working in the market as long as decisions do not require additional resources from the firm.

We conclude from this discussion of commitment decisions that additional commitments will be made in small steps unless the firm has very large resources and/or market conditions are stable and homegeneous or the firm has considerable experience in other markets with similar conditions. If not, market experience will lead to a stepwise increase in the scale of the operations and of integration with the market environment. Steps will also be taken to correct imbalance with respect to the risk situation in the market. Market growth will speed up this process.

Empirical Verification

We think that the general characteristics of the model fit nicely with empirical observations given earlier. In order to validate it empirically we intend to make two kinds of empirical studies. Firstly, we shall make one or two intensive case studies to see if the mechanism can be used to explain empirical situations. In

those case studies, we will try to measure the internationalization variables, market commitment and market knowledge, and investigate how they develop during the internationalization of the
firm.

Secondly, we intend to make comparative studies of the internationalization courses of different firms. Assuming that such factors
as firm size, technology, product line, home country, etc. via
the mechanism discussed above affect the character of the internationalization in different ways, we will investigate whether
firms that differ with respect to those factors also differ with
respect to the patterns of internationalization. Such studies
will require more systematic discussions of the expected influence
of these factors. The present model will constitute the framework of such discussions.

Possible applications

In many countries various programmes to affect foreign trade and
operations are designed and carried out. Still more are discussed.
Usually such programmes are based on models in which prices of
factors and products in different countries are the only explanatory variables. We think that our model can help in giving such
discussions and programmes a better base. An evaluation of a
Swedish export stimulation programme showed that the "export stimulation measures affect firms' export behaviour in different
ways due to differences in their degrees of previous export experience" (Olson, 1975). Our model indicates how such experience
can be expected to affect export behaviour. It also makes it
possible to get a better understanding of foreign investment
behaviour.

We also think that it can be useful in planning and decision-
making in the firm with regard to international operations. Many
firms consider internationalization a promising strategy. There
are, however, numerous examples of firms which have started international operations without success. We think that the importance
of the experience factor is often overlooked. The model indicates
how it is related to other internationalization variables thus
giving a better base for planning and execution of the internationalization process.

And finally we, as other students in the field, hope that our
way of reasoning will add something to the understanding of the
process by which firms go international or even multinational.
Thus, many studies of international trade and investment have
shown that oligopolistic industries are those having the greatest
international engagement. Such features as high R&D intensity,
advertising intensity, and efforts at product differentiation

characterize these industries (Gruber, Mehta, Vernon, 1967 ; Hymer, 1960 ; Kindleberger, 1969 ; Caves, 1971; Vaupel, 1971). Oligopolistic competition, however, lacks explanatory value at the firm level ; we have to look for other features to explain variations in the level of international involvement among the several firms in a given oligopolistic industry (Horst, 1972 ; Knickerbocker, 1973). Perhaps our model of the internationalization process can help in giving a part of this explanation through stressing the importance of some factors affecting the decision making process.

Bibliography

→ Aharoni, Y. (1966), The Foreign Investment Decision Process,Boston.

→ Behrman, J. (1969), Some Patterns in the Rise of the Multinational Enterprise, Chapel Hill.

Carlson, S. (1974), Investment in Knowledge and the Cost of Information, Acta Academiae Regiae Scientiarum Upsaliensis, Uppsala.

Caves, R.E. (1971), International Corporations : The Industrial
Economics of Foreign Investment, Economics, vol. 38.

→ Cyert, R.M. & March, J.G. (1963), A Behavioral Theory of the Firm,
Englewood Cliffs.

Forsgren, M. & Kinch, N. (1970), Företagets anpassning till förän-
dringar i omgivande system. En studie av massa- och pappers-
industrin, Uppsala.

Gruber, W., Mehta R. & Vernon, R. (1967), The R&D Factor in International Trade and International Investment of the United
States, Journal of Political Economy, February.

Horst, T.O. (1972), Firm and Industry Determinants of the Decision to Invest Abroad : An Empirical Study, Review of Economics
and Statistics.

Hymer, S. (1960), The International Operations of National Firms:
A Study of Direct Investment, doctoral dissertation, Mass.
Institute of Technology.

Håkansson, H. & Wootz, B. (1975), Supplier Selection in an International Environment - an Experimental Study, Journal of Marketing Research, February.

Hörnell, E., Vahlne, J.E., & Wiedersheim-Paul, F. (1973), Export
och utlandsetableringar, Stockholm.

Johanson, J. (ed.) (1972), Exportstrategiska problem. Stockholm.

Johanson, J. (1970), Svenskt kvalitetsstål på utländska marknader,
mimeographed licentiate dissertation, Dept of Business Administration, Uppsala.

Johanson, J. & Wiedersheim-Paul, F. (1975), The Internationalization of the Firm - Four Swedish Cases. Journal of Management
Studies.

Kinch, N. (1974), Utlandsetableringar inom massa- och pappers-
industrin. In Vahlne (ed), Företagsekonomisk forskning kring
internationellt företagande, Stockholm.

Kindleberger, C.P. (1969), American Business Abroad. New Haven.

→ Knickerbocker, F.T. (1973), Oligopolistic Reaction and Multinational Enterprise. Boston.

Lipsey, R.E. & Weiss, M.Y. (1969), The Relation of US Manufacturing Abroad to US Exports. A Framework for Analysis, Business
and Economics Section Proceedings. American Statistical Association.

Lipsey, R.E. & Weiss, M.Y. (1972), Analyzing Direct Investment
and Trade at the Company Level, Business and Economic Section
Proceedings. American Statistical Association.

Olson, H.C. (1975), Studies in Export Promotion. Attempts to Evaluate Export Stimulation Measures for the Swedish Textile and
Clothing Industries. Uppsala.

Penrose, E. (1966), The Theory of the Growth of the Firm.Oxford.

Pfeffer, J. (1972), Merger as a Response to Organizational Interdependence, Administrative Science Quarterly, 6.

→ Vaupel, J.V. (1971). Characteristics and Motivations of the US
Corporations that Manufacture Abroad, mimeographed, Boston.

Williamson, J. (1966). Profit, Growth and Sales Maximization,
Economica, 33.

MULTINATIONAL CORPORATIONS AND HOST GOVERNMENT RELATIONSHIPS: A COMPARATIVE STUDY OF U.S., EUROPEAN, AND JAPANESE MULTINATIONALS

Anant R. Negandhi
*International Institute of Management, Science Center Berlin
and Graduate School of Business Administration,
Kent State University, Ohio, U.S.A.*

B.R.Baliga
*Graduate School of Business Administration,
Kent State University, Ohio, U.S.A.*

Introduction

Recent years have witnessed a growing controversy, both at home and abroad, over the role of multinational corporations in international business. They have come under fire at home for exporting jobs and technology abroad.[1] They have had to simultaneously confront host government accusations for exploitation of local labor, demanding higher payments for royalties for obsolete technology and patents, using monopoly power to crush competition,and using their monopolistic power to gain favorable rates for large financial credits[24]. Recently, they have also been accused by host governments for being "instruments of foreign policy of the home government"[3], and this notion has gained a great deal of credibility since the revelations of ITT's political activities in Chile [25]. On the positive side, the multinational corporation has been perceived as "the only institution known to man that can solve today's complex socio-economic problems through integration of economic activity on a global scale". They are viewed as "agents of change and progress.... building, what, for all intents and purposes, must be considered a new world economic system"[17]. In fact, proponents of such views accuse nation states as being impediments to achieving the new beneficial world order [2]. To sum up in a graphic phrase, MNCs are currently being perceived as "The Frightening Angels"[20].

Until recently, studies in the field of international business and multinational corporations were concentrated either on macro-level implications of MNC functioning, (e.g. balance of payments, diffusion of new technologies[11]), or analyzing in detail the functioning of some functional units of the organization, such as marketing [29], finance [23], personnel [8], etc. Very few systematic attempts have been made to analyze the interaction between MNCs and host governments, and other publics in the host countries.

A number of assertions have been made by the academicians and businessmen alike, pinpointing some of the important causes of conflict between the MNCs and the host governments. It has been argued, for example, that the foreign private investor, besides being an "outside intruder", upsets the prevailing status quo in the host country for being :

(a) Larger in size and capital resources[2];
(b) More aggressive in its marketing strategies, and thereby establishing proportionately higher market shares, than the comparable local firms[28];
(c) More sophisticated in its management and technological systems[28] ;
(d) More efficient [17];
(e) More diversified, and hence more visible in the public eye[37].

Although such contentions intuitively sound reasonable and appealing, thus far, such observations have not been empirically verified. The study reported here attempts to do so.

Nature and Purpose of the Study

The following is a comparative study of U.S., European, and Japanese multinationals operating in six developing countries : Brazil, India, Malaysia, Peru, Singapore, and Thailand. The primary objective of the study was to examine the interactions between the MNCs and the host governments. Interactions between MNCs and other agencies (organizations) they dealt with, were also examined in order to obtain a more comprehensive understanding of the dynamics of interactions between MNCs and members of their environments. The study also enabled us to examine similarities and differences in the investment environments of the six countries and their impact on MNC-host country relationships. We also endeavored to examine how the parties involved responded to the changing environment at a particular point in time - in terms of strategy changes, etc. - and what affect this had on their future interactions. We are also interested in determining whether a set of interactions between a MNC and an environment group affected the interactions between some other MNC and environment group. In more specific terms, the study examined the following issues :

1. The nature and kind of conflicts and conflicting issues between MNCs and their host governments.

2. The causes of conflicts between the two parties.

3. The MNCs' response patterns in resolving conflict-based issues.

4. The basic orientations in terms of the MNCs' policies and practices in dealing with the host governments and other groups in the host nations.

5. The personnel policies of the multinationals.

6. The host governments' perceptions of U.S., European, and Japanese multinationals.

7. The host countries' expectations of the MNCs and the MNCs' expectations of the host nations.

8. Controls imposed on MNCs and their response to such controls.

9. The specific contributions made by the MNCs toward the socio-economic development of the host nations.

10. The future of the MNCs as perceived by the multinationals' executives and the host governments' officials.

A space limitation precludes us from reporting the findings in detail. This has been done elsewhere[1]. In this paper, we will analyze only the impact of some of the important attributes of the MNCs (subsidiary) on their relationships with the host government and other publics in these countries. More specifically, the paper briefly analyzes the impact of ownership, equity holding, market power (share), and expectation differences between MNCs and host governments.

Sample and Method

The research sample was drawn at random from various listings of U.S., European, and Japanese MNCs operating in six developing countries – Brazil, India, Malaysia, Peru, Singapore and Thailand. These six countries were chosen to provide diversities in political structures, level of economic and industrial developments, and varied experience with foreign private investors.

Attempts were made to obtain comparable firms from each category of MNC ownership – American, European, and Japanese. A letter seeking their participation was sent out to each MNC drawn from the listings. A total of 124 firms agreed to participate in the study. Senior executives of these firms were interviewed through a structured interview guide prepared in advance (a copy of this is available from the senior author). Some of these interviews were tape-recorded and were later content analyzed.

In addition, a number of government officials and officials of
the Chamber of Commerce and other trade and professional organizations in those countries studied were also interviewed to collect
both the background information on MNC operations and their own
perspectives on the various issues raised by MNC executives.

To provide some perspectives on the nature of the MNCs' host
countries' conflicts, we will first briefly outline the conflicting issues encountered by the MNCs operating in the six developing countries.

Conflicting Issues

Table 1 provides the results of our interviews with the senior
executives of the MNCs concerning the conflicting issues confronting them in the six developing countries. As can be easily
seen from the table, three issues, namely : equity participation,
desire to retain control in the hands of local nationals,and the
utilization of local inputs, dominated the scene. The other
issues, such as : transfer pricing, MNCs' interference with the
host country's socio-economic norms, etc., were not considered
to be major problems.

A similar trend was also observed by the U.S. State Department,
in their analysis of conflicts between U.S. business firms and
host governments, during the period 1960 through 1971[2]. They found
that of the 198 cases of conflicts, 128 were concerned with
equity participation. They also reported that the conflicts on
such issues have been on the rise since 1969.

These results reflect certain fundamental changes in the problems
faced by the international firms. For example, in the early '50s
and '60s, it was widely accepted that a significant proportion
of the problems confronting international firms related to their
difficulties in adapting to the differing socio-cultural norms of
the host societies. During this era, many believed that solving
problems of initial socio-cultural adaptation would create unli-
mited opportunities for the expansion of international business
around the world.

As can readily be seen from Table 1, very few of the MNCs' problems
were related to socio-cultural adaptation. Four of a total of
139 cases of conflicts examined could be traced to socio-cultural
factors. This indicates that host governments are more prone to
defining their problems with foreign investors in economic terms
-- equity participation, management control, expansion of exports,
reduction of imports, use of local inputs, exchange control,etc.

Table 1 : Conflicting Issues Between MNCs and Host Countries
(Interview Responses)

Conflicting Issues	Far East			Latin America			Both Areas			Tot.
	US MNCs	European MNCs	Japanese MNCs	US MNCs	European MNCs	Japanese MNCs	US MNCs	European MNCs	Japanese MNCs	
Equity Participation by Locals	13	14	0	0	0	1	13	14	1	28
Management Control in the Hands of Local Nationals	15	17	13	2	3	2	17	20	15	52
Control on Exchange	2	3	0	0	1	0	2	4	0	6
Control on Imports	3	0	1	0	1	0	3	1	1	5
Expansion of Exports	3	2	2	1	1	0	4	3	2	7
Use of Local Inputs	0	2	0	0	0	0	0	3	0	3
Transfer Prices Pricing Policies	6	6	2	5	2	0	11	8	1	21
Interference by Host Government in Corporate Affairs	2	2	0	0	1	0	2	3	0	5
Contributions to Economic Plans of Host Nations	2	0	0	2	0	0	4	0	0	4
Interference with Socio-Culture Norms	1	0	1	1	1	0	2	1	1	4
Interference by MNCs' Home Governments, in Host Governments Policies	1	0	0	1	0	0	2	0	0	2
	48	47	29	12	10	3	60	57	22	139
Total	114			25			139			

Source : Interview data

Such an attitude on the part of the host governments was evident
in all the six countries studied.

The MNCs' Attributes and Conflicts

In the remainder of this paper, we will analyze the association
between certain important attributes of the multinational corporation, outlined earlier, and the MNC-host-country conflicts.

In order to explore the relationships between the MNCs' internal
attributes and the nature and intensity of conflicts they experienced in the host countries, we created the following four
analytical categories of conflicts :

1. Value conflict was related to the basic belief and value system of a given society. The elements involved in such a conflict went far beyond the actual issues that triggered off
   the conflict.

2. Negotiational conflict had its locus in perception of either
   the host governments, the parties involved, and/or the MNCs,
   in the matter that some basic terms of contract previously
   agreed upon, implicitly or explicitly, had been violated by
   the opposite party. This type of conflict, in our analytical
   terms, was conceived as company-specific, and took place on a
   one-to-one basis.

3. Policy-level conflict had its locus in the basic disagreement
   among the parties with respect to certain policy issues. In
   contrast to the negotiational-level conflict, the policy
   conflict was conceived as industry-specific. In other words,
   a large majority of firms in a given industry were affected
   by such a level of conflict, e.g. price and production controls on pharmaceutical products.

4. Operational-level conflict was generally encountered by the
   MNCs with the task-environmental groups (e.g., consumers,
   suppliers, labor unions, employers) with which the firm dealt
   in its day-to-day operations.

The first three levels of these conflicts were conceived in our
research as interface or inter-organizational conflicts, while
the fourth level of conflict, operational, was regarded as
intra-organizational conflict.

Research Results

Our interviews with the 124 MNCs yielded 102 cases of conflict.
Interestingly enough, of these, only two could be classified as
"value-level" conflict. This finding, as mentioned earlier, indicates that there is an increasing tendency on the part of the
parties involved to be pragmatic and business-like, and to push
other considerations into the background. As these two value-
conflict cases would accentuate the observed differences, it was
decided to omit them for purpose of statistical analysis.

Ownership and Conflict

Table 2 provides an association between the controlling ownership
of the MNC and the level of MNC-environment-unit conflict[3].

Table 2: <u>Conflict versus Controlling Ownership of MNC</u>

	U.S.	European	Japanese
	N/%	N/%	N/%
Negotiational	17/39.5	13/38.2	5/21.7
Policy	16/37.2	15/44.1	4/17.4
Operational	10/23.3	6/17.6	14/60.9
	43/100	34/100	23/100

N = 100

As is evident from the table, the U.S. MNCs have more interface
conflicts, while Japanese MNCs have more operational-level conflicts. However, it is interesting to note that there are no
significant differences between the American and European corporations. In fact, like U.S. MNCs, the majority of European MNCs
also faced negotiational-and-policy-level conflicts; and merely
a fraction of them were plagued with operational problems. In
specific terms, the types of interface problems experienced by
the U.S. and European MNCs centered around the host governments'
requirements for dilution of equity and management control,
reduction or elimination of royalty payments for technology and
knowhow, transfer-pricing policies, etc. The operational problems
faced by Japanese MNCs were : low morale and employee productivity, high turnover and absenteeism, interpersonal conflicts between
Japanese expatriate managers and locals.

Although the American and European MNCs faced similar problems
overseas, they differed in their modes of resolving their conflicts in the host countries.

Equity Holding and Conflict

Both for purposes of monitoring the activities of the multinationals and harnessing them for achieving their own national
socio-economic plans, many developing countries have increased
their demands for local equity participation and staffing of
local nationals at higher managerial positions. Following the
examples set by India and Mexico, such demands, on the part of
the developing countries, have now become a rule rather than an
exception. Most nations now demand majority equity participation,
either by local entrepreneurs, and/or by the government itself
in the foreign ventures operating in their countries. The recently enacted Foreign Investment Regulation Act by the Indian
Government, the regulations enacted by the Andean Pact countries,
and the Malaysian regulation, demanding 40-30-30 ratios in foreign enterprises, exhibit rather striking similarities in their
aspirations and demands of these nations. Such similarities are
not merely accidental. In other words, such similar regulations
represent a growing awareness among the developing countries that
their lot is identical, and that like problems require like solutions.

The multinational enterprises, on the other hand, prefer and
generally insist upon a one-hundred percent ownership and management control of their subsidiaries' operations ; at the very
least, they prefer to retain majority equity and managerial
control.

Given such differences in expectations on both sides, one would,
indeed, expect a certain amount of tension and conflict between
the MNCs and the host nations related to equity participation
and management control. As we saw in a preceding section (Table
1), a large majority of conflicts between MNCs and host governments were indeed centered around these two issues.

In terms of our own study, an overwhelming majority of U.S. subsidiaries (75%) were wholly owned by the parent companies, while
only a fraction of the subsidiaries of the Japanese MNCs were
wholly owned by the parent (26%). European MNCs, as in most
other instances, resembled the American MNCs, two-thirds of them
were wholly owned.[4]

Given these differences in the pattern of equity holding in their
subsidiaries, one could argue that the interface problems faced
by American and European multinationals may be due to their

ownership patterns.   Conversely, one could also hypothesize that
Japanese MNCs have an easier time with the host governments, as
they are willing to settle for minority participation.   Our findings indicate significant confirmatory evidence.   Table 3 shows
that wholly-owned companies have approximately one and a half
times more negotiational-level conflicts with the host countries
than those of the minority-owned corporations.   Our results also
show that the majority-owned enterprises followed a conflict pattern similar to the wholly-owned ones.   The minority-owned companies, however, were not entirely conflict-free.   In other words,
though the minority-owned foreign companies in the developing
countries had complied with equity demands, they were now being
confronted with new demands by the host governments.   These included demands for increase of exports and foreign-exchange earnings,
localization of management control, reduction in prices, etc.
All this suggests that the MNCs should not be naive enough to
believe that complying with host-government demands at one point
in time would result in enduring peace ; rather, they should
anticipate and be prepared to deal pragmatically with newer
demands as and when they arise.

Market Power and Conflict

One of the major concerns of the host nations about MNCs is that
the local industries are being displaced by foreign investors.
There is also a genuine fear that the MNCs could become monopolistic powers, beyond control of the national government.   Behrman
observed that "Although the host country likes improvement of
quality, reduction of prices, increases of wages, etc., resulting
from foreign investment, it may not like to see its domestic
enterprise pushed to the wall"[3].

In other words, a monopolistic or oligopolistic market power of
the multinationals, which could result in a virtual "takeover"
of local enterprises, is actively resisted, not only by the developing, but also the industrially developed nations.   Countries
such as Canada, France, West Germany, and the United Kingdom,
have enacted regulations to discourage such behavior on the part
of foreign investors.   Even the United States, the champion of the
free-entreprise system, has shown concern about the adverse impact
of foreign investments on local enterprises.

Despite such widespread concern over the adverse impact of the
multinationals' market domination in the host countries, our
study did not indicate a significant relationship between the
MNCs' market share and the nature of conflicts in the host countries.   Although a large proportion of the MNCs studied indicated
that their market share was more than 25 percent, their problems
were, in no case, different from those faced by companies whose

market share was minimal. In other words, it appears that,regard-
less of market share, they all were equally susceptible to similar
issues and problems. Of the six countries we had studied, only in
Malaysia, and to some extent in Brazil, did the MNCs' market share
have some impact on the type of problems faced with the government.
The overall relationship, between these two variables was, however,
less striking. This lack of relationship does not imply that the
developing countries are unconcerned about issues of economic
domination by the multinationals. As Table 3 shows, the market
conditions (degree of competitiveness) faced by the MNCs had a
significant relationship with the nature of conflict. Overall,
the firm facing seller's and moderately competitive markets encountered a greater number of negotiational- and policy-level
conflicts than those facing highly competitive markets.

Expectation Differences and Conflict

Psychologists, political scientists, and other social scientists
concerned with the study of human behavior, have argued for quite
some time that actual or imaginary differences in expectations
between two parties involved in an inter-action are likely to
result in a breakdown of communication, and might generate tension
and even conflict between them.

In order to examine whether the differences in expectations led
to a breakdown in communication, and generated tension and conflict
between MNCs and host governments, we collected information on a
variety of items pertaining to the expectations of the MNCs and
the host governments towards each other. Governmental policies,
documents, newspaper reports, and other information gathered
through personal interviews with the MNCs' executives and government officials in these countries, provided additional information
on their expectations toward each other.

Our results indicate a widening gap between the expectations of
the MNCs and the host governments toward each other. Such gaps
in understanding of one another have, indeed, created continuous
tensions and conflicts in the relationships.

In more specific terms, many of the developing countries, in order
to maximize their returns from foreign private investment, have
enacted legislation which requires a majority local equity in
foreign enterprises, higher proportion of local nationals in top
positions, increase of exports and foreign exchange earnings, and
reduction of imports of raw material and spare parts.

Such demands from the host countries have, to some extent, con-
strained the MNCs to rationalize the world-wide productivie capacity they seem to possess. For this purpose, the MNCs on their

part, have made demands on the host countries to provide them
with efficient infrastructural facilities, reduce the bureaucratic
controls and interference in corporate affairs, provide conducive
labor legislation and more flexible expansion policies.

Thus, while the host countries have shown a strong concern over
the displacement of the local firms by the foreign investors, and
demanded the development of local resources, utilization of local
supplies, increase of research and development activities, and
local ownership (equity) in foreign enterprises, the MNCs seem
to have perceived those demands by the host countries as mere
empty noises.

These differences in expectations between the MNCs and host countries are bound to create tensions and conflicts ; our results
show a strong association between these two variables. In other
words, as Table 3 shows, MNCs with larger expectation differences
are more often involved in negotiational-level conflicts with
the host governments than those with smaller expectation differences.

Our results also indicate that, relatively speaking, a greater
number of U.S. MNCs have had larger expectation differences with
the host countries than the European and Japanese MNCs.

Impact of the Other Factors

Our results indicated a very minor impact of such MNC attributes
as size, number of years in operations, the level of technology
utilized, type of industry, and level of diversification on MNC-
host country conflicts. The results are given in Table 3.

Summary and Implications of Results

The assertion that the MNC attributes, such as size of capital
investment, sophistication of technology employed, degree of
diversification, period of operation, size of employee force,and
sales volume would have a significant relationship with the
level of conflict in the host country, fared poorly in the empirical findings. Ownership and pattern of equity holding indicated
a substantial relationship with the level of conflict. The fact
that expectational differences contributed significantly to the
variation in the dependent variable of conflict presents some
very important implications for both the host governments and
the multinational corporations. It was very evident from the
data gathered in the field through depth interviews that both
host government representatives and MNC chief executives had, at
best, only a very diffuse understanding of what they expected of

Table 3: Internal Attributes of MNCs (Subsidiary) and the Nature
        of Conflict

Company Attributes (N = 100)	Nature of Conflict			Level of Significance
	Negotiational	Policy	Operational	
	%	%	%	
Equity holding				
wholly owned	36	36	28	
majority owned	38	27	35	
minority owned	20	60	20	p < .08
Market Share				
more than 60%	40	35	25	
26-59%	33	42	25	
less than 26%	35	27	38	p < .4704
Degree of Competitiveness				
seller's market	70	30	0	
moderately competitive	46	37	17	
highly competitive	25	36	39	p < .05
Expectational Difference (between MNCs and host governments)				
large differ.	54	28	18	
moderate diff.	27	59	14	
little or no difference	21	28	51	p < .003
Number of Employees				
more than 1000	40	31	29	
999 to 400	40	40	20	
399 to 100	19	50	31	
less than 100	17	0	83	p < .0421
Size of Investment				
$ 4.9-$ 3 Mil.	43	31	26	
$ 2.9-$ 2 Mil.	33	42	25	
$ 1.9-$.5 Mil.	20	40	40	
less than $ 500,000	60	40	0	p < .5315

Table 3 (continued)

Company Attributes (N = 100)	Nature of Conflict			Level of Significance
	Negotiational	Policy	Operational	
Period of Operation	%	%	%	
more than 15 years	39	35	26	
6 to 14 years	39	35	26	
less than 6 years	0	50	50	p < .4356
Degree of Diversification				
high—more than 5 products	43	33	24	
intermediate – 2 to 5 products	24	36	40	
low – less than 2 products	24	40	36	p < .3349
Level of Technology				
advanced technology	40	37	23	
intermediate technology	35	31	34	
low technology	20	33	47	p < .4135
Type of Industry				
extractive ind. (petroleum & mining)	70	20	10	
chemical & pharmaceutical	36	29	35	
auto,rubber tires consumer durables	35	38	27	
consumer nondurable (soaps, foods)	11	50	39	p < .10

each other. While most host governments viewed the entry of MNCs
as "the panacea for all economic and social ills", the MNC decision makers viewed their entry primarily in terms of, either,
entry into a potentially large market or in terms of global rationalization of their operations. Any socio-economic benefits that
accrued to the host were viewed as purely incidental to their
main goals.

Our results also showed considerable differences in the modes of
handling conflict by U.S., European, and Japanese multinationals.
A content analysis of field interviews indicated that most of the
American MNCs' executives tended to view the regulations imposed
by host governments with ideological overtones. In contrast,
Europeans and Japanese - especially the Japanese - maintained a
very low profile during periods of stress and conflict. The
Japanese in particular displayed a strong propensity to underplay
any conflict or regulations.

One of the surprise findings of the study was the significant
relationship between degree of market competitiveness and conflict,
as indicated in Table 3. MNCs operating in moderatively competitive and sellers' markets were involved in higher levels of conflict compared to those operating in highly competitive markets.
We can only hazard a guess as to why this is so. It would appear
that firms in the sellers' market were under pressure primarily
from the government - this would account for the significant percentage, 70 percent, of conflicts being negotiated - while those
in competitive markets were under pressure primarily from constituents in the task environment. Firms in moderately competitive
markets would appear to be under pressure from both. The majority
of the U.S. firms operated either in moderately competitive markets, or in highly competitive markets, yet accounted for a significant proportion of interface conflicts.

It appears to us that this finding has important implications for
the American MNC strategy. Rather than adapt a very aggressive
profile, as suggested recently by some, American MNCs would do
better to adopt a lower profile until such time that their contributions to the host can be documented and substantiated. Also,
it appears that U.S. MNC executives have a rather inflated understanding of their leverage (relative to other MNCs and the host
governments), and a proper understanding of it would enable them
to adapt better to the changing host country's environment.

European MNCs would do well to move away from a convergence toward
U.S. practices and shift toward either their original mode (or the
Japanese mode) in terms of the interface/external relation func-
tion.

Japanese MNCs appear to be well placed as far as their handling of interface relations go, though they would do well to learn from the U.S. managerial philosophy of dealing with their task environment.

In conclusion, it may be noted that a significant amount of variation in the dependent variable - 64 percent - remains unexplained. This suggests that probably better predictors of conflict other than the set of internal attributes that we have considered exist. Variables such as the host country's degree of political stability, economic development, extent of differences in political and economic ideology of significant constituents, could be fruitful variables for future research. The firm's management orientation or philosophy and strategy may also account for this unexplained variation in the dependent variable. In our ongoing study, we are attempting to explore this further.

References

1. Anant R. Negandhi and B.R. Baliga : <u>Battle at the Bay : A</u>
   <u>Study of American, European, and Japanese Multinationals</u>,
   1978 (forthcoming).

2. Disputes Involving U.S. Foreign Investment : July 1, 1971
   through July 1, 1973.
   Bureau of Intelligence & Research RECS-6, Washington, D.C.,
   February 8, 1974

3. For the purpose of brevity, we henceforth refer to MNC-host-
   government conflict, and conflicts with various publics in
   the host country, as MNC-environment-unit-conflict.

4. This is in contrast to Franko's study of European multinationals. He reports that a larger number of continental enterprises entering in the developing countries were joint ventures.
   Thus our own sample of European MNCs which were mostly wholly
   owned, might have caused greater similarities between European
   and American MNCs. See L.G. Franko : <u>The European Multi-</u>
   <u>nationals</u>, Stanford, <u>Greylock Publishers</u>, 1976, pp. 120-122.

Bibliography

(1)   AFL-CIO. An American Trade Union View of International Trade and Investment. Washington, D.C., 1972.

(2)   Ball, George. Quote from speech delivered May 5, 1967 to the New York Chamber of Commerce, N.Y., N.Y.

(3)   Berhman, Jack N. National Interests and the Multinational Enterprise, Englewood Cliffs, N.J. : Prentice Hall,Inc. 1970.

(4)   Burtes David, et. al.(eds.) Multinational Corporations-Nation State Interaction : An Annotated Bibliography, Washington, D.C., Foreign Policy Research Institute,1971.

(5)   Dill, Wiliam R. "Environment as an Influence on Managerial Autonomy". ASQ, 2, 407-43, 1958.

(6)   Emery, F.C. & E.L. Trist. "The Causal Texture of Organizational Environment", Human Relations, 18, 21-32, 1965.

(7)   Goffman, E. The Presentation of Self in Everyday Life, New York, Doubleday-Anchor, 1958.

(8)   Gonzalez, R.F. & A.R. Negandhi. The United States Overseas Executive : His Orientations and Career Patterns, East Lansing, Michigan. M.S.U. 1968.

(9)   Heller, R. & Norris Willatt. The European Revenge. N.Y. : Charles Schribner's Sons, 1975.

(10)   Hufbauer, G.C. & F.M. Adler. Overseas Manufacturing Investment and the Balance of Payments. Washington, D.C., U.S. Treasury Dept. 1968.

(11)   The International Corporation and the Transfer of Technology, Paris, International Chamber of Commerce.

(12)   Kahn, Herman. The Emerging Japanese Superstate : Challenge and Response. Englewood Cliffs, N.J., Prentice Hall, Inc. 1970.

(13)   Khandwalla, P.N. "Environment and its impact on the Organization". International Studies of Management and Organization, 2, 297-313, 1972.

(14)   Kobayashi Noritake "The Japanese Approach to Multinationalism", Journal of World Trade Law, Vol. 10, No. 2, March/April 1976.

(15)   Lawrence, P.R. & Jay W. Lorsch. Organization and Environ-
       ment, Homewood, Ill. Richard D. Irwin, Inc. 1969.

(16)   Litwalk, E. & Lydia F. Hilton, "Interorganizational Analy-
       sis : A Hypothesis on Coordinating Agencies". ASQ, Vol.
       6, 395-420.

(17)   Maisonrouge, J. Quoted by Donald M. Kendall, "The Need for
       the Multinational Corporations", in John K. Ryans (ed.)
       The Multinational Business World of the 1980s. (Kent,
       Ohio : Center for Business and Economic Research, Kent
       State University, 1974), p. 22.

(18)   Negandhi, A.R. (ed.), Interorganization Theory (Kent :
       Comparative Adm. Research Institute, 1975), pp. 1-14.

(19)   Negandhi, A.R. and David E. Fry and Claudia W. Fry,
       "Multinational Corporations and Host- Government Conflict"
       A paper presented at the Academy of International Busi-
       ness Meeting in Dallas, December 1974. (A paper availa-
       ble from senior author).

(20)   Negandhi, A.R. and S.B. Prasad, The Frightening Angels : A
       Study of U.S. Multinationals in Developing Countries,
       (Kent : Kent State University Press, 1975).

(21)   Newman, W.H. "Is Management Exportable?", Columbia Journal
       of World Business, Jan./feb. 1970, 7-8.

(22)   Osborn, R.N. & James G. Hunt,"Environment and Organization
       Effectiveness, ASQ Vol. 19, N° 2, 231-246, 1974.

(23)   Polk Judd, Irene W. Meister & Lawrence A. Veit, U.S.Produc-
       tion Abroad and the Balance of Payments (N.Y. National
       Industries Conference Board, 1966).

(24)   Robins, S. & Robert B. Stobaugh. Money and The Multinational
       Enterprise : A Study in Financial Policy, N.Y. : Basic
       Books, 1973.

(25)   Sampson, Anthony. The Sovereign State of ITT, N.Y. : Stein
       and Day, 1973.

(26)   Senate Finance Committee. Multinational Corporation : A
       Compendium of Papers, Washington, Government Printing
       Office, 1973.

(27)   Sethi, Prakash S. Japanese Business and Social Conflict,
       Cambridge, Mass. : Ballinger Publishing Co, 1975.

(28) Servan Schreiber, J.J. The American Challenge, New York,
      Atheneum, 1968.

(29) Stephenson, Hugh. The Coming Clash, London, Weidenfeld &
      Nicolson, 1972.

(30) Terpstra, Vern. American Marketing in the Common Market,
      New York : Praeger Publishing Inc. 1967.

(31) Thompson, James. "Organization and Output Transaction.
      American Journal of Sociology, 68, 309-324, 1963.

(32) Organizations in Action, Chicago, McGraw Hill, 1967.

(33) Turner, Louis. Multinational Companies in the Third World,
      New York : Hill & Wang, 1973.

(34) U.S. State Dept. Disputes Involving U.S. Foreign Investment.
      July 1, 1971 through July 1, 1973. Bureau of Intelligen-
      ce & Research RECS-6, Washington, D.C., Feb. 8, 1974.

(35) Warren, R.L. "The Interorganizational Field as a Focus for
      Investigation". ASQ, 12, 590-613, 1967.

(36) Stephen M. Rose & Ann F. Burgunder, The Structure of Urban
      Reform, Lexington, Mass.:D.C. Heath and Co., 1974.

(37) Yoshino, M. Japan's Managerial System, Tradition and Chal-
      lenge, Cambridge, Mass. : MIT Press, 1968.

STRATEGIC DECISION-MAKING PROCESSES :
PRACTICE OR MANAGEMENT ?

Michel Ghertman
Centre d'Enseignement Supérieur des Affaires

The decision making process of top management in companies is an
area of study attracting a growing interest from government agencies. They are increasingly concerned over their ability to fore-
see companies' reactions to economic measures that they may take
in order to increase the latter's efficiency. In order to predict
these reactions, government planners must possess an adequate
model of the strategic decision-making process. Businessmen are
also interested in the subject, but with a prescriptive orientation, since they want to manage their own decision-making process
in order to increase its efficiency in accordance with the following three criteria :

- increase the viability of decisions taken, by making sure that
  each participant in the process is able to supply the elements
  of information and judgment which he has at his disposal,

- facilitate the implementation of decisions made by avoiding
  intra-organizational tension and conflict,

- reduce the total time spent by top executives in carrying out
  the decision-making process.

What is the most valuable resource a company has if not its top
management's time ? Further what decisions are the most critical
for the company's long term survival if not the strategic choices
taken by its top management ? A better grasp of the strategic
decision-making process, therefore, represents long term advantage
over national or international competitors.

This paper addresses itself to both the descriptive needs of government and the prescriptive needs of companies' top management.
It is the result of the clinical research of a series of decisions
made during the period 1964 to 1974 by one of the foremost French-
based multinational companies, disguised here under the name of

COFRACIS, Compagnie Française de Ciments et Ciments Spéciaux. The
company has a strong presence in almost all world markets through
manufacturing and sales subsidiaries. The only notable exception
before 1970 was the American market where COFRACIS had only limited involvement. The decision-making processes which were analy-
sed fall into two categories : the first relating to the decision
process of each acquisition of American companies and the second
to the formulation of the acquisition strategy in the period 1964
to 1974. The acquisition decision is a relatively rapid process:
in the case of COFRACIS's acquisition activity in the U.S., it
ranged from a few months up to a year. The process culminates in
a very tangible outcome : the purchase of a foreign company or
the abandonment of the project. In contrast, the formulation of
the acquisition strategy is a process extending over a much longer
time period and is much more difficult to identify precisely since
its outcome is not tangible. Only rarely do companies make an
explicit statement of their strategies for a particular moment
in time. It is, therefore, only possible to build statements of
strategy from an ex-post perspective, through the analysis of the
practical activity of the company. It is a question here of
having key documents which aid the analysis of the process which
led to the formulation of the strategy.

In the first section we shall outline the research methodology,
in the second section we shall construct a descriptive model of
each of the two processes. One of these models will show to what
extent the two processes are interdependent. In the third section
we shall propose a system which will enable top management in
companies to manage the decision making process.

Research Methodology

Data collection

Data collection was undertaken in two stages. In the first instance we made a compilation of all the acquisition files in the head
office of the parent company in Paris and of the subsidiary in
New-York. These files contained reports, memoranda, letters,
telex messages, and minutes of meetings, committees and telephone
discussions. The date, the participants, and the content of the
communications were carefully noted. General information on the
company was examined as well as external sources, although the
latter were rare and unsuitable for our purposes. In the second
stage a series of interviews was held with around thirty executives in COFRACIS. They lasted from two to fourteen hours each,
with an average of four hours. These interviews were fairly
unstructured once they were under way. Each participant had the
following questions put to him : when did you first come to hear
or read anything on the American acquisitions ? Through whom ?

Under what circumstances : discussion, meeting, committee, report?
He was then asked to try and reconstruct the sequence of events
as he lived them, insisting on dates, participants and contents.
Some managers had kept their diaries over the years and these
proved to be extremely useful ; others had their secretaries type
up a list of their trips detailing places, dates and contacts.

The treatment of data

The threatment of data was done in two stages. For each event,
defined as an interaction between two or more participants on a
specific date, a card of the following type was recorded :

Exhibit I

Example of the chronological cards

Date	Participants	Type of document	Content	Source of Information
X/X/X	A,B,C	Meeting of X/X/X	Initial study of acquisi- tion of Company Z	Interview Mr. Y

These cards were then classified in chronological order ; if any
contradictory elements appeared, priority was given to written
documents. The multiplicity of sources of data, the range of
written sources, and the number of interviews allowed the construction of a very reliable chronological record. Contradictory data
was extremely rare, since the managers who had difficulty recalling
exact dates, participants, or events did not hesitate to tell
the researcher.

The interpretation of the data

For each of the acquisitions analyzed, a model of the decision
process was built using the theoretical framework set up by Joseph
Bower (1).

Starting from Bower's model and the contribution of his followers
we set up the model which was to act as the starting point for
this research.

Following Ackerman (2) and Gilmour (3), we did not use the initiative, integrative and global phases of Bower's model but instead
the levels of management, which we defined in the following way :

the management of the foreign subsidiary, the headquarters general
management in Paris, and the President of the parent company. For
what Bower calls subprocesses, we used the following phases :

initiative : problem definition and making the initial proposal to
other levels in the organization

impetus : "The force that moves a project towards funding.... the
willingness (of the manager) to commit himself to sponsor a project... he puts his reputation for good judgment on the line"(4)

authorization(5) : the examination of the project by higher echelons of management with the possibility of approval or refusal.

The following exhibit gives a graphic illustration of the model
we set out to test :

Exhibit II

Model of the Process of Formulation of the Acquisition Strategy
tested at Cofracis.

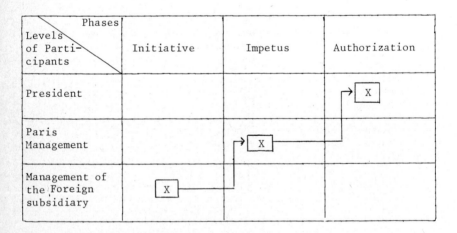

Levels of Participants \ Phases	Initiative	Impetus	Authorization
President			X
Paris Management		X	
Management of the Foreign subsidiary	X		

The boxes filled in with a cross (X) are the equivalents of Bower's
"primary determinant" ; the arrows show the flow of the decision-
making process: initiative comes from the management of the
foreign subsidiary,and is directed toward the general management
in Paris, which in turn acts as an impetus agent towards the President who evaluates the project. Our initial proposition was that
such a model would be an adequate description of both the formulation of the American acquisition strategy and of each decision
making process to buy.

How Strategic Decisions are made

The process of acquisition decisions

This process consists of a sequence of phases of initiative, impetus, and trial which repeats itself until the decision is actually finalized. The following exhibit illustrates this :

Exhibit III

Model of the Acquisition Decision Process at   Cofracis

Phases in the Process / Participants	Initiative Impetus	Trial	Initiative Impetus	Trial
Parent Company President		→ X		→ X
Parent Company Board and Management*				
Management of Foreign Subsidiary	X ⊢		→ X	

N Iterations

* To simplify the model, those two levels have not been included.

The initiative phase consists of problem definition and the issue of the first proposal, as well as subsequent proposals, which substantially modify the content of the first one, to other levels in the organization. This phase is almost always carried out by the management of the foreign subsidiary. It is started by an environmental stimulus, whether this takes the form of either a potential seller or a banking intermediary contacting the foreign subsidiary, or the subsidiary itself getting directly in touch with the potential acquiree.

The impetus phase consists of the involvement of one or more levels of participants to back up the content of a project. In sponsoring a project they are putting their reputation for good judgment on the line(6). This phase is usually carried out by the foreign subsidiary's management, by the Paris head office or by the board of directors. Only rarely was it taken over by the President of the parent company. When this happened, it was to make sure that an option approved by him at a trial phase was, in fact, implemented.

The trial phase is the last of the initiative-impetus-trial sequence. It consists of an assessment by the higher echelons of management with the possibilities that the project is accepted, rejected, or returned for further study. This trial phase introduces a major difference between our model and those of Bower and Ackerman. While their models have only one phase of definition, impetus and authorization, the latter only in Ackerman, our model can have many phases of initiative and impetus because the trial phase need not terminate the decision-making process, it can start a new iteration. There can be many such iterations, as many as the number of trial phases. This phase is the one most usually carried out by the President of the parent company, who holds the essential prerogative of authorization,refusal, or returning the project for further study. This phase is also administered by the Paris management and the board, sometimes alone, sometimes in liaison with the President. It is often after they have administered such a trial phase that the Paris management and board members find it useful to become authors or co-authors of an impetus phase directed to the President. The trial phase is never left up to the foreign subsidiary.

In the process of deciding over acquisitions, the flow of decisions is directed from the bottom upwards, the subsidiary taking the first initiative phase and the President controlling the final phase of the process : the trial phase. It works in the same way for each iteration :the subsidiary is the agent for initiative or impetus towards other levels of participants, while the head-office management and board of directors become agents of impetus towards the President.

The strategy-formulation process

The acquisition strategy is formulated concurrently with the acquisition-decision process. The strategy, either implicit or explicit, which came out of the previous process of acquisition decision serves as an input to the current one, the result of which will either confirm or modify that previous strategy. The strategy-formulation process, evolving over a long time period, therefore,embodies the processes of each separate acquisition decision.

The two processes are thus interdependent. The following exhibit illustrates this phenomenon :

Exhibit IV

Model of the Process of Formulation of the Acquisition Strategy at Cofracis.

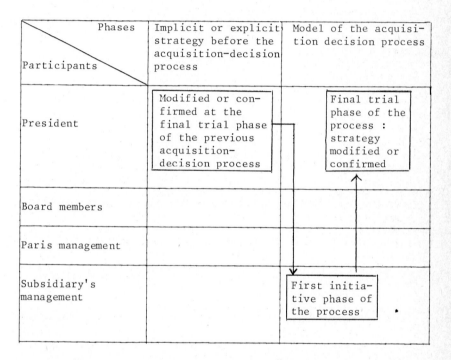

Participants ＼ Phases	Implicit or explicit strategy before the acquisition-decision process	Model of the acquisition decision process
President	Modified or confirmed at the final trial phase of the previous acquisition-decision process	Final trial phase of the process : strategy modified or confirmed
Board members		
Paris management		
Subsidiary's management		First initiative phase of the process

The decision-making flow goes first from the top to the bottom, since it is the parent company's President who gives the final authorization to a strategy when he agrees to the acquisition or he turns it down for reasons which are explained to the foreign subsidiary. The decision-making flow then runs from the bottom to the top when the subsidiary takes up the initiative with new acquisition studies, carrying them through to a conclusion in a varying number of phases of initiative and impetus. The final approval again rests with the President of the parent company.

Cofracis' American acquisition strategy was in fact modified in such a way on two occasions. The first time was in 1964 when a 17% shareholding in CUM was acquired, with first option for the outstanding shares. The financing was provided by the

subsidiary when beforehand the parent company had been expected to
do it by transferring capital from France to the U.S. As a result
of this, the financial element of strategy was changed to a local
source of financing. The second time, in 1969, concerned a central element in the strategy, the size of the initial risk, which
was made explicit at the time of the decision against making a
purchase offer for Industrial Cements (I.C.), a large U.S. manufacturer of specialty cements. When it came to the last trial
phase in the acquisition-decision process, the President of
Cofracis expressed his desire to start with a company smaller than
I.C., in order to be free to make other acquisitions later on.

The dynamics_of_the_decision processes to_buy_:

The dynamics can be comprehended in terms of two variables :

N_I : the number of iterations in each process

N_L : the number of levels of intermediary participants between
the subsidiary and the President.

These two variables are a measure of the degree of decentralization of the decision-making process : the smaller N_I and N_L, the
greater the degree of decentralization. A two by two comparison
of the acquisition decision processes showed that the degree of
decentralization was progressively on the increase during the
acquisition studies, except in the final one. Exhibit V shows
the evolution of this decentralization, measured in N_I and N_L,
for the following activities :

. the attempted acquisition of I.C. in 1969 which did not result
  in an offer of purchase
. contract of purchase of 51% of SCC in 1970
. purchase of 100% of SCC and ICI in 1971
. attempted purchase of Paulian in 1974. The owner did not
  accept the offer
. purchase of Gabbitt and CUM in 1974.

Exhibit V

Evolution of the Degree of Decentralization in the Acquisition
Decision Process

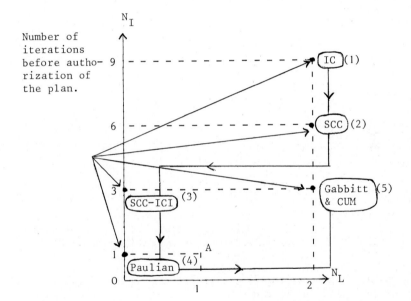

Number of
iterations
before autho-
rization of
the plan.

N_I

Number of inter-
mediary levels
of participants
between the sub-
sidiary and the
President

We arrive in this way at an objectively determined measure of the
degree of decentralization, instead of relying on the subjective
responses of numerous company executives replying to a multiple-
choice scaled questionnaire. The two dependent variables N_I and
N_L which serve as measures of the degree of decentralization are
a function of four explanatory variables :

D_L : the degree of learning about the decision-process to buy

D_C : the degree of confidence of the parent company's President
in the ability of his foreign subsidiary to absorb new
businesses

S_F : the degree of convergence between the subsidiary's proposals
and the parent company's strategy

P_E : the level of perceived environmental discontinuities.

This gives the following relationship :

$$g\ (N_I,\ N_L) = f\ (D_L,\ D_C,\ S_F,\ P_E)$$

The explanatory variables can be measured by the following proxy
variables :

N_D : the number of similar decisions previously undertaken measures the first two variables : D_L and D_C. The larger N_D, the
greater the degree of decentralization.

P_S : the percentage of the elements of the strategy proposed by
the subsidiary that fit that of the parent company measures
the third variable, S_F. The larger the percentage, the
greater the degree of decentralization.

P_E : the level of environmental discontinuities perceived by the
participants in the process is reflected on a binary scale
as being either greater or equal to the level perceived at
the time of the previous decision ; in the first case, it
diminishes the degree of decentralization and in the second,
it has no effect.

This gives the following relationship :

$$g\ (N_I,\ N_L) = f\ (N_D,\ P_S,\ P_E)$$

For COFRACIS, an analysis of the dynamics of the process of deciding on acquisitions revealed an increasing degree of decentrali-

zation. This increase can be explained by the continual growth
of N_D ; a growth up to the 100% level of P_S for the SCC acquisition and its subsequent stabilization at this level ; and zero
influence from P_E except in the Gabbitt-CUM acquisition, as a
result of which there was a decrease in the degree of decentralization.

There was clearly a learning effect in the process of deciding on
acquisitions. This learning phenomenon took place after the
strategy had been made explicit by the last trial phase in the
attempted acquisition of I.C. and during a period in which the
acquisition strategy had not been modified by further purchases
of U.S. firms. This instance illustrates the primacy of the formulation process of the strategy of acquisition, which permeates
and influences the acquisition process.

The evolution of the content of the trial phases

The frequent and repeated occurrence of the trial phases led the
author to make a detailed analysis in order to find out if similar causes lay behind each occurrence. These causes are grouped
into four categories :

- the need for additional information of a general nature on the
  seller or of a more specific nature such as the quality of the
  seller's management team or its tax position. Such information
  could be obtained from the subsidiary, the Paris management,
  or the board.

- the need to delay the decision for reasons of tax advantages,
  better timing in terms of the parent company's strategy, or to
  fit in with the meetings of the parent company's board.

- the need to test the motivation of the subsidiary's management.
  The President may need to probe the strength of the subsidiary's
  commitment to a project for which it has provided the initiative and impetus. This is one of several ways to assess a
  project and its chances of success.

- the need to control the decision-making process for one or more
  of the following several reasons :

  . information or directive given by the President to the
    subsidiary of a stock market, fiscal, or strategic nature
    (percentage of ownership, size of first acquisition)
  . evaluation of the contents of the subsidiary's recommenda-
    tion.

The following exhibit demonstrates the evolution of the frequency
of these various causes of the trial phases for the acquisition-
decision processes which took place between 1964 and 1974.

The analysis of this table becomes more significant if it is contrasted with Exhibit V which shows the development of the degree
of decentralization in the process. The following observations
can be made :

The need to control the decision process is the most frequent
motivation, almost always being present in the administration of
a trial phase : a minimum of two-thirds but practically always
in 100% of these phases.

The need to test the commitment of the subsidiary's management
varies proportionally to the number of trial phase : this need
always accounts for one-third of the number of trial phases.

The two above-mentioned causes vary in direct relation to the
total number of trial phases. This does not hold true for the two
other motivations.

The need for additional information does not have as clear an
evolution as the two other motivations of the trial phases.

Only if the first and last operations (CUM and Gabbitt-CUM) are
excluded, can the growth of the need for additional information
be seen to rise from one-third to two-thirds of the number of
trial phase. Need for additional information is correlated to
the degree of decentralization, which increases during the whole
period, except for the last acquisition decision.

The need to delay varies inversely with the degree of decentralization but much more rapidly. It is very high for I.C. (5 times),
a project which was rejected : occurs only once for the next
acquisition and is non-existent thereafter.

These findings obviously do not have statistical validity. If
they did, however, they would have important implications : the
appearance or absence of certain motivations can give indications
as to whether or not a project is likely to be accepted. Appropriate action can be taken as a result : abandonning the project,
if it is seen to be hopeless, or modifying it in such a way that
it can then be adopted.

Exhibit VI : Summary Presentation of the Evolution of Trial Phases

Acquisition	Date	N° of trial phases	Administrat. of the trial phase	Reasons motivating the administration of a trial phase							
				Need for further informat.	%	Need to delay the decision	%	Need to test subsidiary's motivat.	%	Need to control the dec. process	%
17% of CUM	17/11/64 to 19/3/65	3	President 1 1/2 Paris Board 1 1/2	2	2/3			1	1/3	3	100
IC	19/1/69 to 1/9/69	9	Presid.4 1/2 Par.B. 3 1/2 Manag. 1	3	1/3	5		3	1/3	7	7/9
SCC	17/4/70 to 22/7/70	6	Presid.4 Par.B. 1/2 Manag. 1 1/2	3	1/2	1		2	1/3	4	2/3
100% of SCC, ICI and attempt with CUM	25/10/70 to 12/4/71	3	Presid.3	2	2/3			1	1/3	3	100
Attempt with Paulian	27/4/74 to 13/7/74	1	Presid.1/2 Par.B. 1/2							1	100
Gabbitt and CUM	9/8/74 to 27/10/74	3	Presid.1 1/3 Par.B. 5/6 Managem. 5/6	1	1/3			1	1/3	3	100

How to Manage the Strategic Decision-Making Process

Managing the process of strategy formulation

These recommendations are drawn from the measurement of the degree
of decentralization and are mainly directed to the parent company's
President. A major element of the strategy of acquisition in the
U.S., that of the size of the first acquisition and the progres-
sion of risk which the COFRACIS President was willing to undertake,
was formulated through the refusal to make a purchase offer for
I.C. in September 1969. The I.C. project was the most centralized
process, requiring the greatest number of iterations and of participants, and was the most expensive since it used up the most top
management time, that rarest company resource of all. The project
was not approved after eight months of work during which the subsidiary undertook initiative and impetus phases with an ever
increasing frequency. The cost of the study was high both in
terms of management time and in terms of unfulfilled expectations.
If the management of the foreign subsidiary had not been so dynamic and committed to the prospect of making U.S. acquisitions,
it would have given much less energy to the task or even have
dropped it altogether. This event would have involved a further
opportunity cost and the eventual replacement of the New-York
management. The total cost of formulating the U.S. strategy was
thus so high that it becomes worthwhile to consider how it might
be reduced in similar situations in the future, either for COFRA-
CIS or other multinational companies.

The cost of the decision is measured in terms of the number of
iterations (N_I) and the level of participants between the subsidiary and the President (N_L). These two variables are also used
to measure the degree of decentralization. To reduce the cost
of the decision it is therefore necessary to increase the degree
of decentralization. To do this one must consider the four independent variables which determine N_I and N_L. Of these four, two
cannot be   ~trolled :

D_L : the level of learning about the decision making process,
      measured by N_D the number of previous similar decisions.

P_E : the level of perception of environmental discontinuities.

On the other hand, worthwhile returns can be obtained from S_F :
the convergence between the subsidiary's plan and the parent
company's strategy, measured by P_S, the percentage of the elements
in the plan of the subsidiary which are in line with the parent
company's strategy. It is in this area that our main recommendation lies. We advise :

1. Treat explicitly the formulation of parent's and subsidiary's strategies and the acquisition decision as three distinct problems instead of letting the results of the acquisition decision implicitly determine the strategies without facing the problem of the formulation of these strategies.

2. Consider the three problems at the same point in time in order to determine what are the strategic implications of the components of the acquisition decision - and vice versa. The prescriptive model of exhibit VII shows this recommended procedure in graphic form. It should be compared and contrasted with Exhibit IV.

To implement these recommendations it will still be necessary to prepare a project analyzing the value of the potential acquiree ; furthermore, a statement of the acquisition strategy must be established based on the following conceptual framework :

- The product-market scope considered : should it be similar or different to that of the parent company ;

- The acquisition : is it needed urgently because of a limited number of similar purchase opportunities and strong competition from other buyers or, on the other hand, can it wait until a detailed study has been made which might result in an eventual decision not to proceed ;

- Is one looking for an opportunity to acquire a new technology ;

- Kind of acquisition - production and/or sales ;

- A holding of 100%, a joint venture or a minority holding ;

- Licensing agreements and/or management contracts ;

- Size of the acquisition ;

- Expansion plans ;

- Kind of management to be gained out of the acquisition or kind of management available to replace that of the company under consideration ;

- Mode of financing.

Each of the above items will have to be considered in so far as it is :

- clear, understood, and accepted by all participants

- left ambiguous until the time comes in the near or distant
  future when it needs to be clarified

- left ambiguous and that it is better that it should stay so
  during the ongoing process of the acquisition decision.

This method of approach to be used to manage the two processes
simultaneously will be most effective if it is used first by the
foreign subsidiary at the time of its first phases of initiative
and impetus towards the other levels of participants. The iterations will then have the two documents drawn up by the subsidiary
as a base : the dossier on the seller and the explicit statement
on the acquisition strategy being pursued. In case the President
is not interested in such a system, this need not prevent each
participant, regardless of level, from using the conceptual framework in approaching the acquisition decision. This will allow
each participant to define more closely certain delicate points
in the acquisition proposal and, in strategic terms, to have a
better understanding of the reactions of other participants. The
foreign subsidiary, just as much as the President and his staff,
can engage in this exercise independently. The system will, however, always be more effective if it operates with the agreement
of all participants, as we have recommended. It does not affect
the degree of the President's control over the process : he remains the primary administrator of the trial phases. The final
approval remains as his exclusive prerogative. The option is
always open to him to leave certain elements of the strategy
ambiguous in order to motivate the subsidiary for new initiatives.
There is no question of making this strategy public beyond the
few managers involved in the process : the participants remain the
same throughout. The use of this system allows them to make
explicit any elements of strategy which remain ambiguous. These
elements might well be made explicit in any case, without the
recommended system, but only as a result of an informal process
requiring a larger number of iterations which would, therefore,
be longer, more of a risk, and more expensive. This informal process is a characteristic of present practice while we advocate a
management of this process.

Our recommendation results in the simultaneous study of a foreign
acquisition and its long term implications for the acquisition
strategy. It allows us to master two decision making processes
at the same time instead of leaving the more important of the two
in terms of the long-term health of the firm, the process of strategy formulation, to be the implicit result of a short term decision. The proposed system seeks to resolve, at least partially,
the paradox of general management in companies whose decisions in
the area of long term strategic options are often the result of
a series of discrete short-term decisions. It is probable that
the system could also be applied to several top-management problems
other than solely to cases of overseas acquisition strategy.

Exhibit VII : A Prescriptive Model for the Explicit and Simultaneous Formulation of Group Strategy, Foreign Subsidiary's Strategy and Acquisition Decisions.

Acquisition (or expansion) decision

Phases / Level of participant	Initiative	Impetus	Trial
President			X
Management of foreign+ subsidiary	X	X	
Date	1/1/1977	1/2/1977	1/3/1977
Content	Proposal for acquisition	We put our judgment on the line	Approval, refusal or return for further study

Formulation of the strategy of the foreign subsidiary

	Initiative	Impetus	Trial
President			X
Management of foreign subsidiary	X	X	
Date	1/1/1977	1/2/1977	1/3/1977
Content	Proposal for formulation of ambiguous element of existing strategy	Commitment to formulation	Approval,refusal or delay of proposed element of strategy

Formulation of group strategy

	Initiative	Impetus	Trial
President			X
Group Management	X	X	
Dates	1/1/1977	1/2/1977	1/3/1977
Content	Impact on group strategy	Commitment on impact	Approval,refusal or delay of new element of international strategy.

+ or international vice-president if no subsidiary exists in the country concerned

The last independent variable bearing on the degree of decentralization is D_C : the level of the President's confidence in the ability of the foreign subsidiary's management to take on new business ; this variable is measured by N_D, the number of previous similar decisions already taken. D_C is difficult to control : nothing is more relevant than a team's successful track record on a type of project in order to judge the players capable of a repeat performance. That need for experience, however, makes the first step difficult. For in this situation, the President can analyze the abilities required to take over a new company and check whether or not his foreign management has those abilities which he has identified. Such an analysis is made very risky by the President's lack of knowledge of the potential acquisition. Therefore, both the track record and the analysis of the match between required and available competence are unsatisfactory. As the former is easier to grasp there is no apparent reason to advocate a change of current practice. The only independent variable which can be controlled to improve the two processes is therefore P_S: the percentage of the elements of the strategy proposed by the subsidiary that fit that of the parent.

Managing the process of the acquisition decision

The system already proposed allows a better management of the three processes and consequently of the acquisition decision. The system which follows is concerned only with improving the efficiency of the latter by an analysis of the trial phases and their motivations (Exhibit VI). No statistical study is available for extending the results of this exhibit. Nonetheless the conclusions they enable one to draw seem to be logical. It seems to be the rule that the President seeks to control the process and to test the subsidiary management's motivation in a constant way. Just as it seems to be logical that the need to delay is greater when the strategic choices have not been formulated or previously put into practice. Also, the greater the President's confidence in the subsidiary, the more his requirements focus on information needs. A high frequency of delay and weak information needs can therefore be easily considered by the subsidiary as a pessimistic indication of a proposal's likelihood of acceptance. Conversely, a lower frequency of delay and higher information needs will be interpreted optimistically and quickly confirmed by the project's acceptance. An analysis of the causes of the trial phase will permit the subsidiary to modify the contents of its projects or to adjust the timing of their presentation to the other levels of participants in order to reduce the number of iterations and consequently to increase the efficiency of the process. It is probable that this classification of the different phases of initiative, impetus, and trial, so far as their causes are concerned, will be more difficult for the participants than the formulation of a statement of strategy.

Conclusion

We have seen that foreign acquisition decisions start on the initiative of the foreign subsidiary and are finalized after a series
of iterations of phases of initiative, impetus, and trial, the
last of which, administered by the President, constitutes the clo-
sing of the process. The formulation of the acquisition strategy
arises implicitly from the process of each acquisition decision ;
the initial input to the latter is the implicit strategy that
resulted from the last trial phase of the preceeding acquisition
decision. This practice certainly exists for other types of
strategic decision making such as diversification, capital investment, or the acquisition/sale of a company by the group. Since
the long term options are very difficult to grasp, there is a
strong temptation for management to focus on short term decisions.
However, these decisions themselves have strategic implications
which must be taken into account. In addition, the setting up
of a strategy statement, regularly updated, allows a better orientation for all participants to manage the short-term decisions.
It is for this reason that it is necessary to treat the processes
of strategic decisions and of their strategy formulation together
according to the prescriptive model previously described. This
simultaneous treatment will allow top management to move from the
practice to the management of the strategic decision-making
process. A higher level of efficiency of decisions will be
reached and the firm's competitive advange will be strengthened.

References

(1) Joseph Bower, <u>Managing the Resource Allocation Process</u>,
     Division of Research, Graduate School of Business Administra-
     tion, Harvard University, Boston, Mass. 1970.

(2) Robert Ackerman, "The influence of integration and diversity
     on the investment process", <u>Administrative Science Quarterly</u>
     December 1970, p. 341-351.

(3) Stuart Gilmour "The divestment decision process", unpublished
     doctoral dissertation, Harvard Business School, 1973, Univer-
     sity Microfilm n° 73-15-917, (Ann Arbor, Mich. 1973)

(4) Bower, <u>op cit</u>, p. 68.

(5) This expression comes from Ackerman, <u>op cit</u>.

(6) This confirms the conclusions reached by Joseph L. Bower,
     <u>op. cit</u>., p. 68.

TRANSFERS OF TECHNOLOGY WITHIN THE MULTINATIONAL ENTERPRISE

Georges P. Leroy

Associate Professor.
Faculty of Management, McGill University

Research in the 1960's has brought forward the link between technology and the multinational enterprise to the point that as Keith Pavitt remarked, it is very difficult to dissociate one from the other. The U.S. multinationals have been found to be most active in industries such as transportation, electrical machinery, chemicals, and machinery, other than electrical. These are the top four in terms of research and development intensity[1]. These four industries accounted in 1970 for 2/3 of U.S. manufactured exports and 58% of U.S. direct investments in manufacturing[2]. By comparison, Japan's foreign direct investment in these four industries accounted for only 31% of its total, while textile, lumber pulp, steel, and non ferrous metals represent 56% of Japanese investment. These are clearly industries that are not leaders in technological development. Their success indicates that firms that are capable of developing internationally are not necessarily in high technology industries, but they have to be leaders in their own fields, and they have probably been able to assume leadership particularly in high technology industries.

Since the end of the 1960's the emphasis in MNE research has turned from one focusing on their innovative capacity and the challenge this represented, to one concerned with their role as an agent of development. This concern was raised in a number of developed countries such as Canada, as well as developing countries in Latin America and Asia. It led to a number of studies on (1) gaps in technology by the OECD, (2) the choice and source of technology by the United States, and (3) the impact of the MNE on a variety of host country policies[3].

This research was funded by the Samuel Bronfman Foundation, and by a grant from the Ecole des Hautes Etudes Commerciales in Montreal.

Main issues in technology transfer

Three central issues have emerged regarding the ability of the MNE to foster host country development.

The first issue concerns the adequacy of the technology transferred. The argument is that a number of products are too sophisticated for the stage of development the country is in, leading to excessive price, and maintenance problems.[4] Many firms have found that some degree of adaptation to the host country environment was desirable, but it is argued that product modification may not be sufficient, rather the product should be re-designed. The MNE has three basic product choices : a) sell the same, or a similar product internationally ; b) sell a product it sold at some earlier stage of development ; c) sell an appropriate product. This last choice has sometimes been referred to as intermediate technology.

The technology selection decision should be made in view of one or several goals wanted by the host government : import substitution or export promotion to relieve a balance of payments deficit ; the creation of additional jobs; or, the improvement of living standards.

Some developing countries rather than choosing an intermediate technology want the most modern one even it means higher costs. The choice is based on their desire to be competitive internationally by turning out up-to-date, quality products. Examples of this sort are the packaging of integrated circuits in South-East Asia.[5]

The second issue related to the efficiency of the MNE in the transfer process. This efficiency can be defined in terms of the selection of the appropriate mode of transfer and the rate at which the MNE transfers the innovation in a variety of markets. The MNE is able to choose among alternative transfers such as export, or direct investment ; but it is increasingly pressed to accept the involvement of a third party in licensing or joint ventures or the setting of turnkey operations.

The third issue concerns the conditions under which the host country gets access to the technology. The sale of technology is a complex transaction by the sheer or true nature of the "product" or package involved. The complexity of the transfer within the MNE has been studied only recently.[6] The cost of this package is difficult to assess as it includes not only payments for the right to use the patents and know-how, but also for a number of technical assistance services. The contract may limit the responsibility of the MNE to provide drawings or it may go as far as guarantee the quality of the output to the host country entity.

In this paper we present a number of findings related to the second issue, the efficiency of the transfer process from the managerial point of view. Particular attention was paid to the speed and the pattern of transfer within the MNE, as well as the characteristics that influenced them. No attempt is made to relate it to the host country policies, as such a study would have required work in numerous countries.

The nature of technology transfer

Technology can be viewed as an input to the production process. It concerns "knowledge" about physical relationships systematically applied to useful purposes.[7] It encompasses not only knowledge of the process or product patent, but also various complementary aspects of know-how necessary in order to start production. Technology can also be viewed in a broader context as including some "hardware" aspects (e.g. blueprints of plants, machinery, and equipment) ; and some "software" aspects (e.g. managerial techniques).

The nature of the technology package being transferred should be adapted to the needs of the recipient firm thus making the analysis amenable to a matter of case study. This approach has been used recently by Behrman and Wallender in their interesting analysis of a number of transfer of production technology within multinational enterprises.[8]

In our analysis we use the later and broader definition of technology. Looking at the diffusion of product innovations we are concerned by the inter-country diffusion of technology on the firm's (or producer's) side. This transfer may involve both hardware and software aspects as it is depicted in the table below :

Table 1 : Nature of Technology Transfer

- Production techniques (blueprints, machinery, equipments)	hardware transfer
- Marketing techniques (sales, distribution,pricing,promotion)	software transfer
- Finance techniques	software transfer
- Personnel techniques	software transfer
- General management	software transfer

This inter-country diffusion of technology can take a variety of alternative paths that correspond to particular multinational product strategies implemented by the firm. We showed in an

earlier study that close to twenty paths were used indicating the
ability of firms to select a proper strategy among the feasible
set. However, more than half of the strategies, 58%, correspon-
ded to three paths.[9] These three paths described below relate to
the introduction of a product developed in the parent country of
the firm, and its transfer to one of the host countries.

1) Export only from the parent country where the product was developed and initially marketed. This path corresponds to multinational product strategy no. 7. (abbreviated MPS 7).

2) Export from the parent country followed by manufacturing in the
   host country where the product is in demand.(abbreviated MPS 1)

3) Direct manufacturing in the customer's host country, by-passing
   the export stage (abbreviated MPS 8).

Other paths implemented for products developed in the parent
country include for example export from a third country, or imports into the innovating country as the international product
cycle model suggests. Furthermore, we identified a number of
paths corresponding to products developed in one of the host countries.

Framework of the study

Our objective is to look at a number of characteristics of the
international transfer process within the MNE. A number of studies have looked at the speed of inter-country diffusion of
process innovations. One study by Georges Ray reported on the
introduction of ten new processes showed not only the time lag of
each country behind the pioneer country, but also the years required to produce a given percentage of an industry output with the
new techniques.[10] But Ray was not concerned with the agent doing
the transfer and therefore, it is not possible to distinguish the
cases where this international diffusion occured within an MNE
or between independent firms. He found that the three factors
that appeared to have the most significant influence on diffusion:
(1) the advantages of the new as compared with the existing "traditional" process in terms of overall profitability, (2) the attitude of management to the adoption of the new technique and (3)
the access to capital. He concluded that "the least tangible
factor is, however, likely to have the greatest impact on the
application of any new technique – the attitude of management".
We may expect the MNE to be a leader in the diffusion process,
although that is likely to depend on particular management policies of the firm.

A later study by John Tilton on the diffusion of technology in

semi-conductors sheds some light on firm behavior. He looked at
how a number of U.S. firms entered that industry and transferred
their technology to various European countries and to Japan[12].

One of his main findings relates to the diffusion to Europe. He
observed that in the 1950's European firms committed considerable
resources to be leaders in the diffusion of semi-conductors in
Europe. However, during the 1960's they were late in using more
recent silicon and planar techniques and they lost a sizeable
segment of the market to new American subsidiaries in Europe.
Tilton argued that new foreign subsidiaries have an edge over
local firms because of greater access to the state of the art of
technology.

It appeared from the above studies that the role of MNE was particularly important in certain industries, but we learned little
about how MNE introduced their products in a variety of markets.
Therefore, in this research rather than focus on the transfer from
country A to B (which would be only one of the transfers acted
upon for a particular product) we decided to look at the sequence
of introductions of a particular product in different countries.
This gives a better perspective as to how the firm views international product transfers (which we called multinational product
strategies). The observed pattern that we call a strategy was
not always viewed as such by managers, thus raising the question
of organization and attitude of management of those firms. We
looked upon the pattern of innovation-diffusion as being influenced by various characteristics related to the product characteristics, the country where it was introduced, and the firm policies.

Research methodology and data base

This study of the characteristics that affected the pattern of
innovation-diffusion was conducted in five MNEs coming from a
variety of industries from electronics to farm machinery. In
each firm a number of products were selected in order to analyze
in detail the pattern and speed of product transfers internationally throughout the product's life. These products were selected on the basis that they represented a new product for the firm,
that they had gone through the various product life stages, and
that they covered the various product lines of the firm. In total
52 products were analyzed. This selection is arbitrary in view
of the fact that the firms manufactured several thousand products.
Thus our study is exploratory in nature, as it tries to relate
the product strategy selected to a number of characteristics that
influenced manager's choice.

The data base consisted of a product questionnaire administered
by personal interviews to product managers or international product coordinators of the five firms. This data was collected as
part of a larger study at the product line level[13]. For those 52
products the speed of diffusion across countries is expressed in
market lags and production lags between the country of initial
marketing and the country in which the product is eventually introduced. The market lag for a given product introduced in country X
is defined as the time lag between its initial introduction in
the parent country of the firm and its introduction in country Y.
Similarly, production lag is defined as the time lag between the
initial production in the country of origin, and the start of
production in country Y. A product introduced in several host
countries is likely to show different lags.

Results of the research

The findings of the study categorized by firms appear quite intri-
guing. Table 2 shows that the average market lag for the electronics firms is 1/10 that of the aluminium manufacturer and 1/6
that of the toiletries manufacturer. One is tempted to explain
these lags by suggesting that the electronics industry is a dynamic one, with a high rate of innovation while the other firms
belong to more traditional industries. The nature and the structure of the industry no doubt plays a role in explaining the
differences. An adequate explanation must incorporate other factors besides the industry. We have tried to capture some of those
considerations in looking at three types of characteristics,
product, country and firm characteristics, and their impact on
product innovation diffusion.

1. Product characteristics

It was felt that the type of product, whether a consumer or industrial good, could account for some of the differences in the beha-
vor observed above. The product selection contained 12 consumer
products having an average market lag of 33.7 months, in contrast
to only 10.1 months for the 40 industrial products (see Table 3).
This marked difference is to some extent due to the fact that
consumer goods are in general sensitive to cultural variables and
usually require some modifications.

This "consumer goods vs industrial goods" categorization of products appears to affect not only the speed of diffusion, but also
its pattern. One can see from Table 4 that consumer products have
a higher likelihood to be introduced internationally by direct
manufacturing close to the market (MPS 8). This probably means
that product modifications are often best determined and implemented in close contact with customers.

Table 2 : Market lags and production lags by firm for the 52 selected products

Type of operations of the firm	Electronics firm (Hewlett-Packard)	Agricultural machinery (Massey-Ferguson)	Aluminium manufacturer (Alcan Aluminium)	Visual communication equipment manufacturer (Dymo Ind.)	Toiletries and personal manufacturer (Gillette Co)
Average market lag of the firm (in months)	4.7	21.7	55.8	5.0	30.1
Average production lag of the firm (in months)	36.0	64.0	62.0	6.0	50.0

Source : Survey data compiled by the author.

Note :   The average lag of the firm represents the lag between the country where the product was initially introduced and any other country over all the products selected in this firm and all the countries it was diffused to. Lags are expressed in months.

Table 3 : The type of product as it related to the speed of
diffusion (market lags)

CONSUMER PRODUCTS	Total market lag for all countries (in months)	Number of observations	Average market lag (in months)
Alcan	590	10	59
Dymo	60	8	7.5
Gillette	362	12	30.2
Total	1.012	30	33.7 (=1.012/30)
INDUSTRIAL PRODUCTS			
Hewlett-Packard	367	78	4.7
Massey-Perguson	826	38	21.7
Alcan	24	1	24
Dymo	39	7	5.6
Total	1.256	124	10.1 (=1,256/124)

Source : Survey data compiled by the author

Note : In total 156 (30 + 124) observations were gathered from
the 52 products. On average each product was diffused in three
"countries". The "countries" we looked at are USA, Canada, Europe,
Japan, Latin America. For further details see Table 7.

One could also hypothesize that the choice of a pattern of diffusion in a particular country is affected by the degree of novelty
of the product as perceived by the firm.   It takes a smaller risk
of failure in foreign markets if it has already marketed a similar
product or product line at home.

We measured the novelty of the product of the firm along two
dimensions : the performance novelty and the technological novelty.
A product may be a technological novelty for the firm and yet
represent a smaller degree of novelty in terms of performance
relative to the previous products marketed by the firm.   For example shifting from carbon to stainless steel blades required a
major technological change but was not perceived by managers as
involving a big change in performance.   The figures on table 5
suggest that the degree of novelty of performance has a positive
influence on the market lag in product diffusion.   The average
market lag for new products is 18.4 months while it is only 2.7
months for products with minor modifications in terms of performance relative to the previous product the firm was marketing.

In exploring the variation in market lags further, a similar
question was asked regarding technological novelty of the product,
as this could have been a delaying factor from the manufacturer's
point of view.   Technological novelty refers to the degree of new-
ness inherent to the production process, leading the firm to delay
entry into international markets until it feels the reliability
of the product has been tested in the market place.

Table 5, however, indicates that the degree of technological
novelty does not appear to be an obstacle to rapid international
diffusion of products. Some firms pointed out that six months were
sufficient to make any changes if necessary, therefore technological novelty did not act as a constraint.   This result,however,
is influenced by the fact that half of the observations classified
as "totally new" in terms of technological novelty come from the
electronics firm with the fastest diffusion rate. Some additional
factors, such as the perceived attributes of the innovation (compa-
tibility, complexity, triability) as well as the easiness in
communicating the key product features may also have a bearing on
the diffusion, but they were not incorporated in this study.

The technological novelty of the product can also have an effect
on the pattern of innovation-diffusion selected by the manager.
The hypothesis is that rather than delaying the entry of its product, in international markets up until such time as the market can
support production, the manager may export before producing abroad
or export instead of producing close to the market. Using data on
diffusion from the U.S. or Canada to Europe (see Table 6), we can
observe that managers prefer to use a strategy of diffusion such
as export only (i.e. MPS 7) or export followed by production

Table 4 : The type of product and product strategy implemented

| Product strategy | Type of product | | Proportion of consumer products (1)/(1)+(2) |
	Consumer (1)	Industrial (2)	
A) Diffusion from U.S./Canada to Europe			
Strategy MPS7 (export only)	0	17	0.0
Strategy MPS1 (export & invest)	3	7	.3
Strategy MPS8 (direct invest)	4	1	0.8
B) Diffusion from the U.S./ Canada to Japan			
Strategy MPS7 (export only)	2	16	.1
Strategy MPS1 (export & invest)	2	7	.2
Strategy MPS8 (direct invest)	1	0	1.0
C) Diffusion from any country to any other			
Strategy MPS7 (export only)	5	65	.1
Strategy MPS1 (export & invest)	7	14	.3
Strategy MPS8 (direct invest)	8	2	.8

Source : Survey data compiled by the author.

Note : Numbers in the body of the table correspond to the number of times a particular product strategy was observed.

Table 5 : Market lags related to the degree of novelty of the product.

A) Degree of novelty of performance

	Totally new	Major modifications	Minor modifications
Average market lags (in months)	18.4	16.8	2.7

B) Degree of technological novelty

	Totally new	Major modifications	Minor modifications
Average market lags (in months)	12	13.4	25

Source : Survey data compiled by the author.

Note : Numbers in the table correspond to the average of the market lags obtained for the 52 products analyzed.

abroad (i.e. MPS 1), rather than direct production (i.e. MPS 8).
Exporting appears to be viewed as a way to develop the market and
reduce uncertainty.

2. *Country characteristics*

The international strategy of the firm in terms of production and
marketing is closely related to the specificities of the market.
The pattern of demand is affected by numerous factors : economic
ones such as the stage of economic development, industry conditions such as competition, cultural aspects such as consumer
attitudes, and legal patterns such as local product standards.

In response to the anticipated demand pattern the firm will decide
which countries to enter and how. The firm faces the dilemma of
whether to adapt to or to standardize its approach in the various
markets.

We can see from Table 7 that market lags that expressed the speed
of entry into various countries are generally quite short. The
average lag is 14.6 months, or just over a year.

Two firms stand out as having very short market lags, Hewlett-
Pakcard and Dymo Industries. The electronics products are in
general quite standardized and it appears to be a characteristics
of this high technology industry to have rapid diffusion of its
products. Tilton reported that the lags for a number of semi-
conductors innovations ranged from one to three years. Our findings may indicate a trend toward faster diffusion among developed countries than we observed in the late 60's. The slower diffusion of products for Alcan is an exception to the trend.

There are, however, important differences among countries. In
the electronics field we found the smallest spread of all, with
market lags ranging from 1.6 months to 7 months, while in farm
machinery market lags range from 24 to 68 months.[16]

We looked at the introduction of products in important markets of
the world, the European countries and Japan. Those countries
follow rapidly the innovating country. When we compared our findings with those reported by Hufbauer for synthetic rubber and
man-made fibers, and the diffusion of 10 new processes reported
by Georges Ray, we observed even faster diffusion than they did[17].
This tendency reflects probably one of the strength of the multinationals, that is their ability to organize fast international
diffusion of products.

We observe that the diffusion is slower in Latin America and Australia as those markets lag in terms of development behind Europe
and Japan.

Table 6 : Novelty of the product as it relates to the product strategy implemented (Diffusion from the U.S. or Canada to Europe).

A) Degree of novelty of performance

	Totally new		Major modifications		Minor modifications
$R = \dfrac{MPS\ 8}{MPS\ 1\ +\ MPS\ 7}$	1/9	<	1/3	>	0

B) Degree of technological novelty

$R = \dfrac{MPS\ 8}{MPS\ 1\ +\ MPS\ 7}$	1/12	<	1/8	<	3/7

Source : Survey data compiled by the author

Note   : Figures in the table correspond to the frequency of implementation of the product strategies. The ratio R relates to the number of observations corresponding to strategy MPS 8 (direct investment), relative to the number of observations corresponding to both strategies MPS 1 (export + investment) and MPS 7 (export only).

Table 7 : Market lags by firm and by country (in months)

Firm	USA	Cana-da	Euro-pe	Japan	Latin America	Average lag by firm	USA	Cana-da	Euro-pe	Japan	Latin America	Average lag by firm	Total lag by firm
Hewlett-Packard	-	3.5	6.1	7	1.6	4.9	2	3.9	0	3.5	4.2	3.3	4.7
Massey-Ferguson	0	-	24	42 (Aus-tralia)	68	47.2	11.5	5	0	11.8 (Aus-tralia)	28.6	14.1	21.7
Alcan Aluminium	60	-	51	39	94	55.1	0	24	94	-	-	59	55.8
Dymo Industries	-	0	5	0	6	4.6	5	5	0	8	6	6	5
Gillette	-	7	23	56.6	34.6	30.1	-	5	-	-	6		30.1
Average Market Lags (weighted)	60	4.1	14.5	17.2	19.7	15.8	8.3	6	94	9	20.6	12.2	14.6

Note : The lags are average lags for the firm or the country over the various products. Market lag is the time lag (in months) between the first introduction and the product in one country (country X) and the introduction in another (country Y). The "countries" at the top of the table are Y countries, where the product was diffused to "_" means not applicable as by definition there is no lag for the country of initial introduction. The blank space for Gillette indicates that no corresponding observation was selected.

The competitive forces appeared to have some influence on the
intercountry diffusion. In a few cases it was found that competi-
tition was keener in Europe. The product was not only developed
to suit the European standards, but introduced in Europe first.
In general, one would hypothesize that as the intensity of competition facing a product is stronger, the firm will act faster, thus
resulting in shorter market lags. Table 8 presents the data for
the fifty two products using manager's own appraisal of the general (worldwide) intensity of competition. Three firms, Hewlett-
Packard, Massey-Ferguson and Alcan appear to agree fairly closely
with the hypothesis. In view of the fact that few cases fell in
the "low intensity of competition" category, our interpretation of
the data has been complemented by interviews that appeared to
confirm the hypothesis.

For Hewlett-Packard one would have expected a market lag greater
than 3.3 whenever there is low competition but as we shall see
below another factor overrides the competition effect.

Competition not only affects market lags, but also the particular
path of diffusion selected. Our expectation is that the greater
the competitive situation, the more likely the firm is to produce
close to the market. From a marketing view point, which includes
feedback, visibility and market aspects, this would appear to be
a desirable state. The data in Table 9 confirm that the "export
only" strategy is preferred when competition is low.

In fact, the views that were expressed in the interviews are very
much along the lines that extremely competitive activity in a
market represents an opportunity for profits as opposed to a
threat of losses. Whereas a classic analysis would suggest no
commitment of investment resources in a competitive market before
a market share has been achieved, the firms here in fact tended
to do the opposite. They appear to meet the competition head on.

Firm characteristics

A study of the pattern of innovation diffusion implemented by a
few firms for a selection of their products leads not only to a
grasp of some of the variables that are critical for success in
one industry (i.e. for one product), or in a given country, it
also permits to look at the behavior of the MNE as the actor for
such transfer. An MNE may not be the first to commercialize a
product, but it may be the first to invade a number of markets and
capture a significant share in those countries. For example we
may contrast the strategies of Honda, Renault, and General Motors
in the sub-compact cars segment of the market. Renault waited
3 years to introduce the Renault 5 to the U.S., while Honda introduced the Honda Civic practically simultaneously in both Japan and

Table 8 : Market lags related to the intensity of competition.

		Average market lags (in months)				
		Hewlett-Packard	Massey-Ferguson	Alcan Alum.	Dymo Ind.	Gillette
Intensity of competition for this product	high	3.5	11.6^{x}	33.8	9	40
	med.	10.5	20.1	36	6	10
	low	3.3	-	78	2.5	0

Source : Survey data compiled by the author.

Note   : Lags are expressed in months
         x excludes one implement which had a very high lag

Table 9 : Competitive situation as it relates to the product
strategy selected

	Intensity of competition		
	High	Medium	Low
a) Diffusion from the U.S./Canada to Europe			
Strategy MPS 7 (export only)	1	4	12
Strategy MPS 1 (export & invest)	5	1	4
Strategy MPS 8 (direct invest)	2	1	1
Sub-total	8	6	17
Frequency of MPS 7	1/8=.12	4/6=.66	12/17=.70
b) Diffusion from the U.S./Canada to Japan			
Strategy MPS 7 (export only)	3	3	12
Strategy MPS 1 (export & invest)	3	1	5
Strategy MPS 8 (direct invest)	1	0	0
Sub-total	7	4	17
Frequency of MPS 7	3/7=.23	3/4=.75	12/17=.70

Source : Survey data compiled by the author.

Note   : Numbers in the body of the table refer to the number of
        observations falling in that category.

the U.S., and General Motors put the Chevette on the U.S.
market (after developing it in Brazil and Europe) with the result
that Honda started first on the U.S. market, two years ahead of
its competitors. As stressed by Robertson :

"marketing strategies can guide and control to a considerable
extent the rate and extent of new product diffusion."[18]

The planning and organizational characteristics of the firms studied differed markedly, with the consequence that the international transfer of products was achieved in a variety of ways. This
is illustrated below with two opposite cases called firm A and
firm B.

Firm A develops high technology intensive industrial products,
that are standardized on a worldwide scale. Product development
and specifications were until six years ago the responsibility
of headquarters in the parent country, who exported products to
foreign subsidiaries through the international division. The
subsidiary abroad would ask for the transfer of production whenever this was economical from their point of view. Often the
transfer had implications for the parent product division that
resulted in delays, that were perceived by the subsidiary as a
lack of responsiveness from the parent. For example, rather than
taking into account worldwide product specifications, the parent,
being a profit center, would develop a product based on the specifications of its own parent country market. For transfers to
other countries, some adaptations are necessary if the firm does
not want to be less competitive. However, by transferring production abroad the parent product division lowered its output and
revenues together with its allocation of development expenses.
Thus, acting as a profit center, it was induced to delay production transfers. Delays in the transfer of production were such
that production lags of two years were very common. In reaction
to these inefficiencies the company reorganized into worldwide
product divisions thus resulting in efficient coordination of
domestic and international markets which in turn led to increased
sales, and reduced production lags to 3 to 6 months.

Firm B is a manufacturer operating in an industry using "mature"
technology. It integrated forward a decade ago and is now a
manufacturer of consumer and industrial products. While it used
to have much of its primary technology centrally controlled in the
parent country, it has now decentralized its operations of fabri-
cation into a number of independent geographical areas. Each
country being a profit center, managers have to be persuaded that
a particular technology is a good investment for them. Since
transfers of products or of technology are not decided centrally,
it is necessary to employ worldwide product group coordinators
to help perform the communication and persuasion functions.

Success of a product in one country is in fact a condition for being adopted elsewhere. Products being generally developed for one particular market need to be adapted to suit other markets. This means longer diffusion lags and may also lead to some duplication in development.

Whether a given firm can be satisfied by following a pattern similar to firm B will depend on the nature of the product it manufactures and how it may be affected by competitor's strategies. Few of B's manufactured products are traded internationally, as technical norms vary from country to country. This also results in different planning outlook. For firm A the concept of multinational planning is a reality, the worldwide product manager considers alternatives on a worldwide basis. For firm B, the pattern of diffusion is the result of the series of "independent" country manager's decisions. As the nature of the planning task differs, the linkages between subsidiaries are in one case an integral part of the structure, while in the other they are accomplished informally by committees.

The firm, if it wants to be efficient, is likely to adopt an organization structure that reflects the particular product's technology and the external environment (customer's and geography) it is faced with.

Our findings relating the firm's structure to the pattern of product diffusion are worthy of in depth examination by management. The business policy literature has paid little attention to the timing of strategy, which is a crucial factor in the firm's success. The only study on strategy and structure in an international business context was done by Stopford and Welles.[19] For U.S. based MNE they found that worldwide product divisions were associated with firms emphasizing new products. They measured new product intensity by the ratio of R&D expenses to sales. If we assume that high R&D expenditures are related to a high rate of product diffusion, their findings are consistent with ours. Eventhough this assumption could not be tested with their data, it appears plausible for electronics and chemicals. However industries dealing with consumer products appear to exhibit a fast rate of product diffusion together with low R&D expenditures. It is likely that both high complexity of the product and fast diffusion of new products impose great demands on communications between the parent and its foreign subsidiaries. The electronics industry is probably the most demanding one in view of the technological complexity of its products, the variety of components and the rapidity of commercialization on a world scale[20].

Conclusion

The role of the MNE in international technology transfer is a crucial one in many respects as they are dominating a variety of industries. This transfer of MNE skills is taking various forms depending on the product itself, the country involved, and the firm's objectives. Thus it appeared worthwhile to limit the investigation to a selected number of products in a few firms. This study, albeit of an exploratory nature, suggests a number of observations regarding the pattern and speed of international transfers.

1. International transfer is related to a number of product related characteristics. We found that industrial products were adopted faster internationally than consumer products, the later being more susceptible to adaptation that limited the use of exports as a rapid way of introducing products internationally. The degree of novelty of performance of the product appeared to slow-down the diffusion of the product, while the technological novelty of the product for the firm appeared not to influence the diffusion pattern. However, new technological products were more often introduced by exports, thereby leaving more flexibility to the firm.

2. Country related characteristics, such as the size of and type of demand influenced the speed at which MNE introduced products. In highly developed countries such as Europe, North America, or Japan we found very short time lags. Competitive pressures induce firms to try to introduce products practically simultaneously. This was particularly true for products that could be standardized.

3. The firms differed markedly with respect to their organization of the international transfers. High technology and rapid diffusion appeared to be more compatible with the centralization of responsibilities in a worldwide product manager ; more "mature" industries, with products that often needed some adaptations led the firm to decentralize, adopt an area organization, that resulted in transfer slow-down. This later aspect, relating the technology transfer to the planning and organization of the firm appears particularly important as firms will be increasingly pressed to react promptly in order to capitalize on their innovations.

Footnotes

1. William Gruber, Dileep Mehta, and Raymond Vernon, "The R and D Factor in International Trade and International Investment of United-States Industries", Journal of Political Economy, February 1967, pp. 20-37. See also Raymond Vernon, Sovereignty at Bay, Basic Books, 1971.

2. Multinational Corporations in World Development, United Nations, N.Y. 1973, p. 151.

3. The Impact of Multinational Corporations on Development and on International Relations, Report of the Group of Eminent Persons, United Nations, N.Y. 1974, pp. 66-73 ; and a series undertaken by the OECD under the general title Gaps in Technology, 1967.

4. For a discussion of this issue see Keith Pavitt, "The Multinational Enterprise and the Transfer of Technology", in the Multinational Enterprise, J. Dunning (ed.), George Allen and Unwin Ltd., London 1971.

5. Keith Pavitt, op.cit., pp. 84-85.

6. Jack N. Behrman and Harvey W. Wallender, Transfers of Manufacturing Technology within Multinational Enterprises, Ballinger Publishing Co., Cambridge, Mass. 1976.

7. James Brian Quinn, "Technology Transfer by Multinational Companies", Harvard Business Review, November-December 1969, p. 148.

8. Jack N. Behrman and Harvey W. Wallander, op.cit.

9. The full variety of product innovation-diffusion paths,called Multinational Product Strategies (MPS) is presented in Georges Leroy : Multinational Product Strategy : A Typology for Analysis of Worldwide Product Innovation-Diffusion, New York, Praeger Publishers, 1976. See in particular chapters 2 and 6.

10. George F. Ray, "The Diffusion of New Processes", Intereconomics, no. 11, 1969, pp. 356-358.

11. Ibid, p. 358.

12. John Tilton, International Diffusion of Technology : The Case of Semi-Conductors, Washington, D.C., The Brookings Institution, 1971.

13. Georges Leroy, op.cit. The study included the 30 product li-
    nes of the five firms in order to cover adequately their acti-
    vities. The investigation of 52 products from those products
    lines allowed a better grasp of the specificity of each pro-
    duct.

14. Robert D. Buzzell, "Can you Standardize Multinational Marke-
    ting?", Harvard Business Review, November-December, 1968.

15. Tilton, op.cit., pp. 28-30.

16. The reader may wonder why Hewlett-Packard is introducing its
    products faster in the Latin American market (market lag =
    1.6 months) than in Europe (market lag = 6.1 months). The
    reason is a number of products were not introduced in Latin
    America, therefore the market lag is infinite, however, infi-
    nite lags were not counted. This explains the apparent discre-
    pancy.

17. G.C. Hufbauer, Synthetic Materials and the Theory of Interna-
    tional Trade, Harvard University Press, 1966 ; and C.G.Ray,
    "The Diffusion of New Technology : A Study of Ten New Proces-
    ses in Nine Countries", National Institute of Economic Review,
    no. 48, May 1969.

18. Thomas S. Robertson, "The New Product Diffusion Process" in
    Bernard A. Marvin (ed.), American Marketing Association Pro-
    ceedings(Chicago : American Marketing Association, June 1969),
    p. 86.

19. John M. Stopford and Louis T. Wells, Managing the Multinatio-
    nal Enterprise, Basic Books, Inc., New York, 1972, pp.41-42.

20. For further details on the electronics industry, and in Hew-
    lett-Packard in particular see G. Leroy op.cit.pp.73-86.

IDENTIFICATION, EVALUATION AND PREDICTION OF POLITICAL RISKS FROM AN INTERNATIONAL BUSINESS PERSPECTIVE

Hans Schöllhammer

University of California, Los Angeles
and
International Institute of Management, Berlin

Multinational firms account at present (1976) for almost 15 percent of the aggregate gross national products of the western
world ; their total foreign investments are in excess of 320
billion dollars and the aggregate market value of the foreign
assets under their control is very likely about four to five times
as large. The value of these assets is affected by various risks,
i.e. the probability of a loss, that can be broadly classified
as economic and political risks. This separation is certainly
open to question since there can exist a close interdependency
between the factors that constitute economic and political risks.
A distinction is, nevertheless, appropriate since political risks
stem from changes in (assumed) policy positions whereas economic
risks are associated with changes concerning market, competitive,
and technological factors that diminish the firm's effectiveness
and profit potential. In addition, the actors responsible for
political risks becoming an actuality are more easily identified
than those forces which are responsible for the economic risks
becoming an actuality.

Economic risks have traditionally received close attention and
business executives dispose over a fairly well developed instrumentarium for coping with these risks. For example, market
research, demand analysis, forecasting and planning techniques are
all designed to deal essentially in a quantitative and objective
manner with the economic risks that individual firms face. In
contrast, procedures for identifying, evaluating and forecasting
political risks in a systematic and objective manner have not
yet been developed to a desirable extent. For example, an empirical investigation on the approaches of U.S.-based multinational
firms toward political risks showed that "no executive offered
any evidence of a systematic evaluation of political risks, involving their identification, their likely incidence, and their
specific consequences for company operations"[1). At the same time,

there exists a wide spectrum of evidence that executives of multinational firms have a high risk aversion and that they consider
political risks as among the most important factors affecting
their locational strategies and foreign investment decisions[2].

Because of the elusive, intangible, highly uncertain nature of
political risks, the executives' concern with these risks tends
to be subjective, intuitive, and haphazard rather than objective
and systematic.

The Increasing Significance of Political Risks

In a subjective manner executives of multinational companies are
well aware of the importance of paying close attention to the
changing patterns of political risks. Governmental interference
and regulations of business operations have increased noticeably
during the past two or three decades practically anywhere in the
world. With the spectacular growth of foreign investment activities by multinational firms and an attendant rise in nationalism,
home and host countries alike have adopted various restrictive
measures against the operations of these firms. The rational
for the worsening political climate for multinational companies
is the presumed power potential of these firms. In this regard
a wide range of charges have been made against multinational
companies[3], some of which are purely emotional and lack empirical
verification, others are undue generalizations from a particular
case. For instance, it is alleged that multinational companies
use their power to jeopardize the effective application of national economic policies, that they evade national controls, that they
cause distortions in the competitive structure, that they contribute to disturbances in international monetary relations, that
their profits are excessive, that they evade taxes, that they
engage in questionable ethical and political practices, etc. In
addition, the extraterritorially applied policies of the home
countries in such fields as antitrust, export controls, or reporting requirements suggest to some that multinational firms can be
used as tools of the home governments to interfere in the domestic
affairs of another state. The result of all these considerations
is that governments almost anywhere are attempting to tighten the
controls over multinational firms and to regulate their operations
very closely.[4] As a result, political risks are generally on the
rise and multinational firms can ill afford to ignore them.

The Meaning of Political Risks

The term political risk has a complex meaning and various authors
who dealt with this phenomenon from the perspective of multinational business operations have characterized it in differing

ways. There are those who equate political risks with political
change and political instability[5)]. A somewhat modified version
of this view holds that political risk is the result of political
change that affects business sales and profits negatively[6)].
Franklin Root defined political risks similarly as "possible
occurance of political events of any kind that cause a loss of
profit potential and/or assets in international business operations[7)]. Essentially the same characterization is used by Handel
and West who define political risk as "the risk or probability of
occurance of some political event(s) that will change the prospects for the profitability of a given investment"[8)]   A rather
broad characterization has been advocated by Stefan Robock who
states that "political risk in international business exists (1)
when discontinuities occur in the business environment, (2) when
they are difficult to anticipate,and (3) when they result from
political change. To constitute a "risk" these changes in the
business environment must have a potential for significantly affecting the profit or other goals of a particular enterprise"[9)].
Robock proposes to focus on the political risk phenomenon from
three perspectives : a) the causes of risk such as social unrest,
disorder, xenophobic attitudes ; b) the groups or actors through
which political risk can be generated such as government and its
operating agencies, parliamentary opposition groups ; c) the
effects or manifestations of the risk such as confiscation, expropriation, operational restrictions.

This diversity in definitions suggests that the political risk
phenomenon can be viewed from various perspectives and in greater
or lesser detail. The same situation exists in practice. In spite
of the professed importance that executives of multinational companies attach to an identification of potential political risks,
these risks are generally not examined with the same quantitative
rigor that applies to the economic risks. The reason for this
state of affairs is that politicak risks, i.e. the existence of a
political situation and the possible occurance of politically-
oriented events that affect the prosperity of a firm's operation,
cannot be ascertained directly. Political risks can only be
identified and assessed as inference from an array of factors which
indirectly reflect the current and potential future magnitude of
the political risk situation in a given country.

Approaches to the Identification and Assessment of Political Risks

From the management perspective of a multinational firm it is
important to develop an instrumentarium that provides decision-
makers with operational techniques for identifying and evaluating
the current status of the political risk situation in any country
where the firm has or is planning to have operations. In addition,
multinational firms need analytical tools for sharpening their

awareness of changes in the political sphere that might change
the political risk level.

Analyzing the Causality of Political Risks

The most common approach to the identification and assessment of
political risks in an international business context is to investigate an amalgamation of causal factors or conditions which
either directly or indirectly provide an indication of the current
degree of political risk and its potential developments. The
rational of this approach is that the relative absence (or presence) of certain factors or conditions provides a basis for
making an inference about the degree of political risk in a
country in general and the political risk exposure of a certain
investment in particular.

In the literature one finds a wide variety of "checklists" which
suggest the type of factors that a decision-maker might conceivably want to investigate in order to come to some subjective
conclusion about the political risk situation and its developments
in a particular country. Some of these checklists focus on a
relatively narrow set of indicators of political violence or
civil strife such as politically motivated assassinations,
terrorism, sabotage etc.[10]. Most of the checklists are, however,
much more comprehensive and include, apart from political factors
in a narrow sense, socio-economic variables as contributors to
and indicators of a given political risk situation[11]. An example
of such a checklist is given in Appendix 1.

The advantage of analyzing potential risk factors on a very broad
scale is that it can provide a decision-maker with a heightened
awareness of the general political situation in a country and a
better perspective of the political exposure problem. The main
drawbacks of this approach are, however, that for some of these
factors no precise information can be obtained, that many of
them are not quantifyable and that no clear comparative analyses
can be made. In addition, not all factors are of the same weight
as constituents of a political risk situation. Although it is
possible to attach different weight to the various factors, the
weighting itself would be largely a subjective matter and the
resultant political risk assessment an arbitrary exercise of
questionable validity.

A Quantitative Approach to the Assessment of Political Risk : The
Development of a Political Risk Score.

Ideally, a multinational firm should continuously scan the current
political risk situation in any country where it has or plans to
have operations. For this purpose it is essential to focus on a
limited number of manageable variables that can be quantified and

Table 1 : Average Political Risk Scores for Sixty Countries (1948–1967)*

Rank	Country	Degree of Political Strife Related to Size of Population (mill.)	Degree of Political Strife Related to Per Capita Income	Country	Rank
1	Netherland	0.248	0.0013	Norway	1
2	Ivory Coast	0.261	0.0013	Sweden	2
3.	Japan	0.336	0.0019	Switzerland	3
4	Central African Republic	0.370	0.0020	Netherland	4
5	United Kingdom	0.413	0.0020	Denmark	5
6	Brazil	0.429	0.004	Iovry Coast	6
7	Sweden	0.433	0.005	Ireland	7
8	Afghanistan	0.620	0.005	Canada	8
9	Canada	0.640	0.006	Central Afric.Rep.	9
10	Norway	0.645	0.006	Belgium	10
11	Switzerland	0.749	0.007	Uruguay	11
12	Thailand	0.779	0.010	Austria	12
13	India	0.830	0.011	Jamaica	13
14	Denmark	0.893	0.011	El Salvador	14
15	Mexico	0.949	0.012	United Kingdom	15
16	West Germany	1.015	0.027	Costa Rica	16
17	El Salvador	1.042	0.031	Chile	17
18	United States	1.044	0.032	West Germany	18
19	Italy	1.051	0.038	Japan	19
20	Tanzania	1.065	0.038	France	20
21	Belgium	1.141	0.042	Singapore	21
22	Ethiopia	1.316	0.044	Panama	22
23	Uruguay	1.436	0.049	Italy	23
24	France	1.483	0.055	United States	24
25	Ireland	1.566	0.061	Ghana	25
26	Pakistan	1.700	0.073	Hong Kong	26

* Computations were done by the author.

Table 1 (continued)

Rank	Country	Degree of Political Strife Related to Size of Population (mill.)	Degree of Political Strife Related to Per Capita Income	Country	Rank
27	Austria	1.716	0.081	Cambodia	27
28	Cambodia	1.791	0.089	Mexico	28
29	Chile	2.031	0.098	Ecuador	29
30	Ghana	2.235	0.113	Afghanistan	30
31	Ceylon	2.577	0.132	Brazil	31
32	Jamaica	3.048	0.158	Tanzania	32
33	Ecuador	4.170	0.162	Venezuela	33
34	Malawi	5.114	0.169	Peru	34
35	Peru	5.335	0.184	Thailand	35
36	S. Korea	6.005	0.201	Ceylon	36
37	Costa Rica	7.886	0.380	Zambia	37
38	Hong Kong	8.057	0.429	Malawi	38
39	Nigeria	8.852	0.545	Argentina	39
40	Sudan	9.380	0.661	Ethiopia	40
41	Burma	11.148	0.861	Tunesia	41
42	Singapore	11.180	0.980	Dominican Rep.	42
43	Mozambique	12.414	1.167	Mozambique	43
44	Venezuela	16.332	1.270	Sudan	44
45	Panama	16.577	1.284	Taiwan	45
46	Phillipines	17.819	1.451	Bolivia	46
47	Argentina	18.760	1.604	Pakistan	47
48	Zambia	21.914	1.623	S. Korea	48
49	Taiwan	23.457	1.780	Colombia	49
50	Uganda	23.864	2.071	Uganda	50
51	Colombia	27.789	3.528	Malaysia	51
52	Tunesia	41.720	3.602	Phillipines	52

Table 1 (continued)

Rank	Country	Degree of Political Strife Related to Size of Population (mill.)	Degree of Political Strife Related to Per Capita Income	Country	Rank
53	Congo – Kinshasa	49.286	3.883	Burma	53
54	Bolivia	64.363	3.999	India	54
55	Dominican Republic	71.733	6.060	Nigeria	55
56	Kenya	79.274	6.311	Cameroon	56
57	Malaysia	114.820	8.249	Kenya	57
58	Cameroon	154.485	9.393	Congo-Kinshasa	58
59	Indonesia	296.191	14.427	Algeria	59
60	Algeria	296.805	315.039	Indonesia	60

that is twice as high as the score of another country does not necessarily mean that its political risk is twice as high. It is also necessary to interpret the political risk scores in the light of the economic potential that the countries offer from the perspective of a particular firm. Since most investment decisions are based on analysis of anticipated cash flows and net returns, it is suggested that the political risk scores can be used as discount factors in a cash flow analysis. This simply suggests that a higher political risk might be compensated by a higher return, or a lower political risk might make a lower net return still acceptable.

The scores in Table 1 are based on data from 1948–1967, and they thus reflect an average, long-term political risk level of the individual countries. In order to assess a country's current risk situation, the scores should be calculated for individual years of the most recent past. This procedure also enables one to detect trends in the political risk development of individual countries. It is, however, not recommended to use a simple trend analysis to forecast political risks. Forecasting political risks is an integral part of any political risk analysis ; it is, however, a more complex endeavor than ascertaining the current level of political risk.

Forecasting Political Risks : An Analysis of Potential Political Changes

The essence of wisdom is concern with the future and the essence of effective business management is systematic planning. In the context of a multinational firm the planning effort must include forecasts of the economic, technological, competitive conditions as well as of the political environment of countries or regions where the company has or plans to have operations. Forecasting of economic and technological developments is widely practiced since reasonably well developed techniques and concepts are available for this purpose. In contrast, forecasting political developments and associated risks is done in a very haphazard and subjective manner which amounts to little more than educated guesswork.

Traditional Approaches to Forecasting Political Changes

Most executives of multinational firms when asked about their approach to forecasting political risks indicate that they try to develop a certain sensitivity for and awareness of political developments and that they reach conclusions about future political risks on this basis. Most of the existing literature on this subject recommends a similar, relatively unstructured approach. For example, Stefan Robock suggests that "the task of political

forecasting involves four basic steps : First, an understanding
of the type of government presently in power, its pattern of political behavior and its norms for stability ; second, an analysis
of the multinational enterprise's own product or operations to
identify the kind of political risk likely to be involved in particular areas ; third, a determination of the source of the political risk ; and fourth, to project into the future the possibility of political risk in terms of probability and time horizons"
[14]. The culmination of this effort is a probability analysis
of essentially radical political changes that Robock [15]
Stobaugh[16] and Lloyd [17] exemplified in a similar manner.

The shortcoming of this approach is that it does not provide any
objective, quantifyable criteria for carrying out the projective
risk assessment. Any forecast of political risks is then largely
a subjective, discretionary matter depending on the awareness and
risk-orientation of the executives who have to make a decision.

A Causality Approach to the Forecasting of Political Change and
Political Risk.

The development of a tool for predicting political risks requires
an understanding of the factors that cause political changes and
a testing of the relative predictive validity of these factors
on the basis of historical data. For this purpose it has been
hypothesized that any political change causes some degree of
uncertainty and risk and that the frequency and severity of political changes are precipitated or at least facilitated by a series
of causal factors in the political and socio-economic sphere.
The author has built a conceptual scheme to help in the forecasting of political risk. It is illustrated in Table 2.

The pivotal link in this conceptual scheme are political changes
as reflected in a) executive transfers, i.e. a change in the
office of the national executive from one leader or group to
another ; and b) executive adjustments, i.e., a modification in
the membership of a national executive body. In all countries,
be they democratically governed or in an autocratic fashion,
executive transfers and executive adjustments and the related
policy changes are ultimately the result of conditions in the
political, economic and social sphere.

The author made a multiple regression analysis involving numerical
data for sixty countries (same countries as in Table 1) for the
years from 1948 to 1967[18] with executive transfers and executive
adjustments as dependent variable and the indicated causal factors
as independent variables revealed that the following variables are
statistically significant (at the .10 level) :

Table 2 : Forecasting Political Risk : A Conceptual Scheme

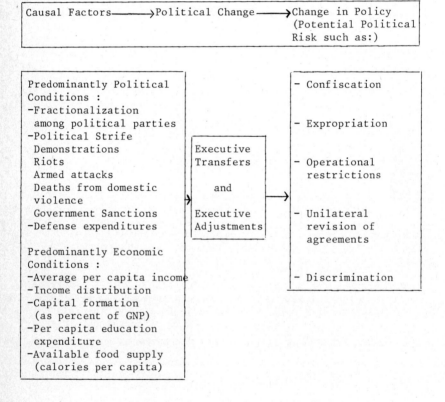

Causal Factors⟶Political Change⟶Change in Policy (Potential Political Risk such as:)

Predominantly Political Conditions :
-Fractionalization among political parties
-Political Strife
 Demonstrations
 Riots
 Armed attacks
 Deaths from domestic violence
 Government Sanctions
-Defense expenditures

Predominantly Economic Conditions :
-Average per capita income
-Income distribution
-Capital formation (as percent of GNP)
-Per capita education expenditure
-Available food supply (calories per capita)

Executive Transfers

and

Executive Adjustments

- Confiscation

- Expropriation

- Operational restrictions

- Unilateral revision of agreements

- Discrimination

Predominantly Political Conditions :	Computed T - Value
Fractionalization among political parties	2.617
Political Strife	
Demonstrations	2.891
Riots	2.055
Armed attacks, violent deaths, government sanctions	1.980
Defense expenditures	1.991

Predominantly Economic Conditions :	
Per capita income	− 2.159
Sectoral income distribution (GINI index)	− 1.769
Capital formation	2.090
Food supply (calories per capita)	3.003
Multiple correlation coefficient	.665
F-value for analysis of variance	3.879
Standard error of estimate (actual versus predicted political change)	9.712

Other variables that were tested such as ethnic and linguistic fractionalization were statistically not significant as indicators of political change and policy changes.

These results provide some evidence that political changes and related political risks can be predicted by analyzing a relatively small number of conditions on which quantifyable, up-to-date information is available. All indicated relationships, with the exception of per capita income and income distribution, are positive, i.e. the greater the individual variable the greater the potential for political change and political risk. A high per capita income and a relatively high equality in income distribution tend to reduce incidents of political change. Expressed differently, the lower the per capita income in a country and the greater the inequality in income distribution, the greater the potential for political change.

Summary and Conclusions

The proper identification, assessment and prediction of political risks is an important aspect in planning and managing multinational business operations. While foreign investments by multinational companies have increased at an unprecedented rate during the past fifteen years, the hospitability and the general political climate

for these investments has declined. Once an investment has been
made the transfer of assets in case of a worsening political climate can be very sticky. For this reason it is at least as important to monitor the current and future political risk situation
as it is to analyze the economic risks. Decisions on the deploy-
ment of corporate resources must be made from the perspective of
the economic and political risks on the ultimate preference function of the enterprise.

For the objective analysis and the projection of essentially economic risks there exists a reasonably well developed and widely
used instrumentarium. In contrast, for the assessment and projection of political risks executives of multinational companies
use rarely a systematic, comparative approach and hardly any
quantitative data. As a result they reach intuitive, subjective
conclusions about the political risk situation that amount to
little more than educated guesswork.

Most of the existing publications on analyzing and forecasting
political risks in an international business context stress that
executives should develop an awareness of a wide spectrum of
factors that might conceivably have an impact on the political
risk situation in a given country or region and then to draw
rational conclusions. The basic disadvantage of this approach
is that on many of the suggested factors a decision-maker may not
be able to get any reliable information and even if information
is available, it may be of a qualitative nature that can only be
interpreted in a subjective, intuitive manner.

The main purpose of this study is to propose a quantitative, comparative approach to the identification and prediction of political risks that uses a smaller number of variables on which reasonably up-to-date information is readily available. It is advocated that from the perspective of managing a multinational enterprise the current political risk situation can be ascertained by
monitoring periodically five variables on a country by country
basis where the company has or plans to have operations : protest
demonstrations, riots, armed attacks, deaths from political violence and governmental sanctions. The quantitative indicators on
these variables can be added up and related to a country's size
of population or the average per capita income. The resultant
scores or ratios provide executives of multinational firms with
an indication of the comparative political risk in the investigated countries and a basis for observing political risk developments over time. Inferences drawn from these scores can lead
to a more objective, systematic assessment of political risks and
a better risk management.

In order to forecast the political risk situation this study proposes to focus on factors that tend to increase or facilitate the
potential for political change. The greater the prospects of
political change, the greater the potential political risk. Based
on an extensive statistical analysis of historical data this
study suggests that executives of multinational firms can assess
future developments in the political risk situation of a country
by investigating current political cleavages, changes in the
fractionalization among political parties, the development of
incomes and the income distribution situation. A continuous and
systematic monitoring of these factors will sensitize multinational firms about potential political changes and increases or
decreases in the political risk.

References

(1) Franklin R. Root, "U.S. Business Abroad and the Political
     Risks", <u>MSU Business Topics</u>, Winter 1968, p. 24.

(2) See, e.g.,Yair Aharoni, <u>The Foreign Investment Decision
     Process</u>, Boston: Harvard University, 1966, p. 39 ; Peter D.
     Bennett and Robert T. Green, "Political Instability as Deter-
     minant of Direct Foreign Investment in Marketing", <u>Journal
     of Marketing Research</u>, Vol. 9 (May 1972), pp. 182-186 ;
     Robert T. Green, <u>Political Instability as a Determinant of
     U.S. Foreign Investment</u>, Austin : The University of Texas,
     p. 11 ff ; Hans Schöllhammer, <u>Locational Strategies of Multi-
     national Firms</u>, Los Angeles : Center for International
     Business, 1974.

(3) See, e.g. Hugh Stephenson, <u>The Coming Clash : The Impact of
     Multinational Corporations on Nation States</u>, New York :
     Saturday Review Press, 1972 ; Richard J. Barnet and Ronald
     E. Müller, <u>Global Reach : The Power of the Multinational
     Corporations</u>, New York: Simon & Schuster, 1974 ; Robert
     Gilpin, <u>U.S. Power and the Multinational Corporation</u>,
     New York : Basic Books, Inc. 1975.

(4) See, e.g., Rainer Hellmann, <u>Kontrolle der multinationalen
     Unternehmen</u>, Baden-Baden : Nomos Verlag, 1974.

(5) See, e.g., Robert T. Green, "Political Structures as a Pre-
     dictor of Radical Political Change", <u>Columbia Journal of
     World Business</u>, Vol. 9, No. 1 (Spring 1974), p 28 f.

(6) Antoine W. van Agtmael, "How Business has dealt with Politi-
     cal Risk", <u>Financial Executive</u>, January 1976, p. 27.

(7) Franklin R. Root, "Analyzing Political Risks in International
     Business", in A. Kapoor and P. Grub, eds., <u>Multinational
     Enterprise in Transition</u>, Princeton : Darwin Press, 1972,
     p. 57.

(8) Dan Haendel and Gerald T. West, <u>Overseas Investment and
     Political Risk</u>, Philadelphia : Foreign Policy Research Insti-
     tute, 1975, p. XI.

(9) Stefan H. Robock, "Political Risk : Identification and Assess-
     ment", <u>Columbia Journal of World Business</u>, Vol. 6, no. 4
     (July 1971), p. 7.

(10) See, e.g., Rudolph J. Rummel. "Dimensions of Conflict Beha-
     vior within and between Nations", Yearbook of the Society
     for General Systems Research, Vol. 8, 1963, p. 25 ff ;
     Charles Tilly and James Rule, Measuring Political Upheaval,
     Princeton : Center for International Studies, Princeton
     University, 1965 ; Ivo K. Feierabend and Rosalind L. Feiera-
     bend, "Agressive Behavior within Politics, 1948-1962 : A
     Cross-National Study", Journal of Conflict Resolution, Vol.
     10 (September 1966), pp. 249-271; Ted Gurr, "A Causal Model
     of Civil Strife", The American Political Science Review
     Vol. 62, 1968, p. 1104 ff.

(11) See, e.g., Robert B. Stobaugh, "How to Analyze Foreign
     Investment Climates", Harvard Business Review, September-
     October 1969, pp 100-108 ; Herbert Cahn, "The Political
     Exposure Problem : An Often Overlooked Investment Decision"
     Worldwide P & I Planning, Vol. 6, no. 3(May/june 1972),
     pp. 16-22 ; Bruce Lloyd, "The Identification and Measurement
     of Political Risk in the International Environment", Long-
     Range Planning, Vol. 7, No. 6 (December 1974),pp 24-32 ;
     Antoine W. van Agtmael, "How Business has dealt with Politi-
     cal Risk", Financial Executive, January 1976, pp 26-30, and
     by the same author "Evaluating the Risks of Lending to
     Developing Countries", Euromoney, April 1976, pp 16-30.

(12) An excellent data base is Charles L. Taylor and Michael C.
     Hudson, World Handbook of Political and Social Indicators,
     2nd ed., New Haven :Yale University Press, 1972. Some
     additional data can be obtained on magnetic tape from Inter-
     University Consortium for Political Research, Ann Arbor,
     Michigan. See also C. Taylor and M. Hudson, Guide to Resour-
     ces and Services, 1976-77, Inter-University Consortium for
     Political and Social Research, the University of Michigan,
     Box 1248, Ann Arbor, Michigan, 48106, 386 pages. This guide
     lists all kinds of publications including data sources on
     political and social indicators.

(13) The definitions of these variables (adn the statistical
     data that were used in the subsequent analysis) are from
     Charles L. Taylor and Michael C. Hudson, op. cit.,p. 66-70.

(14) Stefan H. Robock, op. cit., p. 16.

(15) Ibid., p. 17

(16) Robert B. Stobaugh, op.cit., p. 108.

(17) Bruce Lloyd, op.cit., p. 30.

(18) For recent years one could use the data from varying sources
     listed in C.Taylor and M.Hudson, Guide to Resources and Ser-
     vices, op.cit.

Appendix 1 : Country-related Factors Affecting the Political Risk:
*   A Checklist(1)*

Internal Relationships

Historical Perspectives
- Origin of national political institutions - indigenous versus
  foreign roots.
- Constitutionality of government
- Record of governmental stability
- Stability of political parties
- Prevailing political ideology and characteristics of the econo-
  mic system
- Clarity, uniformity of legal prescriptions
- Past record of foreign investments
- Past record of expropriation of foreign-owned assets
- Past record of unilateral breach of agreements or commitments

Form of Government
- Democracy
  One party rule or coalition among political parties
  Ideology, aims, strength of opposition parties
  Strength of communist party

- Dictatorship
  Degree of popular support
  Degree of opposition

- Military regime
  Degree of popular support
  Degree of opposition
  Rivalries among military commanders
  Relationships between civil servants and military

Governmental Effectiveness
- Quality of political leadership
- Performance of civil service
- Governmental sensitivity to social programs and social reforms
- Degree and form of corruption among government authorities and
  civil servants.

Homogeneity Versus Heterogeneity
- Sense of national unity
- Ethic, linguistic, religious, political fractionalization
- Relationship among factions
- Separatist movements

---

(1) This checklist was made up by the author. Similar checklists
    can be found in A.W. van Agtmael, Financial Executive and
    Euromoney, op. cit.

Relationship between Civil Authorities and Military
- Mutually supportive
- Neutral
- Antagonistic
- Possibility of a military coup

Intensity and Persistence of Civil Strife
- Protest demonstrations
- Political strikes
- Riots
- Mutinies
- Politically motivated arrests
- Scope and intensity of governmental sanctions
- Guerilla activities
- Civil war

Sources of Internal Political Conflicts
- Political discrimination
- Religious, ethnic, linguistic, political, economic cleavages
- Degree of inequality in income distribution
- Economic scarcities
- Ban on political activities
- Governmental restrictions of civil liberties and harrassments

External Relationships

International Political Relationships
- Membership in political or military alliances
- Existing treaties of friendship, commerce and navigation
- Leverage of foreign powers

International Economic Relationships
- Magnitude of foreign trade
- Direction of trade
- Major trading partners
- International monetary relationships
- International indebtedness
- Balance of payments situation
- Degree of economic integration with other countries

International Economic Restrictions
- Restrictions on foreign investments
- Restrictions on the international transfer of goods, capital,
  personnel

Discriminatory Practices against Foreign Interests

ORGANIZATIONAL STRUCTURES AND MULTINATIONAL STRATEGIES OF CONTINENTAL EUROPEAN ENTERPRISES

Lawrence G. Franko

Center for Education in International Management, Geneva

Throughout the growth and spread of their multinational operations, Continental European enterprises maintained highly personalized relations with their foreign manufacturing subsidiaries (Siemens, 1957 ; Kocka, 1969 ; Degussa, 1973: 39; McKay, 1970). Even at the beginning of the 1970's, the most important bonds between center and periphery in European multinational systems were still the personal relationship between presidents of parent companies and presidents of foreign ventures.

The personal nature of parent-foreign subsidiary relationships in Continental enterprise has come to be known as the mother-daughter form of organization. Its structure can be illustrated in chart form as in Figure 1. The mother-daughter reporting relationships ran from parent president to foreign subsidiary presidents and was almost always accompanied by a domestic organization in which functional heads for production, sales, research and finance reported to (or served on the same managing board as) the parent president. Domestic operations outside the parents' main industry were often handled by subsidiaries whose presidents also reported to the parent head.

The mother-daughter relationship was the most common international organizational form used by large Continental multinational enterprises at the start of 1971. It was used alike by firms with many and with few foreign manufacturing operations. Table 1 shows that 25 of the 70 large enterprises for which organizational histories could be developed used the mother-daughter form. Twenty-one of the firms organized along mother-daughter lines had manufacturing operations in more than seven countries ; one company maintained mother-daughter relationships while manufacturing in 17 nations.

In the past, the mother-daughter organization had been even more common. In 1961, only nine enterprises were using alternative structures.

Reprinted by permission of the publisher from The European Multinationals, Harper & Row, 1976.

Figure 1 : Basic Features of the Mother-Daughter Organizational
Structure.

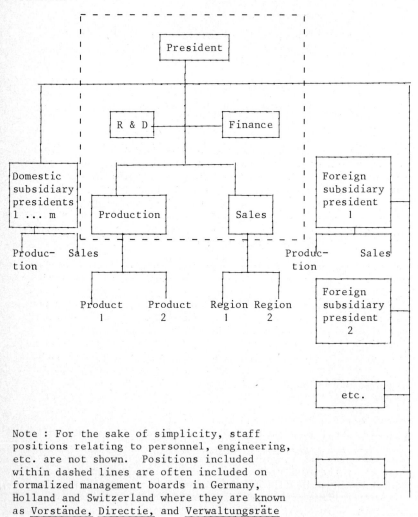

Note : For the sake of simplicity, staff
positions relating to personnel, engineering,
etc. are not shown. Positions included
within dashed lines are often included on
formalized management boards in Germany,
Holland and Switzerland where they are known
as Vorstände, Directie, and Verwaltungsräte
respectively.

American multinational enterprises had followed a very different
organizational evolution. President-to-president relationships
similar to the mother-daughter sort were often used by American
firms during the early stages of their foreign manufacturing experience (Stopford and Wells, 1972 ; Franko, 1971B). But American
enterprises with such a structure rarely managed networks of manufacturing operations spanning many countries. More than 60% of
the American enterprises in the Comparative Multinational Enterprise Project abandoned president-to-president, personalized
reporting structures in favor of another organizational form before they had established their fifth foreign manufacturing subsidiary (Stopford and Wells, 1972: 21). None of the American
multinationals had even maintained president-to-president reporting relationships beyond ten foreign manufacturing subsidiaries.

American terms do not, however, quite correspond to the behavior
which typically occurred in European company systems. The mother-
daughter relationship was less a formal organizational structure
based on written rules, procedures, and reporting relationships
than it was a structural surrogate based on career, social,
friendship and family ties.

MANAGING THE MOTHER-DAUGHTER RELATIONSHIP

The nature of the mother-daughter, parent-subsidiary relationship
in the Continental multinationals can be glimpsed in a number of
ways. One way is to contrast the management practices in firms
maintaining this relationship with those in firms which abandoned
it. Tables 2, 3 and 4 present managers' perceptions of the role
played by written job descriptions and rules, standardized reporting periods and formats, and the use of expatriate home-country
managers in relationships between headquarters and foreign manufacturing subsidiaries. These tables are based on questionnaire
and interview responses provided by 35 Continental enterprises.

Despite the great international spread of the seven mother-daughter
firms that responded to the questionnaire (six of the seven were
manufacturing in more than nine foreign countries), none ascribed
a major role to written rules and procedures in the control of
international operations. In contrast, 12 of the 28 firms with
alternative structures, as seen from Table 2, indicated that
written rules and procedures played a major role in managing
foreign operations. Whereas mother-daughter firms used little
standardization of reporting periods and document formats, most
of the firms with other structures had a high degree of standardization, as can be seen from Table 3. The mother-daughter firms
employed a higher proportion of home-country expatriates as presidents of foreign manufacturing subsidiaries than did firms with
alternative structures. Table 4 shows that this contrast held

Table 1. Large Continental European Enterprises Classified by
International Organizational Structures and Geographical Spread,
1971.

Structure	Enterprises Manufacturing in :			Total number of firms
	Less than seven countries	Seven to ten countries	More than ten countries	
Mother-daughter	5	9	12	25
International division	1	5	5	11
World-wide product	4	6	14	24
Area and world-functional	0	0	3	3
Mixed and matrix	0	0	6	6
Total	10	20	40	70

Note : Data concerning organizational structure was not obtai-
nable for all 85 Continental enterprises in the Comparative
Multinational Enterprise study. Some enterprises which were
classified as having world-wide product or area structures had
one or two subsidiaries reporting to parent firms along mother-
daughter lines.

Table 2. Continental Multinational Enterprises, Classified by International Organizational Structure and Role Played by Written Job Description and Rules in Controlling Foreign Manufacturing, 1972.

Structure	A minor role	A major role	Total number of firms
Mother-daugher	7	0	7
Other	16	12	28
Total	23	12	35

Notes : All enterprises manufactured in more than seven countries. See appendix A for questions and method of classification.

Table 3. Continental Multinational Enterprises Classified by
International Organizational Structures and Standardization of
Reporting Periods and Documents of Foreign Manufacturing Subsi-
diaries, 1972.

Structure	Degree of standardization		Total number
	Low	High	of firms
Mother-daughter	6	1	7
Other	4	22	26
Total	10	23	33

Notes : All enterprises manufactured in more than seven countries.
See appendix A for questions asked and method of classification.

Table 4 : Continental Multinational Enterprises, Classified by International Organizational Structure and Percentage of Home Country Nationals as Presidents of Manufacturing Subsidiaries in Various Regions, 1972.

Structure	Region of Subsidiaries and Percentage of Home-Country Expatriate Subsidiary Presidents :									Total Companies Responding
	North America :			Europe:			Less Developed World:			
	0-33%	34-67%	68-100%	0-33%	34-67%	68-100%	0-33%	34-67%	68-100%	
Mother-daughter	2	0	5	0	3	5	2	1	6	9
Other	8	1	4	11	8	4	6	8	7	23
Total	10	1	9	11	11	9	8	9	13	32

true whether the comparisons were for foreign operations in North
America, Europe, or the less developed countries.

Although the data presented in Tables 2, 3 and 4 relate to only
about half of the Continental European multinational enterprises
maintaining the mother-daughter structure in 1973 (the year in
which the questionnaire was circulated), there is little doubt
that the patterns shown by these data applied just as well to
firms not providing information. Our questionnaire was complemented by press descriptions of mother-daughter relationships in non-
responding enterprises which read, for example, like : "all the
74 subsidiary companies report to the president, who attempts to
see each company head twice a year. These are largely informal
visits". The president of this enterprise went on to remark
"I meet the managing director and his production people. We talk
about his problems and whether the parent company can do anything
to solve them". The contrast could not be more complete between
the management practices of the Continental European multinationals using the mother-daughter form and the archetypical American
multinational with job descriptions, "bibles" of rules, and frequent use of local nationals as foreign subsidiary presidents
(Vernon, 1971 ; Franko, 1973; Van Den Bulke, 1971).

Control and constraint

Although managers in firms with mother-daughter structures often
spoke about the great independence of foreign subsidiary presidents, the kind of autonomy granted was rarely of the sort exercised by subsidiary presidents in American multinationals during
the so-called autonomous subsidiary phase of their earliest
foreign operations. Few of the traditionally organized Continental multinationals considered their foreign, tariff or non-tariff-
barrier factories as portfolio gambles, made to insure against a
feared, but incalculable penalty for not investing (Stopford and
Wells, 1972: 20). When European managers described their mother-
daughter organizations, they invoked analogies of control systems
used in Roman or feudal times (Cvetkov, 1972). Like Roman pro-
consuls sent out to govern the colonies after being educated as
good Romans, subsidiary managers in many Continental firms were
given foreign responsibilities only after years spent absorbing
the values and practices of the parent company. The absorption
process was facilitated by the fact that many of the foreign managers were of the home-country nationality, as Table 4 indicates. Indeed, they often came from families long established in
headquarters' cities. Written rules and reports were unnecessary
in most circumstances, for headquarters managers could usually
predict how their foreign presidents would act : it was said
that managers in one enterprise "simply would not do things not
in the group interest". Consequently, foreign subsidiary

presidents were often allowed great autonomy -- but within precise, yet unwritten constraints. Five mother-daughter organizations examined in depth were able to achieve nearly total world-
wide standardization of policies relating to product mix and
diversification, product quality, brand names, product design and
formulae, external versus internal financing and personnel promotion and reward systems. This occurred without anything resembling a system for reporting and control.

As long as constraints were respected and divident checks appeared
when anticipated, the center rarely interfered with -- or even
asked for much information from -- foreign subsidiaries. When
information was transferred, it often travelled on lines established by friendship and acquaintance, and in a manner showing little
concern for the principle of unity of command (or "one man, one
boss") (see also Lombard, 1969: 38 ; Schollhammer, 1971: 354).

Rationale of the mother-daughter structure

The possible reasons for the lengthy use of the mother-daughter
organization by Continental enterprises are numerous. Some
managers suggested, for example, that enterprises with the bulk
of their foreign subsidiaries in Europe could maintain the mother-
daughter relationship simply because of the relatively short geographical distances involved. There was, however, no observable
relationship between Continental firms' propensities to concentrate foreign manufacturing in Europe as of 1971 and the likelihood of their having mother-daughter structures.

Alternatively, managers suggested that multinational companies
with narrow product lines could maintain the mother-daughter
structure longer than highly diversified enterprises. A priori,
they felt it was easiest to maintain a simple, personalized relationships among component parts of a relatively simple (one- or
few-product) multinational enterprise. It is difficult to imagine
a president transferring much information among 74 manufacturing
subsidiaries during twice-yearly visits in all but the most specialized firm. In practice, however, fewer than half of the
Continental European multinational enterprises employing the
mother-daughter structure in 1971 had narrow product lines in
their foreign production operations, as one sees from Table 5.

But how were Continental enterprises able to maintain mother-
daughter structures in the face of considerable geographical
spread and product diversity (while American firms adopted alternative structures)? It may have been partly because European
managers (unlike American managers) usually spent their working
lives in one firm (Franko, 1973; Stopford, 1972: 87, Schollhammer,
1971: 355). If managers' loyalty to company objectives is a

Table 5 : Continental Multinational Enterprises, Classified by
Structure and by Foreign Product Diversity, 1971.

Structure	Total Number of Firms with Production in Seven or More Countries	Number of Firms Classified by Foreign Product Diversity		
		None	Low	High
Mother-Daughter	21	3	6	12
International Division	10	3	5	2
World-Wide Product	20	1	6	13
Area and World-Functional	3	1	2	-
Mixed and Matrix	6	-	2	4
Total	60	8	21	31

function of time spent in the firm, then there is some margin of substitutability of personalized for impersonal means of achieving organizational cohesiveness (Galbraith, 1969 : 12). Nonetheless the evidence argues that this margin was too narrow to allow mother-daughter structures to be maintained under all pressures : despite the nearly life-long tenure of their managers, firms such as Switzerland's Nestlé and Ciba-Geigy, and Germany's Siemens, Bayer and Basf had shifted to alternative structures by 1971.

It is conceivable that many Continental mother-daughter enterprises were able to obtain some cohesion throughout their multinational systems by avoiding joint ventures with foreign partners. Table 6 points out that mother-daughter enterprises were particularly prone to have wholly owned foreign manufacturing subsidiaries.

Perhaps the most powerful forces behind the long predominance of mother-daughter relationships were the barriers to trade (public and private) which kept national markets separate from one another, and thus limited the need for cross-border communication in most Continental European multinational systems. The greatest contrast between the mother-daughter structure and the alternative structures sketched in Figures 2 and 3, lies in the fact that none of the managers in the mother-daughter organization has strictly supranational responsibilities, whereas there is an explicit recognition of cross-border responsibility, coordination and communication in all the alternatives to the mother-daughter relationship. In organizations in which decision-making power is held by the head of an international, a world-wide product or an area division, chiefs of national subsidiary units can no longer lay claim to a status in their fiefdoms nearly equal to that of the mother-company president ; national desires and interests must go through an international filter before they can obtain the attention of the parent president. The mother-daughter structure was a logical organizational counterpart to the economic behavior of international combines of subsidiaries held together by common ownership, but not by a supranational strategy. Organizational behavior was but the reflection of the tariff, non-tariff and cartel barriers to trade which kept national markets economically separated from one another.

Before World War II, in the thick of the negotiable environment, only one Continental enterprise managed relations with foreign subsidiaries through a supranational structure, even though 14 enterprises manufactured in more than seven countries by 1938. By 1968, the year when tariffs reached zero within the EEC, 12 enterprises had moved to structures with supranational centers of responsibility ; by 1971 the number was 39.

Table 6 : Continental Multinational Enterprises, Classified by
Organizational Structure and Percentage of Wholly Owned Foreign
Manufacturing Subsidiaries, 1971.

Structure	Percentage of Subsidiaries wholly owned :			Total Number of Firms
	0-32%	33-49%	50% or more	
Mother-Daughter	6	6	9	21
International Division	4	2	4	10
World-wide Product	8	6	6	20
Area and World-Functional	0	2	1	3
Mixed and Matrix	0	4	2	6
Total	18	20	22	60

Note : All enterprises manufactured in seven or more countries.

Figure 2 : Basic Features of Organizational Alternatives to the Mother-Daughter Structure .

1. The international division structure

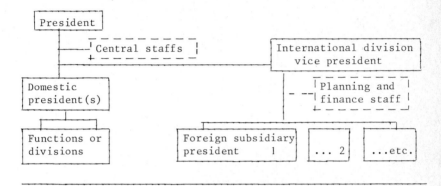

2. The world-wide product structure

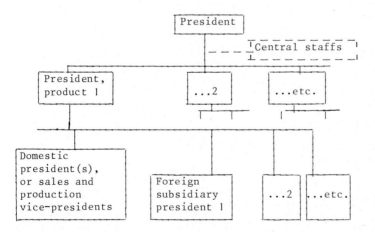

3. The area structure

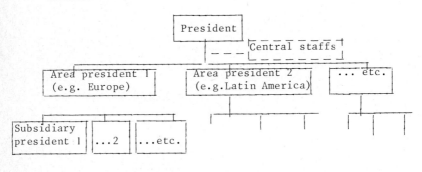

4. The world-functional structure

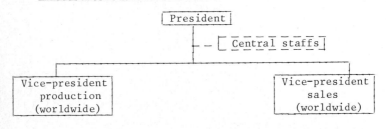

5. A mixed structure

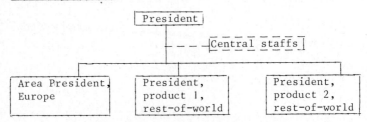

Figure 3 : Matrix Structures for International Operations

1. The Philips Matrix

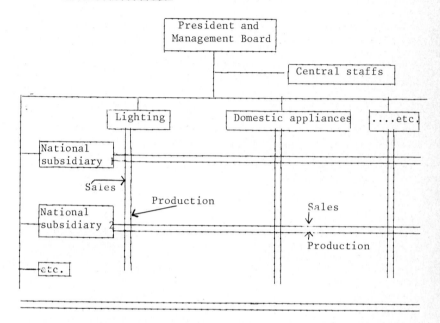

2. The Ciba-Geigy Matrix

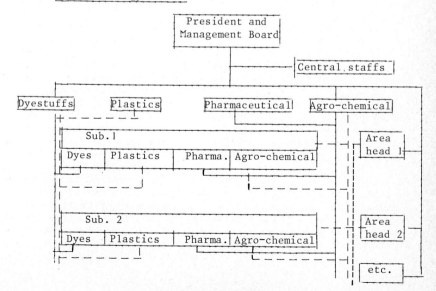

In a world of separate markets, the Continental firms ignored the American paradigm of international structure following a company strategy of international product diversification or geographical dispersion (Stopford and Wells, 1972; Franko, 1971B). I.G. Farben, for example, produced in 13 countries and in eight industries (counting chemicals and drugs as one industry) on the eve of World War II, yet the mother-daughter structure sufficed.

The separation of markets by trade barriers eliminated most possibilities of production specialization and trade inter-dependence among the foreign subsidiaries of Continental European multinational enterprises. This in itself minimized the need for cross-border communication about delivery times, payment terms, product specifications and quality. Since there were few transfers of goods, there was little need for discussion about transfer prices, much less about the distortions these could cause on subsidiary or parent income statements when transfer prices were set without taking due account of their repercussions on profitability throughout the multinational entity.

Separation of markets was a necessary condition of the use of the mother-daughter structure on a large scale. The sufficient condition was provided by the nature of the material-substituting or process innovations being carried into foreign productions by many Continental enterprises (Franko, 1975: ch. II).

Firms engaged in the pioneering of new products, like most American multinational enterprises, needed considerable cross-border communication within the organization as they spread new products around the globe in product-cycle fashion, even in the absence of an interdependent flow of goods within the multinational system. Customer demand for new products, unlike that for synthetics or old products produced with new processes, tends to be price inelastic (Vernon: 1966 ; Hirsch: 1967). Before deciding to purchase new products, customers require information that is not supplied in a price quotation; they ask questions about the function of the product, its reliability, where can it be used, and where can it be serviced. For sales in foreign, second markets to grow, marketing information such as this must be transferred from the market of innovation to subsequent markets. As the American multinationals learned, organizational structures assigning supranational responsibility are important means of transferring marketing information from first to second markets.

The tendency of Continental European firms to spread international production of goods with relatively high price elasticities implied that little regular transfer of marketing information was necessary. When a trade barrier was to be jumped, there occurred a relatively unique, discrete need for technical communication. The technical knowledge necessary to starting new plants or

introducing new processes and synthetics could be circulated
among production departments on a non-formalized basis.

To the extent that Continental enterprises could reach a negotiated modus vivendi with local or international competitors the need
for subsequent international transfer of technical information was
reduced. When steady-states of nationally compartmentalized markets could be reached, the personalized hierarchy of the mother-
daughter relationship did not need replacement by structures
designed for a more efficient supranational transfer of information. Indeed, an efficient transfer of information represented
a positive danger in such circumstances : it facilitated local
competitive initiatives, which in turn could result in the un-
doing of the laborious negotiations necessary to the formation of
most cartels.

Organization change

Enterprises with U.S. operations

The Continental enterprises with the largest and most successful
operations in the United States led the movement away from the
mother-daughter structures. The competitive nature of the American market virtually ensured that the leisurely pace of personal,
unsystematized mother-daughter communications would lead to
frustration on both sides of the Atlantic (Franko: 1971 A, ch.III;
Franko: 1971 C). Table 7 indicates that nine of the ten Continental multinationals that abandoned the mother-daughter relationship before 1968 manufactured in the U.S. ; eight of those
nine had American subsidiaries with more than $ 50 million in
sales in 1970.

A direct connection between U.S. operations and changes in system-
wide organizational structures was often perceived by the managers
of the enterprises, although not always in economic terms. Philips
of Holland, and the Ciba predecessor of Ciba-Geigy of Switzerland,
traced the breakup of their mother-daughter relationships shortly
after World War II to the influence of managers returning to
headquarters operations from wartime exile in America (Bouman,
1956). The move by American firms to organize their domestic
operations by product divisions, begun in 1921 by Du Pont and
General Motors, was building toward the wave of reorganizations
that engulfed the majority of large American firms during the
1950's (Rumelt, 1974). Philips and Ciba managers brought back
to Europe the product-division concept, which its emphasis on
assigning profit responsibility for operating decisions to managers of self-contained business units. They adapted it to Swiss
and Dutch proclivities for group management by substituting collegial responsibility for American-style individual responsibility.

Table 7: Continental European Multinational Enterprises, Classified by Importance of US Manufacturing Operations in 1970 and
Abandonment of Mother-Daughter Structure.

	Abandons mother-daughter structure:		Not abandoned	Number of firms
	Before 1968	Between 1968 and 1971		
Companies with US manufacturing sales exceeding $ 50m (1970)	8	7	6	12
Companies with US manufacturing sales less than $50m (1970)	1	10	9	20
Companies having no US manufacturing (1970)	1	12	6	19
Total	10	29	21	60

Note : Any company with fewer than 20% of foreign subsidiaries
reporting on mother-daughter lines was counted as having abandoned
that relationship.

Ciba did this by forming division boards ; Philips assigned joint
divisional responsibility to co-equal technical and commercial
managers. Philips further adapted the divisional concept into the
matrix structure shown in Figure 3 by confronting the two co-
equal technical and commercial managers of product divisions with
yet other co-equal technical, commercial and financial managers
responsible for all products within individual nations. But
Philips and Ciba then applied the notion of product responsibility
not only to their domestic markets as the Americans were doing --
perhaps since Holland and Switzerland were so small -- but also
to international operations.

Nestlé adopted the area organizational structure even before
World War II, a move related to the importance attached even then
to the transfer of marketing information within that Swiss multinational. The marketing information being transferred had to do
with product pioneering undertaken in the U.S. both by Nestlé and
by its American competitors (Heer, 1966: 140, 165-168).

Managers of the U.S. subsidiary of one of the first German firms
to have abandoned the mother-daughter structure mentioned the
effect of the relative non-negotiability of the U.S. market on
their -- and their parent's -- operations. These managers indicated that they had implored the German headquarters to allow
them to divisionalize in the U.S. during the first decade in which
manufacturing had taken place in that market, but that the German
parent had insisted that U.S. operations be organized along functional lines like those of the parent. The U.S. managers, however,
found the functional organization a serious handicap to a speady
response to competition, because no one was responsible for both
the sales and production functions of the subsidiary's numerous
products. Partly as a result of the difficulties encountered by
its U.S. subsidiary, the German parent eventually replaced its
mother-daughter organizational structure. The company simultaneously moved from functional to product-line responsibility for
its highly diversified domestic operations, allowed the U.S. subsidiary to divisionalize by product, and linked domestic with
U.S. and other foreign operations by means of an international
division.

The connection between important U.S. operations and international
organizational change was not universal, as Table 7 shows. Six
of the 21 enterprises with large American manufacturing subsidiaries had not abandoned the mother-daughter form by the end of
1971. Yet, had the cutoff date for Table 7 been the end of 1972,
the table would have shown that four of these six companies were
no longer structured along mother-daughter lines.

Competition in Europe

A need for international communication resulting from product
pioneering or competitive experience in America was not the only
cause of reorganization of international operations by Continental
European enterprise.   Competition was beginning to break out in
Europe in many sectors by 1968.   Tariffs within the EEC disappear-
ed.   Penetration of Continental markets by American multinationals
was becoming considerable in the motor vehicle, electrical, machinery, and rubber sectors (Franko, 1975: ch. VI, Table VI.7).
Cooperative habits in the chemical industry were being attacked
by Italian firms bent on taking market share away from older oligopolies and by EEC and German government antitrust actions.

The multinational enterprises of Continental Europe with their
main base of activities in competitive industries, followed the
venturers to the United States in adopting supranational structures (Capital, 1971: 66 ; Hennemann, 1971: 221).   Table 8 classi-
fies the Continental European multinationals by their main industry and their propensity to abandon the mother-daughter structure.
The enterprises whose main sectors of operations were in the more
competitive categories were considerably more prone to reorganize
by 1971 than were the enterprises based in the less competitive
iron, steel, and non-ferrous metals industries.   The exceptions
to the rule, such as the three motor-vehicle and parts producers
which retained the mother-daughter structure, can be explained
by the fact that almost all their foreign manufacturing operations
took place in highly protected (usually LDC) markets.

The role of competitive pressure in promoting the adoption of
supranational structures is again suggested by the classification
of Continental multinational enterprises by their headquarters
country and their 1971 international organizational structures
shown in Table 9.   Table 9 also compares the 1971 structures of
Continental multinational enterprise to the structures of British
and American multinationals.   The fact that small, internationally open Holland and Switzerland had the lowest proportion of firms
retaining the mother-daughter structure (next to the United States)
again suggests that supranational responsibility was especially
necessary for those buffeted most by the winds of international
competition.

The sequence of change

Unlike American multinationals, the Continental enterprises that
adopted supranational organizational structures typically did so
only after achieving a relatively large geographical spread of
manufacturing operations.   Moreover, when the Continental multinationals changed their organizational structures, they did so
in a very different sequence than that followed by their American

Table 8 : Continental European Multinational Enterprises Classified by Main Industry of Operations and International Organizational Structure, 1971.

Industry	International structure				Total number of firms with information available
	Mother-Daughter		Other		
	Number	%	Number	%	
Food	0	0	1	100	1
Wood and Paper	0	0	2	100	2
Chemical and Drug	4	24	13	76	17
Petroleum	0	0	5	100	5
Rubber	1	33	2	67	3
Glass	0	0	2	100	2
Iron and Steel	5	83	1	17	6
Non-Ferrous Metals	3	100	0	0	3
Non-Electrical Machinery	2	40	3	60	5
Electrical Machinery	3	30	7	70	10
Motor Vehicles and Parts	3	50	3	50	6
	21		39		60

Note : Main industry of operations refers to the two-digit, US
Department of Commerce Standard Industrial Classification (SIC)
industry, which accounted for the largest proportion of enterprises' worldwide sales.

Table 9 : International Organizational Structures of Multinational Enterprises based in Continental Europe, the United Kingdom and the United States, 1971.

Country of Parent System	Mother-Daughter	International Division	Product	Area and World-Functional	Matrix and Mixed	Total Known
Belgium–Luxemburg	1	–	3	–	–	4
France	3	4	5	1	–	13
Germany	9	3	6	–	2	20
Italy	3	1	1	1	–	6
Netherlands[+]	0	1	1	–	2	4
Switzerland	2	–	2	1	2	7
Sweden	3	1	2	–	–	6
Total Continentals	21	10	20	3	6	60
United Kingdom[++]	8	12	8	1	19	48
United States[+++] (170 multinationals, 1968)	0	90	30	17	25	162

+   Data for multinational enterprises based in the United Kingdom was supplied by Dr. John Stopford of the London Business School.

++   Unilever is included with United Kingdom firms in this tabulation

+++   Data for the United States is from Stopford and Wells, 1972.

Some enterprises which were classified as having international division, world-wide product division, or area structures had one or two subsidaries reporting to headquarters alongs mother-daughter lines.

Figure 4 : International Organizational Evolution of Multinational
Enterprise

Continental Multinational Enterprise

International structures

Domestic structures	Mother-Daughter	International Division	Global structures

Functional

Divisional

(4)   (4)   (2)   (1)   (1)   (1)   (27)   (1)   (1)

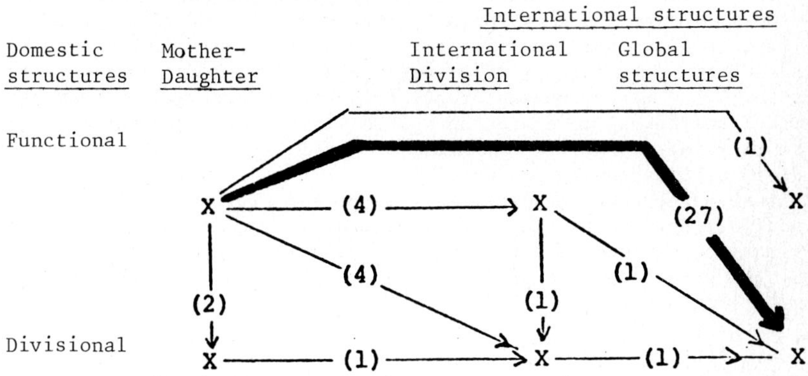

American Multinational Enterprise

International structures

Domestic structures	Mother-Daughter	International Division	Global structures

Functional

Divisional

(56)   (10)   (8)   (88)   (16)   (42)   (75)   (49)   (14)

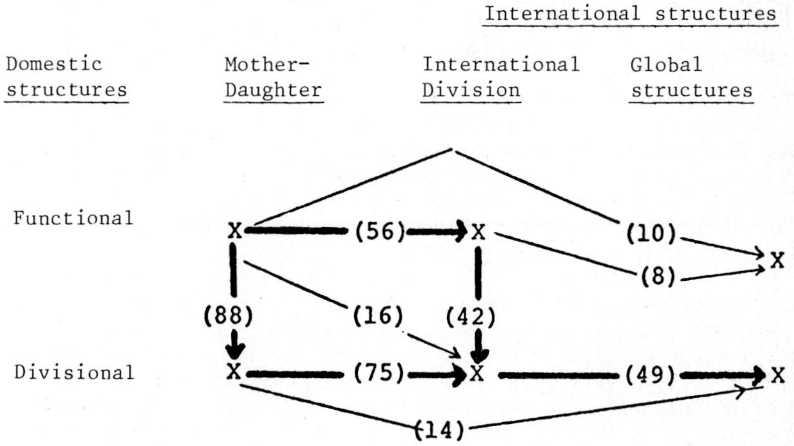

Sources : For Continental Multinational Enterprise : CEI-Harvard
Comparative Multinational Enterprise Project. For US Enterprise,
Stopford and Wells, 1972, p. 28.

counterparts.

Figure 4 contrasts the organizational evolution of Continental
European multinationals with that of American multinationals. One
sees that most Continental firms simply skipped the international
division phase passed through by nearly 90% of the 170 American
multinationals surveyed (Stopford and Wells, 1972: 21-28). In
addition, Continental enterprises, in all but three cases, undertook both domestic and international reorganization simultaneously. Continental moves to the "global" forms of organization
(world-wide product, area, mixed or matrix structures) accompanied
divisionalization by product at home. In contrast, more than
three-quarters of the American enterprises classified as multinational saw fit to change their domestic structures from functional to divisional forms prior to adopting one of the so-called
global structures (Stopford and Wells, 1972: 28 ; Fouraker and
Stopford, 1968).

The disinterest of Continental enterprises in anticipating international structural change by domestic structural change can be
traced to the fact that Continental companies' home-country markets were among the most negotiable parts of their international
orbit -- rather than among the least, as in the case of the U.S.
firms. Changes in the competitive environment facing Continental
enterprise worked their way inward from the periphery of the
U.S., then to other European operations, toward the center.

In the competitive environment of their home market, American
firms adapted their structures to meet the needs of their product-
diversification strategies (Chandler, 1961). In practice, this
means the American firms having diversified their product lines
at home, forsook the functional structure for a divisional structure before they became involved in foreign operations (Chandler,
1961; Fouraker and Stopford, 1968).

In Continental Europe, structure did not follow strategy until
there was a change in the competitive environment (Franko, 1974).
The average Continental European enterprise was actually more
likely to be diversified both at home and abroad than was the
average American multinational (Franko, 1975: ch.I, Table I.11).
Whereas 16% of American multinationals had all their domestic
operations in one industry, only 11% of Continental multinationals
were similarly undiversified at home. While 35% of the American
multinationals had their foreign operations in one industry, only
16% of the Continental multinationals were undiversified abroad.
Had structure followed strategy in the Continental European environment, one would have expected nearly universal use of the
product-division structure (Franko, 1974; Thannheiser, 1972;
Pavan, 1972; Pooley-Dyas, 1972).

Moves to global structures

Once Continental multinational firms began to face internationally competitive environments, Continental structures became con-
gruant with domestic and international product-diversification
strategies.

When organizations were changed, enterprises with highly diverse
foreign product lines adopted world-wide product structures. Nine-
teen of the 20 Continental European multinationals that moved to
world-wide product structures were managing foreign operations
in several industries, as shown by Table 5.

Area structures -- or their near cousin, world-wide functional
structures -- were adopted by three firms by 1971, all of which
had little foreign product diversity, and all of which were manufacturing in more than 14 countries. Like the American multinational enterprises that adopted the area structure, Continental
multinationals with specialized product lines moves to defend
themselves against the onslaughts of competition, not by abandon-
ing the products to which they had a long commitment, but rather
by building an organization permitting the exploitation of all
possible economies of multinational scale. The organizational
means to achieve such economies was the centralized coordination
of operations in particular geographical areas. Centralized coordination sometimes culminated in the elimination of general management responsibility for individual countries and the adoption
of world-wide functional structure (Franko, 1971B : ch. III).
Such coordination could permit economies of scale in marketing,
since successful promotion and product-differentiation methods
could be rapidly diffused around the multinational system. Area
coordination could also facilitate the use of unexploited economies in finance and production when competitive pressures made
"rationalization" necessary.

The experience of one Continental enterprise which was taking
tentative steps in 1972 toward grouping its mother-daughter subsidiaries into areas, illustrates in microcosm how international
competition could render traditional parent-subsidiary relationships absolete for companies having relatively narrow product
lines. The enterprise had no foreign production outside its main
industry and had maintained mother-daughter relationships with
its foreign subsidiaries over 60 years of multinational operations.
It had long been among the leaders in an industry in which firms
had traditionally maintained relatively co-operative relations
in operations outside of the antitrust-conscious United States.
During the 1950's, tariff barriers and more-or-less gentlemanly
rivalry urged the enterprise into production in Latin America.
At the time manufacturing commenced in Latin America, trade among
the foreign subsidiaries in the system occurred only sporadically.

Trade for the enterprise had previously meant exports from the
home country – until such time as local governments forced production. Since transfers of goods among subsidiaries were rare,
the prices at which transfers took place were set by individual
daughter-company presidents, often without consulting or inform-
ing the mother company. After start-up, one of the Latin American
daughter companies placed a small order for some intermediate
component goods with one of its sister manufacturing subsidiaries:
the sister, wishing to tend to its own protected national market,
and not wanting to be bothered by small orders from a distant land,
intentionally set a transfer price at an exceedingly high level
with the aim of discouraging such bothersome orders. For more
than 15 years, however, the Latin American subsidiary refused to
be discouraged. It was not aware that it was being charged a
penalty price, and, as local economic growth proceded in a highly
protected market, it could sell increasingly large volumes of its
protected manufactures incorporating the excessively priced intermediate.

In the late 1960's, however, a relatively small American newcomer
to the industry, seeing the wide gap between its costs (calculated
on a basis which took into account the interdependence of the
firm's world-wide operations), and prices in the Latin American
country, also jumped the tariff barrier, set up production, and
cut prices. The subsidiary of the European enterprise then saw
its sales' growth rate start to decline, despite efforts to differentiate its product on the basis of its long experience and
technical competence in the industry. It was gradually forced to
meet its competitor's prices. The mother company, no longer
receiving the dividends and statements of earnings to which it
had been accustomed, decided that local management was not being
zealous enough in cutting costs. Taking advantage of the approaching retirement of the subsidiary manager, headquarters sent another expatriate out from the center with orders to show more profit. The new president promptly began to cut local costs by embarking on a no-new-hiring policy. When locally reported profits
were not restored, first managers, and then employees were let go.
The Latin American country was, however, facing severe unemploy-
ment and under-employment problems. The firings were received
with mass protests by workers, great unrest among remaining personnel, and more than one attempt on the life of the new subsidiary president.

Only after these disagreeable events did subsidiary managers note
that the subsidiary was maintaining sales volume by taking a loss
on the good incorporating the imported component with its penalty price. The multinational system as a whole had been making a
considerable profit out of the Latin American business ; it showed up, however, as a particularly pleasant profit in the subsidiary that exported the intermediate goods, and as a loss on the

books of the importing operation. Because of the mother-daughter
organizational structure of the company, each national subsidiary
was treated as a portfolio holding unconnected to the rest of the
multinational system, with the result that neither headquarters,
nor either of the two subsidiaries in question had a complete
picture of profitability- or even the cost and price elements
composing system profit.

As management recognized the fact of international interdependence of company parts, they realized that the organizational structure of the enterprise needed to reflect this interdependence.
When neither governments nor firms could isolate national markets
from one another and prevent competitive entry, an organization
designed for supranational co-ordination became necessary.

References

Bouman, P.J., <u>Anton Philips of Eindhoven</u>, Weidenfeld and Nicolson, London, 1956.

<u>Capital</u>, "Management-Beratung McKinsey - Die Jesuiten der Deutschen Wirtschaft", March 1971.

Chandler, Alfred, <u>Strategy and Structure</u>, M.I.T. Press, Cambridge, 1961.

Cvetkov, Pierre, "Le Contrôle de la Société Générale sur les Principales Enterprises Belges et ses Mecanismes", <u>La revue nouvelle</u>, November 1972.

Degussa, <u>Aller Anfang ist schwer</u>, Degussa, Frankfurt-am-Main,1973.

<u>Financial Times</u>, "Synthetic Fibre Safeguards", June 19, 1973.

Fouraker, Lawrence E. and Stopford, John M., "Organizational Structure and the Multinational Strategy", <u>Administrative Science Quarterly</u>, no. 13, no.1, June 1968.

Franko, Lawrence G., <u>European Business Strategies in the United States</u>, Business International, S.A., Geneva, 1971 A.

Franko, Lawrence G., <u>Joint Venture Survival in Multinational Corporations</u>, Praeger, N.Y., 1971 B.

Franko, Lawrence G., "Strategy + Structure - Frustration = Experience of European Firms in America", <u>European Business</u>, Autumn 1971 C.

Franko, Lawrence G., "Who Manages Multinational Enterprise?", <u>Columbia Journal of World Business</u>, Summer 1973.

Franko, Lawrence G., "The Move Toward the Multidivisional Structure by European Organizations", <u>Administrative Science Quarterly</u>, December 1974.

Franko, Lawrence G., "<u>The Other Multinationals : The International Firms of Continental Europe</u>", Harper and Row, London and N.Y., 1975.

Galbraith, Jay R., "Organization Design : An Information Processing View", unpublished Ms., M.I.T., Cambridge, Mass., October 1969.

Haber, L.F., The Chemical Industry, 1900-1930, Clarendon Press, Oxford, 1971.

Heer, Jean, Reflets du Monde, 1866-1966, Présence de Nestlé, Château de Glérolles, Rivaz, Suisse, 1966.

Hennemann, Friedrich, Organisationstruktur und Produktion in Ausland, Universität Karlsruhe (West Germany), 1971.

Hirsch, Seev, Location of Industry and International Competitiveness, Oxford University Press, London, 1967.

Kocka, Jürgen, Unternehmensverwaltung und Angestelltenschaft am Beispiel Siemens 1847-1914, Ernst Klett Verlag, Stuttgart, 1969.

Lombard, Andrew J., Jr., "How European Companies Organize their International Operations", European Business, July 1969.

McKay, J.P., Pioneers for Profit, Foreign Entrepreneurschip and Russian Industrialization, 1885-1913, University of Chicago, Chicago, 1970.

Pavan, Robert J., Strategy and Structure of Italian Enterprise, unpublished D.B.A. thesis, Harvard Graduate School of Business Administration, Boston, 1972.

Pooley-Dyas, Gareth, Strategy and Structure of French Enterprise, unpublished D.B.A. thesis, Harvard Graduate School of Business Administration, Boston, 1972.

Rumelt, Richard, Strategy, Structure and Financial Performance of the Fortune "500", 1950 - 1970, Harvard University Press, Cambridge, 1974.

Schollhammer, Hans, "Organization Structures of Multinational Corporations", Academy of Management Journal, Vol. 14, no. 3, September 1971.

Siemens, G., History of the House of Siemens, vols I and II, Karl Alber Verlag, Freiburg/Munich, 1957.

Stopford, John M. and Wells, Louis T., Jr., Managing the Multinational Enterprise, Basic Books, N.Y., 1972.

Thannheiser, Heinz, Strategy and Structure of German Enterprise, unpublished D.B.A. thesis, Harvard Graduate School of Business Administration, Boston, 1972.

Van Den Bulke, D., Les investissements industriels étrangers dans l'économie belge, Université de Gand, Gand, 1971.

Vernon, Raymond, "Some Tentative Hypotheses on the Behavior of
    European-based and Japanese-based Multinational Enterprises",
    Manuscript for a conference on Multinational Enterprises,
    Agnelli Foundation, Turin, Italy, June 1971.

Vernon, Raymond, "International Trade and International Investment
    in the Product Cycle", Quarterly Journal of Economics, May
    1966.

OWNERSHIP AND CONTROL OF FOREIGN OPERATIONS

John M. Stopford
Professor of International Business
London Business School

Klaus O. Haberich
Ph.D. candidate
London Business School

In 1974, the Indian government announced new legislation to reduce
to 40 per cent the share most foreign companies could hold in
Indian firms. Other forms of control have also recently been announced, such as the Brazilian Post Office's decision to buy tele-
communication equipment only from companies whose majority is in
Brazilian hands. Both highly developed countries such as Canada,
and developing countries such as Nigeria and Indonesia are evolving legislation to limit the foreign ownership of companies.
Such laws have, to be sure, long been on the statute book in some
countries : Sweden has had them in some sectors of her economy
since the 19th century. What is new is the accelerating pace at
which such legislation is spreading around the world.

Constraints on ownership policy have become, short of outright
denial of entry or expropriation, the most widely used means of
controlling the so-called multinational corporations (MNC). Even
the United States Congress has felt sufficiently threatened by the
inward-directed investments following the dollar devaluations to
discuss limits to foreign ownership. This type of legislation
raises a number of crucial questions both for the managers of MNC's
and for governments. Will enforced joint ventures contribute more
to the local economies than might have been expected under conditions of unrestricted foreign ownership ? Will MNC's simply withdraw or refuse either to reinvest or to enter countries introducing such legislation ?

The research on which this paper is based was funded in part by
the Ford Foundation, to which grateful acknowledgement is made.

Reprinted by permission of the published from the Journal of
General Management, Vol.III, nr.4, Summer 1976.

The list of such questions and attendant speculation seems endless.
Part of the difficulty of assessing the likely impact of regulating
ownership is the dearth of information about the MNC's current
ownership policies and practices. Despite an extensive literature
on individual cases[1] and surveys in particular countries[2], few
aggregate data on the factors that condition MNC's global policies
are available. One exception is a study of 187 U.S.-based MNC's
that indentified strong relationships among the firm's strategy,
its industry, and ownership policy[3]. The purpose of this paper is
to provide data on the ownership policies of 83 British-based MNC's
in a form comparable to those in the United States study. Joint
ventures for which all the partners were foreign to the country
of the venture's activity were excluded in both the United States
and the British studies. Attention is focussed on arrangements
where the equity is shared between foreign and local interests.

The Parent Companies

By the end of 1970, the 83 British-based manufacturing parent
companies examined here had established or acquired over 7.000
affiliates abroad, of which more than 2.500 were engaged in local
manufacturing. All the firms were ranked in the top 150 of the
Times 1000 survey for 1970, and all owned 25% or more of at least
three manufacturing companies abroad. Foreign controlled firms,
and non-manufacturing firms were excluded from the analysis,
though Royal Dutch/Shell and Unilever were included. In 1970
these British firms employed approximately 1,5 million people
abroad. Their overseas sales, excluding exports from the United
Kingdom, amounted to over ₤ 22.000 million – probably three-
quarters of total overseas manufacturing output of British-owned
companies.

Apart from being primarily concerned with manufacturing activities,
these firms were exceedingly diverse in nature : their sales in
1970 ranged from under ₤ 100 million to over ₤ 6.000 million ;
they represented virtually every sector of British manufacturing
industry ; their involvement in international business varied from
Bass Charrington's recent small exploratory investments to the
long-established global systems of such firms as Dunlop or Reckitt
and Colman.

The overall propensity of the parent company to work with partners
has also varied widely. Contrary to the much-repeated statements
that both British and United States firms insist where possible
upon wholly owned affiliates, many have actively sought partners.
Whether by design or by force of circumstance, most of the 83 British firms had partners in at least some of their overseas manufacturing affiliates.

Table 1 : MNC's Classified by Percentage of their Foreign Manufacturing Affiliates that were Joint Ventures[*]

Percentage of MNC's Foreign Manufacturing Affiliates that were Joint Ventures	British MNC's (1970 Data) %	United States MNC's (1966 Data) %
None	5	18
1-20	14	24
21-40	38	23
41-60	29	20
61-80	12	9
81-100	2	6
	100%	100%
Number of MNC's	83	187

[*] Excludes affiliates in India, Japan, Mexico, Pakistan, Spain, Sri Lanka.

Sources : For United States MNC's : J.M. Stopford and L.T. Wells, Managing the Multinational Enterprise (London : Longman 1972), Table 7-1.

For British MNC's : London Business School Multinational Data Bank.

Table 1 shows that almost half of the British firms had partners
in at least 40 per cent of their affiliates at the end of 1970.
The 187 United States firms, also shown in Table 1, had a somewhat
lower proportion of joint ventures, but even they did not in general conform to the stereotype. The table, like most that follow,
excludes affiliates located in six countries – India, Japan,
Mexico, Pakistan, Spain, Sri Lanka – where government has for some
considerable time closely controlled ownership choices. Most of
the analysis is concerned with activities where the MNC has been
able to choose among alternative policies.

Despite the diversity of owernship practice, some common strands
of policy are apparent among firms pursuing similar investment
policies in similar countries. In order to disentangle some of
the major and interrelated forces influencing choices of ownership policy, the analysis that follows proceeds on a step-by-step
basis progressively excluding special cases. The analysis is
limited to manufacturing affiliates. The owernship of oil wells,
mines and other purely extractive operations deserves separate
and detailed examination beyond the scope of this article. Affiliates concerned solely with selling, transportation, and other
non-manufacturing activities are also excluded.

Historical Perspectives

Data on the ownership of foreign affiliates at the end of 1970
provide merely a snapshot of a field of long-distance runners.
From the time each firm started abroad, strategies have been adjusted with consequent effect on the desirability or otherwise
of partners in the management of the overseas factories. As their
fortunes have fluctuated, some firms have sold affiliates,created
or acquired new ones ; others have issued part of the affiliate's
equity on the local stock exchange or bought out their erstwhile
partners. Changes in government policy have also affected the
firm's propensity to work in partnership, sometimes under duress.

Despite the continuous and shifting interplay of forces affecting
ownership policy, a long-term trend towards a more frequent use of
partnership arrangements is apparent. As Table 2 shows, 90 per
cent of all manufacturing affiliates established before the end
of World War 1 were wholly owned. During each subsequent decade
that percentage fell steadily to 64 per cent during the 1960's.
Data on some 2.800 overseas affiliates of United States firms show
the same trend.[4]

Several interdependent factors provide some clues as to the reasons for this trend. First, early entrants to international investment such as Dunlop were typically strong leaders in an oligopoly and able to insist on outright ownership. Frequently the

Table 2 : British MNC's Ownership of Foreign Manufacturing Subsidiaries, by Period of Entry[+]

Period of Entry	Total No. of Subsidiaries	Ownership at Time of Entry		
		Wholly owned %	Majority owned %	Minority owned %
Before 1919	50	90	10	--
1919-30	117	78	9	14
1931-40	73	74	12	14
1941-50	86	72	13	15
1951-60	333	68	17	15
1961-70	1291	64	17	19

+ Excludes affiliates that were sold, expropriated or otherwise
  lost to the parent system before 1970 : also excludes affiliates in India, Japan, Mexico, Pakistan, Spain, Sri Lanka.

++ Figures are percentages of total number of affiliates in each
   period.

availability of suitable partners who could contribute to the new
ventures was distinctly limited when they created industries new
to the countries in which they invested. Over time however competitors appeared, often with superior technology, to erode the
power of the oligopolies. Second, many firms like Reed Paper with
strong domestic market positions delayed their entry abroad until
well after the end of the Second World War. Lacking knowledge of
local market conditions and wishing to catch up on their entren-
ched international competitors, they frequently turned to local
partners to speed their entry. Third, many firms for long limited
their foreign ventures to Commonwealth countries. Only recently
have they begun to range more widely and have turned to local
partners for help in learning about new markets. Fourth, legislation to limit foreign ownership has become more widespread.

There have been, to be sure, countervailing forces at work. Policies to rationalise and integrate previously independent production centres have on occasion been implemented at the same time
as local partners have been bought out. Adopting area-based structures of management has also been closely associated with buy-out
policies.[5] Data on the incidence and importance of such policies
in British-based MNC's are scarce. Yet it seems clear that taken
together they did not have a significant impact on the general
historical trend before 1970.

Legal Ownership and Management Control

Before one may usefully explore the data in greater depth, some
problems of terminology need to be resolved. Tables 1 and 2 considered ownership to be a function of whether one or more partners were directly involved in the management of the affiliates.
Considering owernship in this way ignores the fact that many are
owned only indirectly by the parent company.

Table 3 shows typical chains of ownership of affiliates. Affiliates A1 and A2, for example, are wholly owned by the Australian
holding company, of which in turn 75 per cent is owned by the
parent company. Although these two affiliates have no partners
directly engaged in their management, the parent group does not
own all their equity. The examples shown in Table 3 are relatively simple and restricted to four links in the chain of legal
ownership. In practice many large firms have more than four links
in the chain for some parts of their business. Further compli-
cation is introduced in situations where, for legal and tax
reasons, portions of the equity of an affiliate are shared among
several other affiliates.

For the purposes of assessing an MNC's ownership policy, the
existence of these chains must explicitly be recognised. Legal

Table 3 : Hypothetical Example of Structure of Legal Ownership of Foreign Affiliates

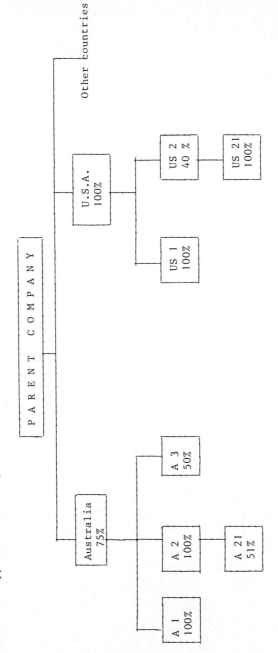

Note : Percentage figures in each box refer to the percentage of the voting equity held by the affiliate's immediate parent.

ownership, defined by the equity attributable to the parent company, is used here for this purpose. The arithmetical rule for
calculating the attributable percentage is modified for a chain
of ownership in which each link is at least majority owned. Thus,
for example, affiliate A21 in Table 3 is considered to be majority owned even though only 38 per cent of its equity is attributable to the parent. Legal ownership is not always directly equivalent to control.[6]

Other factors, to be sure, impinge on the affiliate and affect
the ability of the central office to exercise control. Some
combinations of government legislation and licensing procedure
can virtually isolate a wholly owned affiliate from its parent's
control. There are times when a parent can exercise effectively
absolute control over a minority-owned affiliate.

One set of circumstances, where legally defined ownership is
clearly not a good indicator of management control, needs explicit recognition. Where the parent has sold a minority portion of
an affiliate's shares on the local stock exchange, seldom has
absolute control been seriously dissipated ; the local shareholders are typically too dispersed to provide an effective voice
in management. There are of course exceptions to this general
rule.

Of the roughly 2.500 manufacturing affiliates studied, over 350
were clearly identified as being subject to these circumstances.
Most were concentrated in a few countries and a few industries.
To avoid distortion in the analysis and to facilitate comparisons
with the U.S.-based MNC's, for which such local stock exchange
behaviour is rare outside Canada, the appropriate adjustments
to the category of legally defined ownership were made.[8] The
adjusted figures are referred to under the heading of management
control. They provide the basis for most of the analysis that
follows.

Policies Favouring Joint Venture Partners

Some strategies of international expansion so stretch the firm's
ability to expand their resources that they may turn to partners
who can provide the needed resources in return for some of the
control. Many firms in extractive industries have collaborated
with local partners in their manufacturing investments so as to
ensure their access to markets for their raw materials. Firms that
have widely diversified their product lines have used partners as
sources of the additional skills, especially marketing, necessary
to develop their new lines.

Among the major U.S.-based MNC's in 1966 it has been shown that
those operating overseas in four or more industries collaborated
with partners nearly twice as frequently as did those concentrating their activities within a single industry. The same test
applied to British-based MNC's revealed no such distinction. Quite
why there should be such a disparity in behaviour between the
two groups of firms is not entirely clear. Part of the answer
concerns the acquisition and merger behaviour of the British-
based MNC's during the 1960's. In many instances, diversification was accomplished by buying other British firms that had previously developed important overseas investments. For example,
Wiggins Teape had created a large international network of paper
interests long before being purchased by British American Tobacco
in the late 1960's. Any measure of BAT's ownership policy in
1970 is weighted by the early Wiggins Teape policies, not those
of BAT for the management of their new paper interest. Few instances of equivalent magnitude were recorded among the U.S.-
based MNC's.

In order to avoid this problem, the analysis was restricted to
the development of "diverse" product lines after their acquisition. Diverse lines were those that a) were in industries quite
distinct from the major lines in terms of technology or type of
market, and b) accounted for less than 2 per cent of overseas
turnover. One hundred and seventy-four affiliates manufacturing
products that met these requirements were identified.

As Table 4 shows, very few of these "diversified" affiliates were
wholly owned. Even though they were unimportant compared to the
main businesses, these product lines have received considerable
attention : nearly 10 per cent of all foreign affiliates were
created to manage their international expansion after initial
acquisition. Just as has been the case for U.S.-based MNC's,
partners have clearly been a major source of additional resources for the development of these peripheral businesses.

Table 4 also shows that British-based MNC's have been more ven-
turesome in product policy in the Commonwealth and have worked
with partners there more frequently than elsewhere. Again the
reasons are not clear. One line of speculation concerns the
typical central policy restricting an affiliate's products to
those made at home. In some firms that central policy has been
relaxed to a degree unknown among U.S.-based MNC's. Indeed, there
are instances where an affiliate has been permitted to enter any
potentially profitable business. Such permission is likely to
be granted more readily in countries - predominantly Commonwealth
- where the affiliate has previously gained considerable experience. Metal Box provided a recent example when it made its first
move into glass containers, not in Britain, but in Nigeria. Metal
Box's knowledge of the Nigerian container market was added to the

Table 4 : British MNC's Management Control of Foreign Manufacturing Affiliates, Classified by Location and Product Diversification, end 1970[+]

Management Control	Affiliates in Diversified Products[++]		All Other Affiliates	
	Commonwealth %	Non-Commonwealth %	Commonwealth %	Non-Commonwealth %
Absolute	25	34	68	67
Majority	21	27	17	13
Minority	54	39	15	20
	100%	100%	100%	100%
No of Affiliates	110	64	1107	793

[+] Excludes affiliates in India, Japan, Mexico, Pakistan, Spain, Sri Lanka ; also excludes extractive firms.

[++] See text for definition.

technological resources of a Japanese glass company in a consortium that included the Nigerian Industrial Development Bank to form the country's first major glass bottler.[9] Territorial experience combined with a willingness to diversify overseas can produce innovative partnerships.

Portfolio Investments

Many large international investors have very small shares of some foreign companies that have been acquired in a variety of ways. Some represent the conversion of royalty agreements into an equity sharing arrangement. Other are the legacy of selling small affiliates to larger local competitors. Associated Portland Cement Manufacturers (APCM), for example, acquired a 10 per cent holding a Gemstar, a large Belgian-controlled Canadian producer of building materials in exchange for APCM's small Canadian offshoot. Yet others are held by such bodies as the Tobacco Securities Trust, in which some MNC's have a stake. Overseas assets acquired by such means are largely peripheral to the firm's main strategies of investment and control. Using the convention of defining direct investments in terms of a holding of more than 25 per cent of the voting equity, holdings of 25 per cent or less - portfolio investments) are excluded from the analysis that follows.

There are however two types of portfolio investment that have a direct bearing on the strategy of the firm. First, arrangements in vertically integrated industries such as the consortium refineries mentioned earlier are often tied to management contracts for at least one member of the consortium. The proportion of the shares held by each member is frequently well below 25 per cent. Second, there are investments of the type dubbed "an exchange of hostages". These investments are made, sometimes on a reciprocal basis, by major firms in an international oligopoly. They are designed, inter alia, to restrict or at least control areas of competition or to provide a mechanism for the exchange of technology. BICC in Britain and General Cable in the United States, for example, each hold roughly 20 per cent of the other's stock. The existence of such "hostages" means that the exclusion of all portfolio investments also excludes some aspects of international management policy.

Policies Favouring Absolute Control

Within the mainstream businesses of the manufacturing firms there are various strong reasons why some firms insist upon unambiguous control. These reasons fall into two broad categories. First, there are reasons related to the nature of the business and the

strength of the firm to insist upon control. Leadership in a
technology-based industry where frequent transfers of information
to affiliates are needed to ensure continued competitiveness is
an example. Second, there are businesses where the only resources
a partner could bring to a joint venture are those resources already possessed by the parent system in abundance. Marketing-
intensive businesses and very large, long established affiliates
fall into this second category.

Location Factors

When firms are choosing where to locate new manufacturing facilities, critical considerations are the size of the local market
and the economic health of the local economy. The larger the
market, the greater the incentive both to invest and to aim for
a wholly owned affiliate.

Table 5 shows that affiliates in the United States had the highest incidence of absolutely controlled affiliates, followed by
the developed Commonwealth[10] and the advanced European countries.
These are the high-income territories with the largest markets for
the products of the MNC's. They are also the markets demanding
the most transfers of new technology. Furthermore, many of the
customers in these markets are themselves multinational and able
to buy from more than one affiliate. These factors all provide
both pressure and incentive for the parent company to exert absolute control.

The frequency of joint ventures in Europe is undoubtedly influenced by the fact that many of the firms started investing in
Europe as late as the mid-1960's and were subject,as suggested
earlier, to all the uncertainties of the new boy. Some erstwhile
joint venture partners had already been bought out by 1970 and
more since then, so it is possible that the pattern of British
investments in Europe will come to resemble that in the United
States.

Affiliates in smaller, less developed countries had a lesser
impact on the performance of the firm as a whole, generally required little transfer of new technology, and were more frequently
joint ventures. The propensity to accept partners was markedly
higher in the less developed Commonwealth. Lingering ties of
Empire and a residual population of expatriate British and Bri-
tish-trained local nationals may be part of the reason. Emerging
legislation to limit foreign ownership in Nigeria, Zambia and
other ex-colonies also had an effect by the end of 1970.

In interpreting Table 5, the reader should remember the adjustments made to arrive at the figures for management control.Defined

Table 5 : British MNC's Foreign Manufacturing Affiliates in Commonwealth and Other Territories, Classified by Management Control, end 1970[+]

Control Management	U.S.A. %	Commonwealth[++] Advanced %	EFTA EEC %	Rest of World %	Commonwealth Less Developed %
Absolute	84	78	71	63	50
Majority	6	13	12	20	33
Minority	10	9	17	17	17
	100%	100%	100%	100%	100%
Total No of Affiliates	86	801	449	235	255

+ Excludes affiliates located in India, Japan, Mexico, Pakistan, Spain, Sri Lanka ; excludes extractive firms, diverse affiliates, and portfolio investments.

++ Australia, Canada, New Zealand, Rhodesia, South Africa.

on a purely legal basis, the percentage of wholly owned affiliates in the developed Commonwealth drops from 78 to 50 per cent,
far lower than in other regions except the less developed Commonwealth. The reader should also note that over half the affiliates
(and perhaps as much as three-quarters of the value of the investments) were concentrated within the Commonwealth. The bias in
investment location introduced by political and cultural ties has
been enormous.[11] Per capita income effects and size of market are
not, of course, the whole story. Nevertheless, the data suggest
that they are powerful influences on management thinking about
ownership policy.

Large Affiliates

Just as foreign investment is concentrated in relatively few
industries, so the overseas production of British-based MNC's is
concentrated in a relatively few, very large affiliates. Among
all the affiliates of the non-extractive firms included in this
study, 177 were known to have had sales exceeding Ł 10 million
in 1970. A few, like BAT's United States affiliate Brown and
Williamson, were major firms in their own right with sales far in
excess of Ł 100 million. Some were portfolio investments. This
handful of firms accounted for sales of over Ł 7.500 million, of
which Ł 5.100 million was attributable to their parents on an
equity accounting basis.[12]

Table 6 shows that policies favouring absolute management control
were exercised more forcibly as the size of the affiliate increased. None of the very largest of the affiliates – those with sales
of over Ł 40 million – in the Commonwealth were owned outright.
They were all firms with shares widely distributed locally. By
contrast, most of those absolutely controlled outside the Commonwealth were also wholly owned.

Many of these very large affiliates were located in the high-
income markets discussed above. One might conclude therefore that
the trend shown in Table 6 is a function of location, not size.
The two factors cannot entirely be separated. Yet more detailed
tabulations show that within the high-income countries, large
affiliates are more frequently wholly owned than smaller ones.
In other words, the two factors may be considered as mutually
reinforcing.

Because much of the success of so many firms' international strategy rests on the success of their largest foreign affiliates, it
is perhaps no surprise to find that size and absence of partners
were related. Besides, these affiliates were of a scale sufficient to support their own wide array of specialist activity
without help from a partner. In some cases the managing directors

Table 6 : Relative Importance of Manufacturing Joint Ventures,
Classified by Size of Affiliate, end 1970[+]

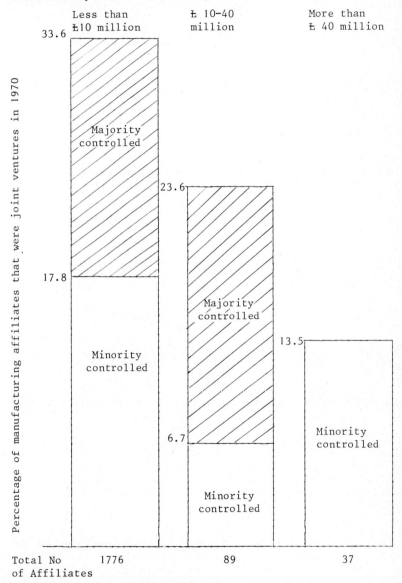

Total No   1776   89   37
of Affiliates

+ See Table 5 for data excluded.

of these affiliates had a seat on the parent company's board. In
other cases they were managed separately from the main systems of
organisation and control, and subject to special procedures. Homogeneous systems and policies for ownership and control are not
appropriate within the international groups of affiliates of
greatly varying size and strategic importance.

Global Investors

Leadership in any industry has been associated with both the
preference for and insistence upon wholly owned affiliates. Leadership may be based upon distinctive skills in research and development, in marketing, or in the administration of large-scale
systems. Among the firms studied, some had based their international expansion upon one or more of these skills. They had
developed on a global basis strong competitive positions in industries associated with oligopolistic competition. These "global
investors" are distinct in many respects from the rest, which have
in the main concentrated their efforts within the Commonwealth.

Global investors were identified as those in 1970 with less than
half of their international sales in the Commonwealth and local
manufacturing on at least four continents. Sixteen of the non-
extractive firms met these simplistic conditions. As it turned
out they were also firms with distinctive strengths of the types
already discussed. Most, like Dunlop, were among the early pioneers of international investment, though a few were relatively
recent entrants to the global game in research-based industries.
Some were among the giant firms of the world, whereas others like
Reckitt and Colman, were of more modest proportion.

Table 7 shows the differences in ownership policy for the two
groups of firms in Commonwealth countries and elsewhere. As might
be expected, the global investors' policies appeared insensitive
to the location of the affiliates. By contrast, Commonwealth-
based investors showed an increased preference for partners outside the Commonwealth where they were weakest. These differences
also held true within each of the regions shown in Table 5. Both
in relation to competitors and to governments these global investors exhibited a greater willingness and ability to insist upon
absolute control.

These firms, to be sure, were not the only category with a low
tolerance of local partners. The most research-intensive and the
most advertising-intensive firms were equally averse to joint
ventures[13]. Most of these firms were also global investors but
some had remained primarily within the Commonwealth. To an important degree the category "global investor" can be taken to connote
international competitive strength. With due allowance for some

special cases, the remainder of the firms studied were weaker
relative to their international competitors.

Compared to the United States firms the 16 global investors had a
slightly lower proportion of joint ventures, measured on the basis
of management control. Measured on the basis of purely legal
control they had strikingly similar percentages in all three categories of ownership. The strong implication is that when equally
strong competitively, British firms adopt ownership policies of
the United States variety. It is the weaker British firm that
has relied more frequently upon local partners abroad.

Countries Investing Upon Joint Ventures

Some countries have for a considerable time insisted upon the
foreign investor sharing ownership with local partners. Six
countries - India, Japan, Mexico, Pakistan, Spain and Sri Lanka -
are generally considered to have had more dirigist ownership policies than others. The ability of a government to implement its
policies depends upon its bargaining strength. Judging by the
data in Table 8, these six governments have had some success in
their bargaining ; they have ended up with local participation in
a larger proportion of the foreign-owned affiliates than is
generally the case elsewhere.

The low number of affiliates in Japan, Spain and Mexico suggest
that the countries pay some penalty for insistence on their policies in that firms have refused to consider investment on the
available terms. Most of the affiliates in Japan, for example,
are accounted for by half a dozen of the global investors. It
may also be the case that many of the firms would not have considered investment in these countries on any terms. Yet the United
States experience also suggests that refusal to invest has been
a factor. In India, Pakistan and Sri Lanka the position is
different, because of historical ties. Here many British firms
invested during Colonial or immediate post-Colonial days and most,
pace the Sri Lanka expropriation polices, have remained.

Cross-sectional data for 1970 must, of course, be placed in an
historical perspective. Most of the ownership laws in these six
countries were implemented after the Second World War. Table 9
shows the marked difference in the initial ownership percentages
between those entering before 1950 and those later on. Added to
the data in Table 9 is the fact that many affiliates, initially
absolutely controlled, have reduced the share held by the parent.
Such evidence provides an impression of the strong impact of
legislation upon the foreign investor.

Table 7 : Relative Importance of Manufacturing Joint Ventures Among British MNC's.

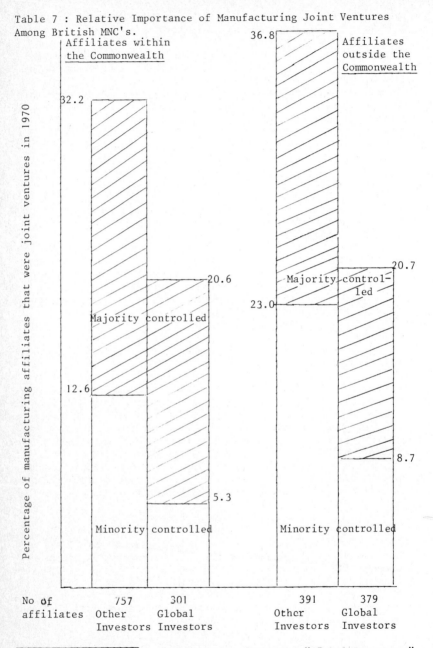

+ MNC's Classified by whether or not they were "Global Investors" end 1970.

Table 8 : Management Control of British-Owned Manufacturing Affiliates, Classified by Country of Incorporation, end 1970

COUNTRY OF INCORPORATION

Management control	Japan %	Spain %	India,Pakistan & Sri Lanka %	Mexico %	Other less developed countries %
Absolute	5	23	33	46	57
Majority	18	25	30	15	27
Minority	77	52	37	39	16
	100%	100%	100%	100%	100%
No of affiliates	22	48	132	26	548

Table 9 : Ownership at Time of Entry of British-owned Manufacturing Affiliates in Six Countries[+]

Ownership at Time of Entry	Period of Entry	
	Before 1950	1950-1970
	%	%
Absolute	59	21
Majority	32	28
Minority	10	51
	101%	100%
No of affiliates	41	160

+ India, Japan, Mexico, Pakistan, Spain, Sri Lanka ; excludes
affiliates liquidated or expropriated before 1970.

Table 10 : Changing Location and Ownership Policies for Foreign
Manufacturing Affiliates[+] (1970-1974)

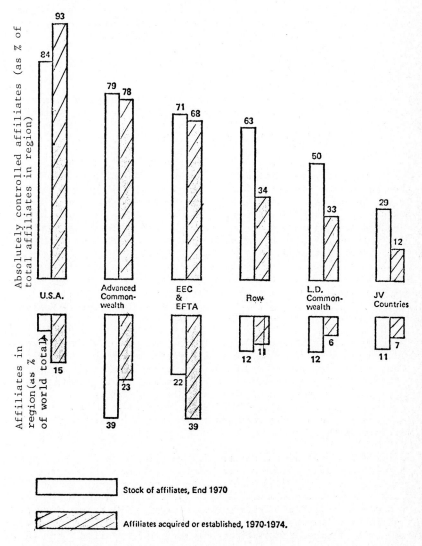

+ Excludes affiliates located in India, Japan, Mexico, Pakistan,
Spain, Sri Lanka ; excludes extractive firms, diverse affiliates,
and portfolio investments.

While Japan has been liberalising the entry conditions for
foreigners in some carefully selected industries, India has been
increasing the severity of the controls. At the same time, other
countries, notably Nigeria, Zambia, Malaysia, Thailand among
others, have been following India's lead. Even advanced countries
such as Australia have begun to introduce controlling legislation
for key sectors of their economies. Although it is too early as
yet to identify how the MNC's have and will be reacting to changes in legislation, some hints are already apparent.

Recent Responses

Few multinationals react to changing legislation in one country
without taking into account changes, both political and economic,
happening elsewhere. Table 10 provides two crude indicators of
how British-based MNC's have reacted to changing world conditions.

Compared to the position at the end of 1970, Table 10 indicates
that, among the 390 affiliates entering the parent systems during
the period, the proportion of wholly owned affiliates has risen
in the United States and the advanced Commonwealth;has declined
sharply in the less developed world ; and has remained static in
advanced Europe. Investors of the "new boy" variety have probably depressed the proportional figures for Europe, though they
have clearly not done so in the United States. These regional
changes have been occurring while the overall historical trend
towards a more frequent use of partners has continued. Calculated on a basis comparable with that in Table 2, the overall
proportion of the new affiliates that were wholly owned declined
from 64 per cent in the 1960's to 55 per cent.

Table 10 shows that not only has the proportion of wholly owned
affiliates declined in the less developed world - where legislation controlling ownership is most prevalent - but also the proportion of all new affiliates in these areas has also declined.
Taken together these two indices suggest that British-based MNC's
have been concentrating their efforts in the developed world and
withholding both management and financial resources from the less
developed world.

That sense of relative concentration is reinforced by some shreds
of evidence about recent changes in the control of affiliates
that were owned in 1970. Table 11 shows that the areas of concentration for new investment are also areas in which the MNC's have
been buying out their partners. For example, EMI bought out all
the minority shareholders in Capital Inc. in order to restructure
the whole of its North American operations. Many firms, including
Cadbury Schweppes, have begun to restructure their European activities on a continental basis and have in the process felt impelled

Table 11. Changes in the Management Control of Foreign Manufacuring Affiliates, Classified by Region, 1971-74[+]

Number of Affiliates where Management Control has been :	U.S.A.	Developed Commonwealth	EEC & EFTA	Rest of World	Less Developed Commonwealth	JV++ Territories
Increased	–	7	21	3	3	4
Decreased	3	22	5	2	18	10

+ Excludes extractive firms.

++ Includes India, Japan, Mexico, Pakistan, Spain, Sri Lanka.

to buy out their erstwhile national partners who could take only
a parochial perspective on the change. At the same time, control
has been reduced elsewhere, mainly in direct response to changing
legislation.

Conclusions

The ownership of foreign manufacturing affiliates and the control
exercised by the British parent company has been influenced by a
number of considerations internal to the firm. The evidence suggests that where the parent company possessed distinctive strengths
in product lines critical to its continued survival, wholly owned
positions have been preferred. Where the resources of the parent
were less distinctive as compared to other international competitors, or where the business was peripheral to the main interests
of the parent, partners were often preferred.

These influences can be interpreted in terms of the management
of transfers between the overseas affiliate and the rest of the
parent company's international system. Transfers are in the form
of inputs to the affiliate : technological and other resources as
well as the supply of components or semi-finished products. They
are also in the form of outputs from the affiliate : products, as
well as dividends and other financial flows. In situations where
the management of some or all of these transfers is needed on a
regional or global basis, absolute control is preferred. Conflicts
with joint venture partners are most acute where the needs of the
affiliate are made subordinate to the needs of the MNC as a whole.
In situations where the need for management control of the transfers is less pressing and greater degrees of local autonomy are
both acceptable and desirable, working in partnership can be not
only less prone to conflict, but also positively desirable in
terms of adding needed resources to the management of the affiliate.

In these respects the British-based MNC's have behaved in a manner closely resembling that of U.S.-based MNC's. The only major
difference has been the greater willingness of the British to
sell part of their affiliates' equity on local exchanges. But
that willingness has largely been restricted to the Commonwealth
and has not unduly diminished the control retained by the parent.
To the extent that many British-based MNC's are somewhat weaker
in terms of technological resources, marketing skills, and even
sheer size they have exhibited a slightly higher propensity to
work with partners abroad.

Ownership and control are also directly influenced by the policies
of host governments. The evidence shows that some governments
have succeeded in implementing policies requiring greater local

participation without causing foreign firms to withdraw in droves.
They may, however, have inhibited some firms from entering at all,
and have biassed the types of new investment in favour of those
requiring relatively few transfers with the rest of the MNC's
systems.

The emerging changes in general investment preference among
British-based MNC's in recent years may, however, prove to have
a significant effect on the outcomes of the MNC/government bargaining. Many British managers increasingly feel impelled to
develop stronger roots in developed economies to offset the problems of controlling a world business from a weakening home base.
This sense may lead some firms to withdraw more readily than
hitherto from smaller, less developed markets as the levels of
local control are raised. The planned sale of Burmah-Shell in
India is an example. In other words, the risk to governments of
losing British investments appears to be increasing.

Set against this risk, however, are two important factors. First,
British firms may become more willing to contemplate management
contracts and licensing agreements, tied perhaps to minority
equity holdings, in areas previously restricted by Board policy
to investments absolutely controlled. The returns from small
investments become relatively more attractive as the calls for
resources in other parts of the world increase. Such alternative
arrangements are much more politically acceptable in countries
actively concerned to control the activities of foreigners.
Second, governments may find that investors from other countries,
especially from Japan, have no inhibitions about accepting even
minority positions. To the extent that they can attract investors from some country with the needed resources, governments
(even and perhaps especially those ex-British Colonies) will not
worry about the risk of losing British investment. Under these
extremely uncertain conditions, sensible policies are likely to
be developed only if both companies and governments are each
willing to understand the position of the other more clearly than
they have in the past.

References

1. An excellent example is Friedman, Wolfgang G. and Beguin,
    Jean-Pierre, Joint International Business Ventures in Deve-
    loping Countries. New York : Columbia, University Press,1971.

2. See for example Tomlinson, James W.C., The Joint Venture Pro-
    cess in International Business. Cambridge : MIT Press, 1970.

3. Stopford, John M. and Wells, Louis T., Managing the Multi-
    national Enterprise. London : Longman, 1972, Part II.

4. Stopford and Wells, op. cit. Table 10-1.

5. Franko, L.G., Joint Venture Survival in Multinational Corpo-
    rations. New York : Praeger, 1971.

6. For the purposes of analysis, absolute control was deemed to
    include equity holdings of 95-100%. Also, 50-50 joint ven-
    tures were included in the minority category.

7. For a fascinating account of the reasons for this share issue,
    see Reader, W., Imperial Chemical Industries : A History.
    Vol. Two. London : Oxford University Press, 1975.

8. Note that much of the United States data were computed for
    the immediate parent links in the chain. Fortunately this
    complication is probably slight, because most U.S.-based
    MNC's have shorter chains of ownership than the British.
    Nevertheless, as in all such comparative work, care must be
    taken to recognise that legal practices differ without neces-
    sarily implying differences in management practice.

9. For an account of the reasoning that led to this consortium,
    see "Giving Africa its own bottles", Financial Times, October
    10, 1975.

10. South Africa is included among the developed Commonwealth in
    view of its past membership and the fact that the country's
    published per capita income figures do not accurately portray
    the development of the white community.

11. For an examination of this bias and its incidence in various
    industries, see Stopford, J.M. "Changing Perspectives on
    Investment of British Manufacturing Multinationals", in
    Dunning, J.H. (ed.), Methods of Servicing Overseas Markets
    (forthcoming).

12. Despite many gaps in the data on affiliates' size, those for
    the largest are considered reasonably complete. Precise fi-
    gures were obtained for 115 and reasonably close approxima-
    tions were provided by companies themselves for the remainder.
    Even so, a few large affiliates may have slipped unnoticed
    through the net. Extractive firms were excluded from these
    calculations, because of the difficulty of obtaining accurate
    figures for the affiliates' turnover.

13. Measured respectively by R & D expenditures of more than 5
    per cent of turnover and by advertising expenditures of more
    than 2 per cent of turnover.

MULTINATIONALS, TRANSNATIONALS AND NOW CONATIONALS

Milton Hochmuth

Centre d'Enseignement Supérieur des Affaires

The Inversion of Multinational and Transnational

A great deal of sound, far more printed word, and an inordinate amount of fury have long centered on the "multinational" corporation. To this complex mass of reasoned (and not infrequently unreasoned) analyses there has been added an equally large dimension of confusion. This confusion was triggered by the Hearings Before the Group of Eminent Persons to Study the Impact of Multinational Companies on Development and International Relations sponsored by United Nations (1). It crystalized when some witnesses before the Group insisted on reversing the previously widely accepted definitions, of multinational and transnational corporations. Speaking for the Andean Pact countries Senor José de la Puente stated ".. the multinational corporation denotes an enterprise in which a number of states participate. The term for corporations operating beyond their frontiers is "transnational". This Andean Pact redefinition was foreshadowed by the testimony before the Group of Senor José Capillo Sainz, Mexican Under Secretary for Commerce, who also used transnational instead of multinational. Later testimony by Professor Joseph Nye, a political scientist, further helped blur the distinction between the two words that had until then become commonly accepted by scholars and practioners in the fields of business administration and management. Nye used the two adjectives interchangeably, slipping from one to the other (2).

Though the "Group of Eminent Persons" included John Dunning a professor of economics and specialist in international business who had himself earlier used the terms "multinational enterprise" and "transnational" in the generally accepted sense (3) the group as a whole consisted mostly of political scientists and economists. Their report to the Secretary General of the U.N. (4) began with the following classic description : "Multinational corporations are enterprises which own or control production or service facilities outside the country in which they are based. Such enterprises

are not always incorporated or private, they can also be co-
operative or state-owned entities". Given the testimony, the
backgrounds of the Group and the political and economic context
within which the U.N. initiated the study (5) it is not surprising
to see this definition followed by : "there is a general agreement
that enterprises should be substituted for corporations, and a
strong feeling that the word transnational would better convey the
notion that these firms operate from their home bases across
national borders". Accordingly, when the Economic and Social
Council adopted the recommendations of the Group and constituted
a permanent Commission to study the impact of multinational corporations the official title given was the "United Nations Commission on Transnational Corporations". However, it is curious that
the "general agreement" to substitute enterprise for corporation
was ignored while the "strong feeling" to use transnational was
seized upon.

In one fell swoop the progress that had until then been made in
clearing the terminological jungle decried by scholars (6) was
effaced and the situation was worse than ever. Reasoned and
scholarly analyses concerning the numerous criteria that could be
considered in defining the envelope of what is a "multinational
firm" were overshadowed by this basic terminological somersault
(7). That it should have occurred during the hearings was particularly regrettable, for an earlier report prepared by the Department for Economic and Social Affairs of the United Nations Secretariat to facilitate the work of the Group placed the U.N. stamp
of approval on a number of definitions reflecting widely accepted
prior practice within the international business and academic
communities (8).

While this turnabout may have seemed logical and satisfactory to
some it has not eased the lot of scholars and others who need an
unambigous set of definition in the pursuit of their every-day
tasks. When the problem was broached with a world-renowned authority on international business he threw up his hands - "too
sensitive to touch". I disagree. The academic community has a
fundamental responsibility to assume leadership in the definition
of concepts.

At the root of the current confusion is the term transnational.
Though, until recently, most French, English and U.S. dictionaries,
even unabridged, did not define multinational; transnational has
long been defined in U.S. dictionaries as "going beyond national
boundries or solely national interests". It is to be noted that
the Andean pact definition is absolutely consistent with this
anglo-saxon definition.

As pointed out by Nye and Keohane (9), Raymond Aron (10) was one
of the first social scientists to define and use the term as part

of a conceptual framework, in his case the theory of international relations. Aron defined transnational as a system or society"... characterized by commercial exchanges, individual migrations, common belief, and organizations which cross frontiers, finally ceremonies and contests open to members of all political unities". This (French) usage paralleled in essence the definition found in U.S. dictionaries. Other political scientists writing on the same subject soon followed Aron's lead (11).

Nye and Keohane defined transnational relations as"... contacts coalitions, and interactions across state boundries that are not controlled by the central foreign policy organs of governments" (12). However, they went on to explain that transnational relations subsumed transnational "interactions" where governments may or may not be involved but where non-governmental actors must play a significant role. Such transnational interactions might or might not in turn subsume transnational organizations. There is a slight contradiction between their definition and their later elaboration that transnational relations, while not necessarily sponsored or initiated by the "foreign policy organs of governments", may certainly be under full or partial control of such organs or of other governmental organs. However, the contradiction is one of nuance...

Having rapidly traced the usage of transnational in the political science context, let us look at its origins in the literature of business administration.

Certainly the first widely disseminated use of the term in this domain was a 1964 article by Donald Kircher, then president of the Singer Manufacturing Co (13). In the article entitled "Now the Transnational Enterprise", Kircher postulated that forces generated by the evolving world economy would bring about the emergence of a new and different form of business organization which he called the transnational enterprise. In his view such enterprises would most likely result from mergers between two large firms from different countries through exchange of stock. Key characteristics of Kircher's transnational enterprise were :

- Ownership of stock spread through many countries
- Manned and managed by persons of many nationalities
- Operations carried out throughout the world politically open
  to it
- Not a holding but an enterprise with a unifying central theme
  (products, fields of interest, etc...)
- International control, that is that the setting of policy at
  the highest level would be shared between representatives of
  the several national ownership groups. Top direction would thus
  not be in the hands of citizens of a single nation.

Kircher cited Royal Dutch/Shell and Unilever as two firms that most closely approached his concepts - both having their roots of policy and control split between Britain and Holland. But he wondered and was vague about the top-management structure of his hypothesized transnational.

Unlike Aron's use of the term, Kircher's did not spread quickly in the literature of management or business administration. One can only conjecture but the most likely reason was the relative paucity of multinationally owned and controlled firms compared to the rapidly growing number of single-nation based firms operating multinationally. It was the latter, under the rubrique "multinational firm", "multinational corporation" or "multinational enterprise" that were getting the lion's share of attention ; public, academic and governmental. According to one source it was David Lilienthal who first used the terme "multinational firm" in a paper delivered in 1960 (14). Though Kircher's usage of transnational was not immediately followed, the concept itself was not ignored by researchers.

Here our quest tends to become complex and it is beyond the scope of this article to attempt to trace the evolution of either terminology or concepts during the 1960's and early 1970's. Suffice to say that the term transnational crops up only infrequently. Instead, when faced with the need to describe the few plurinationally owned and controlled large "multinational firms" some authors resorted to the awkward "international multinational" firm/corporation, "multinationally controlled enterprise" or "multinationally owned enterprise".

Then in 1967, Robinson reintroduced the term transnational in Kircher's sense as one category of international business (15). Because cooperation within Western Europe was spawning an increasing number of plurinationally owned firms (S.A.S., AGFA-GEVAERT, VFW-FOKKER etc.) and plurinational managed public enterprises (European Space Research Organization, European Launcher Development Organization, Concorde SST, etc..) the subject took on renewed interest. Authors in the field of business administration both in the U.S. and abroad began using transnational to describe plurinationally owned/controlled firms. As research efforts were initiated in the U.S. and Europe it was only natural that the term transnational in the Kircher/Robinson sense, by now firmly established in management literature, should be used by researchers (16). And it was this definition that the United Nations ECOSOC secretariat cited in its initial report.

Is the Terminological Problem Important ?

Does it really make much difference which term is used as long as
the text is unambiguous ? Is this really only a semantic problem
of relatively minor importance to students and researchers ? The
answer depends on which discipline one is working in. Political
scientists are basically interested in intra and intergovernmental
relationships. Their interest in business firms as important factors in international relations is relatively recent (17). Moreover their interest is in the firms or organizations as impact
agents rather than on their internal structures. For political
scientists, then, the "multinational" corresponds to an electronic
"black box" whose causal outputs under various inputs are studied
with little concern for its inner circuitry.

Economists have almost uniformily accepted multinational in general usage although they are in the forefront of the discussion
and contention on how to quantitatively define a multinational
enterprise (size, type of operations abroad, relative importance
of foreign to domestic operations, distribution of ownership
shares, etc... etc...). And though the micro-economists do focus
on the teleological analysis of factor input and output of the
firm, they are relatively disinterested in the firms sociological,
psychological, and organizational aspects. Whether a firm's top
management is single-nation based or plurinational is of little
concern to the economist. He is primarly interested in the firm's
relationships with its political contexts, its sector(s) and in
the quantitative relationships between its suppliers, markets and
competitors. As a result economists, like political scientists,
have not found it necessary to differentiate between multinational
and transnational firms.

Understandably, there is also a vast literature on multinationals
in the legal and juridical domain. Here, as in the other fields
the term multinational has been widely used in its prior generally
accepted sense. In the U.S. the term transnational has been employed by legal scholars for many years in the same sense as used
by political scientists, following the dictionary definition.
Professor Philipp Jessup initiated legal use of the term in his
Storss Lectures on jurisprudence at the Yale Law School in the
early 1950's (18). Jessup defined transnational law as including

> "all the law which regulates the actions or events that trans-
> cend national frontiers.... (It) includes both civil and cri-
> minal aspects, what we know as public and private international
> law and it includes national law both public and private.
> Transnational situations.... may involve individuals, corpora-
> tions, states or groups."

Jessup's work ultimately gave birth to the periodic <u>Columbia</u>
<u>Journal of Transnational Law</u> (19).

Jurists are obviously interested in the internal structure of the
firm and the formal basis for attribution of policy control.
However, the juridical questions arising from plurinational ownership and control have almost universally concerned international
joint-ventures and it is the latter term that legal authors use
for this specific set of firms. When they treat the rare international merger they resort to terms such as <u>international multi-</u>
<u>national</u> (20).

It is in business administration and management that the terminological confusion causes the greatest problems. If researchers
and teachers in this area actively use the concepts of the disci-
plines already cited, they also have an important additional
concern - understanding the process of top-management decision-
making. For them the distribution of power and how policy is formulated and implemented are crucial because these factors bear
heavily on success or failure of an organization. Moreover these
factors differ fundamentally between single-nation based multinationals and those that are plurinationally controlled. Obviously
the latter must additionally be endowed with a structural mechanism
that can ajudicate efficiently and rapidly between plural roots
of power and control. Nor are businesses (privately or publicly
owned) alone concerned with this problem. There are numerous
intergovernmental organizations whose purpose is to provide products or services. For these the administrative and management
problems are conceptually identical with those of private enterprises. Organizations such as the European Space Agency (ESA)
or INTELSAT are international organizations fundamentally different from agencies such as the U.N. ; O.E.C.D., or the European
Common Market. If the latter have a commonly agreed on purpose
they have no time constraint on achieving it. Failure to achieve
peace on earth or to solve a critical common economic problem
does not jeopardize the very existence of the organization -
debate and polemic replace decision and action and each partner
goes his own way. ESA and INTELSAT labor under different rules.
Contractors must be chosen, satellites designed, built and
launched, commercial communication links established etc...
Failure to resolve national differences concerning key decisions
or to forge a central strategy in a timely manner causes paralysis,
schedules are delayed, costs rise and failures ensue. ESA's predecessor, the European Launcher Development Organization met its
demise in this manner.

The success of an organization, however measured by its sources
of power, is an elusive goal even in single-national based endeavors. Understandably, then, business and governments alike are
most reluctant to enter into joint international endeavors where

the hazards and complexities are exponentially greater than in purely national organizations. Yet the same inexorable forces that have spawned and nurtured the multinational corporations in some cases leave no alternative to such plurinationally owned or controlled enterprises. Among these forces the following are particularly salient :

- large investments beyond the capability of one firm or one government required for development and/or production (e.g. satellite launchers)

- very high unit costs with limited markets (e.g. CONCORDE)

- the need for world-wide markets to achieve competitive economies of scale (e.g. computers)

- the need to achieve a minimum financial, marketing, research, development and manufacturing size so as to compete effectively with the largest firms in a given sector (e.g. Agfa-Gevaert, Dunlop-Pirelli).

- geography (e.g. the Channel Tunnel).

Note that these criteria could lead to the classic international joint-venture. Such joint-ventures have become very common since the end of World War II and have elicited considerable and wide interest on the part of academic researchers, businessmen and governments. But where these forces - either separately or in concert) compel partners to the marriage altar or lead to temporary "affairs" and where one or more of the partners refuse to lose their identity (by acquisition) or cede dominance (yield national sovereignty), plurinationally controlled enterprises will be created. Whereas the classic joint-venture has the characteristic of being able to survive as a purely national entity even if one of the parent organizations withdraws, this "survivability" is not shared by the organizations central to this discussion. The kinds of plurinationally controlled enterprise of primary interest here are those where "divorce" by the parents would be traumatic, if not impossible. Examples are Royal Dutch/Shell and Unilever to VFW-FOKKER and Agfa-Gevaert in the private sector, weapons programs such as the NATO HAWK and commercial aircraft ventures such as CONCORDE and AIRBUS, the International Moselle Company and the European Space Agency that are government sponsored industrial programs. The list is already long and is constantly growing. Unfortunately the low success and survival rate of these organizations is alarming. UNIDATA (Europe's ill-fated challenge to IBM's supremacy in computers), the European Launcher Development Organization, the Channel Tunnel were failures. The CONCORDE SST was a technological success but appears to be a financial and marketing failure. Even those plurinationally controlled enterprises

that have not failed attest, on examination, to their fragility.
Previous studies have also shown that whether such an enterprise
is intergovernmental or interfirm, public, private, or mixed, the
root of the problem appears to be the lack of an effective mechanism for the strategy level decision-making process (21). Such a
mechanism must not only be able to rapidly reconcile conflict
between the multiple sources of power – it must be able to both
propose action that is acceptable to these higher powers and to
pave the way to timely acceptance of the proposed action. All this
in addition to the usual tasks of coping with unpredictable changes
inside and outside the organization.

The Conational Organization or Enterprise and some Research Concepts

We have now defined a unique category of international organizations. Given the growing importance of this category (its inevita-
bility in certain industrial sectors) coupled with its intrinsic
set of complex and thorny management problems there is a manifest
need for research. How should such research procede ? To begin
with the terminology needs to be disentangled and this category
given a name. From the earlier discussion it is clear that the
erstwhile term transnational is ambiguous. Moreover the latter
has now received U.N. approbation as still another and official
expression for the yet to be precisely defined multinational.
Therefore I propose that the term CONATIONAL be used.

Conational clearly denotes the unique characteristic of the organizations on which this essay is centered : an organization,
private or governmental in which the ultimate power of decision
is shared between centers of power in two or more countries without one country being dominant. As it stands this definition could
include the whole panoply of international organizations whose
objectives are less concrete and which are basically political,
professional, fraternal or informative in nature ; such as the
U.N., O.E.C.D., etc... A conational organization is therefore
further defined as having been assigned the objective of providing
products or services (other than information, regulation or enfor-
cement). Implicit in this definition is that the decisions taken
conationally are binding if the organization is to survive. Furthermore the above definition excludes such organizations as the
European Economic Community, the International Court at the Hague,
etc.

As herein defined conationals may or may not be transnational in
the political science sense. For they may or may not be governmental actors (subject in some degree to the foreign policy organs
of the participating states). In the sense defined by the Andean
Pact countries and now the U.N., conationals, may or may not be

transnational. For it is possible that the conational's activities would be restricted to a single country as is the case for many joint-ventures.

With terminology (but not taxonomy) out of the way, the question arises as to which concepts are the most useful for further research? It was earlier hypothesized that the fundamental problem is achieving an efficient, effective, and if necessary competitive decision-making mechanism in a context of multinationally shared power. There is an abundant literature on the decision-making process at the top-management level of task-oriented organizations. This literature can be roughly divided into two broad categories that have a wide overlap. The first group of authors view the process from the overall strategy or policy formulation and implementation standpoint (22). This perspective is particularly useful in relating the decision-making process to the structure of the organization as a whole ; that is the relationship between the decisional output and the organization's internal human and mechanical linkages which shape and regulate individual choice and action. As such this viewpoint relies (or should rely) heavily on the second group whose models are essentially psychosociological (23).

Certainly the problem of multiple sources of power influencing the top-management decision-making process exists in purely national organizations. Best known examples are banks which are often powerful stockholders or creditors, family groups with large stock-holdings, government agencies or individuals with regulatory power, etc... However numerous these external sources of power or intricate the decision-making process may be in purely national organizations the latter are deeply ingrained and structured with decision-making patterns sensed by all concerned as falling within an accepted envelope. For example we take for granted one chief executive with the ultimates power of choice and decision. That he has motives avowed and ulterior or that he is subject to influence from various centers of power is intuitively understood and accepted. The various techniques for adjudicating and synthesizing decisions and implementing them are also intuitively accepted. These techniques are culture-based in both the formal sense, e.g. organizational structure and law, and in the informal sense, e.g. techniques for the exercice of power, criteria for team cohesiveness, the role and purpose of the organization in the national context, etc.. Whether the famous (and out of context) statement attributed to Charles Wilson, then president of General Motors, that "What is good for General Motors is good for the country" was believed by others or not is not important. What is important is that both Wilson and his critics believed that it ought to be so. Indeed, it is the suspicion that the "multinational" may be better serving its own and its home country's interest than the interest of the host country that lies behind the fear of the "transnational corporation".

Conationals suffer the obverse problem : the fear on the part of
the different national sources of power that what is good for the
conational or the other partner(s) may <u>not</u> be good for their <u>home</u>
interests. As already pointed out the rich panoply of mechanisms
for resolving such problems that exist in purely national organizations are here lacking.

If there is to be one chief from which country will he come ? In
which country will the headquarters be located? What happens when
law, usage, or customs clash ? What happens if the interests of
different national power sources clash on specific issues which
must be quickly decided to prevent loss of funds or even to avoid
disaster ?

Those who organize purely national enterprises, in whatever the
country, consciously and subsconsciously rely on decades and even
centuries of prior practice, law and custom. Designers and executives of conationals,lacking such a framework, quite naturally
seek to apply those methods and constructs developed in the purely
national context. These are quickly perceived as inadequate and
in the absence of precedent it is not surprising that each time
partners from several countries agree to found a joint organization
to accomplish a set of industrial tasks they end up with a different structure. (Less true for classic joint-ventures).

Just how varied the top-management decision making mechanisms
could be has already been pointed out (24). In fact the only
common thread appears to be the elaborate precautions taken to
safeguard the interest and influence of the separate national
centers of power. One obvious result of such measures were either
the carefully circumscribed power of the newly created organization's top-management, a collegial top-management, or both.
Royal Dutch/Shell when founded in 1907 as 60% Dutch and 40% British
is an interesting exception that proves the rule (25). This same
study further showed that these formal restraints on top-management autonomy were only very slowly relaxed over years, if ever.
In newly formed organizations the key managers were of course
carefully selected. They also came out of a cultural and organizational environment in which they had been rared and which permeat-
ed their every fiber. Most importantly they arrived at the
(usually freshly founded) conational with a set of preformed proclivities for their home cultures, the national organizations from
where they came, and their previous national supervisors, colle-
gues and subordinates. In a now classic treatise Philip Selznick
(26) showed that the process of blending the goals of the individual members of any organization into the goals of the overall
organization - that is, the infusing of a homogeneous set of goals
and values, was the crowning and necessary task of good leadership.

This process of institutionalization (Selznick's term) is slow
and takes years and even decades to accomplish. It is also obvious
that if the executive posted to a conational expects to return
"home" after a few years he will never really be able to transfer
loyalty to his conational superiors or place the welfare and values
of his temporary conational organization above his past and probably future "home", from whence spring his ultimate rewards (or
punishments). The study of permanent conationals has shown that a
residual if small amount of national cultural loyalties, as opposed
to conational firm-centered loyalties, continues to remain in
senior executives who have spent their entire careers in the conational environment. This occured in organizations that had been
conational and ably led for many decades (27).

The above discussion provides the researcher with several insights
and suggest relevant concepts concerning conational organizations.
But any research or even better understanding of conationals as a
category stumbles over a signal problem – their extreme heterogeneity.

A Taxonomy of Conationals

Though conationals share in common the problems of time-constrained
task accomplishment and the need for a decision-making mechanism
that can cope with multinational sources of power, they otherwise
differ widely in many respects. Consider for example the governmental INTELSAT on the one hand and UNILEVER on the other. Consequently, before embarking on a study of conationals a necessary
prerequisite is their classification so they can be systematically
studied and compared. On what basis, around which characteristics
should a taxonomy be constructed ?

The formal organizations chosen by conationals in the past have
been so varied and haphazardly chosen that this important and
logical characteristic is difficult to use as a basis for classification. One could begin with type of ownership, whether public,
private or mixed, or possibly with the number of countries involved. Again, one might classify conationals according to the particular conceptual framework of the researcher concerned.

Examination and analysis of several past and existing conationals
have led me to several criteria that can serve as a basis for
classifying conationals (28). These criteria were chosen because
they had both a heavy impact on the efficiency of the strategic
decision-making process and because they permit a logical grouping
of those conationals observed.

Some conationals have been organized with the goal of accomplish-
ing a specific and limited task. Others have continuing missions.

International engineering consortia to build dams, the Anglo-French
Channel Tunnel, the Franco-German telecommunications satellite
SYMPHONIE and the organization to build the CONCORDE SST are
examples of ad hoc conationals. Others such as AGFA-GEVAERT,
UNIDATA (Europe's unsuccessful challenge to U.S. dominance of the
computer industry) or the European Space Agency were founded as
permanent organizations with continuing missions. We have already
mentioned the numerous authors who have shown that the strategic
decision-making process is strongly influenced by the psychosociological factors affecting an organization's members. In turn
these factors have been shown to be strongly dependent on the
planned perpetuity of the organization (28).

An organizational environment in which the key decision-makers
know they will ultimately leave and probably return to their
parent organizations makes it difficult to achieve the building
of esprit de corps, unity of purpose, organizational loyalty,etc.
necessary for a successful organization. Thus whether a conational is ad hoc or permanent appears to be a fundamental criteria
(Figure 1).

Another factor of almost equal importance revealed by this previous research is the degree of government participation in the
decision-making process. Wherever a conational endeavor is sponsored or subsidized by governments the latter usually organize
conational governmental organs to supervise or monitor the industrial agencies charged with the actual tasks. This superposition-
ing of governmental power centers above industrial power centers
affects the decision-making process in two ways. First, the mere
existence of government civil servants in the formal decision-
making chain tends to crystalize and nourish disagreement along
national lines because these representatives are usually careful
to represent the views of their separate national agencies by
whom they are judged. And, because the conational governmental
agencies are normally jealous of their powers of decision and
veto over the industrial agencies (in order to "protect national
funds", insure "equal treatment", etc.) tensions arise between
the governmental and industrial levels which profoundly affect
the overall strategy and ultimately the success or failures of
the endeavor.

Beyond the manifest observation that the mere existence of a
formal governmental decision-making role complicates and slows
down the strategic process it is obvious that the degree of governmental participation and hence its influence can vary considerably
and take many forms. Is there a separate formal conational government agency ? Is it a full-time agency or is it a committee that
meets periodically ?If there is no formal separate agency is there
direct influence by a highly attentive government agency that may
even represent the state as a stockholder ? Analysis of numerous

conationals has led to the choice of three broad categories with decreasing order of governmental influence (see also figure 1) :

A) Endeavors where the governments role in the top level decision-making is institutionalized in the form of full-time conational governmental agencies (CERN, (Centre Européen de Recherche Nuclé-aire), European Space Agency).

B) Endeavors wherein one or more of the home governments is acti-vely involved either because it instigated the conational, provi-ded funds or financial guarantees, or is directly or indirectly a principal customer for the products or services to be produced. However there is no formal full-time conational government agency directly involved in the decision-making process (CFM - 56 jet engine, CII - Honeywell-Bull Computers, both French-US.).

C) Endeavors that are purely private in nature, where governments might be one client among many. Government interest and inter-vention is of the usual kind, on an industry-wide and purely national basis (classic joint ventures, UNILEVER).

A third broad category of the criteria are subsumed under the heading of intensity of industrial collaboration. The implicit hypothesis concerning government participation was that government decision-making is intrinsically slower than classic private indus-trial procedures and that the sharing of decision-making authority between formal government organs and the industrial agencies is likely to be a less efficient if sometimes necessary technique. The hypothesis underlying the criteria of intensity of industrial collaboration is that the closer the different national sources of power are bound together, organically, legally, and financially, the more efficient the strategic decision-making process. Again, based on previous research, four subcriteria have been chosen : (see also figure 1)

1 - Whether or not the task-accomplishing industrial/commercial organization consists of an exclusive set of national firms or a single conational firm. In other words was there competition at the industrial level in seeking the task award ? In the case of the CONCORDE the French Sud-Aviation and British Aircraft compa-nies were exclusive contractors to the two governments. For the HAWK missile system the conational SETEL (Société Européenne de Téléguidage S.A.R.L.) was the sole contractor to the five european governments sponsoring the program. For purely private conationals this sub-category is interpreted to ask whether there is competi-tion between members of the conational in the same product-markets. Neither Royal Dutch/Shell or UNILEVER have subsidiaries that com-pete with each other, with minor exceptions. On the other hand DUNLOPP-PIRELLI parent firms had competing vehicle tires in most of the world markets.

2 - Whether or not there are juridical and or financial ties
between the parent or partner firms. Here, the best known examples without such ties are temporary price-fixing or market-
sharing arrangements and the prewar oil and steel cartels. The
committee of European aircraft companies attempting to reach
agreement on the next generation European civil air transport,
known as the "Group of 6/7" is another example.

3 - Whether there is a "marriage" between the parent firms or
whether the parent firms maintain separate juridical, organizational and financial independence. "Marriage" is defined as
merger in any of these areas. Parent firms may choose to create
conational subsidiaries and/or joint ventures while retaining
complete independence from one another. Examples of "marriage"
are AGFA-GEVAERT and DUNLOP-PIRELLI ; an example of creating a
conational while retaining independence is CIFAS (Consortium
Industriel Franco-Allemand pour la Construction de SYMPHONIE), a
jointly owned conational to develop and construct a communications
satellite.

4 - Lastly there is the criteria of type of conational management.
This criteria is further divided into five sub-categories :

a) Whatever joint decision-making that exists is accomplished
through periodically meeting committees. This is clearly the
weakest form of joint decision-making. Examples are the CONCORDE
(both at the governmental and industrial level) and DUNLOP-
PIRELLI at the purely private level.

b) A formal conational organization without its own means of production. This conational must rely on its parent or other firms
for its output of goods and/or services. Examples are a purely
sales joint-venture, the industrial consortia in the SYMPHONIE
program, or the CFM-56 jet engine program (U.S. General Electric
with French SNECMA).

c) Unity of purpose and formulation of a cohesive joint strategy
is accomplished through the use of key executives common to both
or several parents. At one extreme this could be partially achieved through interlocking boards of directors, however the classic
example in 1976 is AGFA-GEVAERT where the key top managers are
common to both AGFA and GEVAERT. This latter arrangement is
manifestly dependent on the geographic proximity between the two
headquarters. The advantage is a single set of key decision-
makers.

d) A formal conational with its own or separate means of production is next in order of increasing ability to formulate and
implement effective strategy. While the top management of such a
conational must act within the constraints imposed by its multi-

national sources of power, the strategic leeway to chart its own
course is far greater than the type "b" conational mentioned
earlier. The most common form is the classic joint-venture either
in developing or fully developed economies.

e) The most "advanced" form of conational management is where the
various different national industrial, commercial, and managerial
components of the parent firms are merged, creating an inseparable
whole. Such a situation can only result from a complete "marriage"
and even then true merger takes years to accomplish. Here the
best known examples are Europe's two largest firms - Royal Dutch/
Shell and UNILEVER.

Conclusion

A conflation of several world-wide trends makes the creation of
conational organizations increasingly probable. In certain advanced technology sectors the research and development costs required
to achieve a marketable product are becoming so great that single
national industries, even with government support, are less and
less willing or even capable of assuming the financial risks. The
world aerospace industry's gyrations concerning the next civil
air transport are an example. This R & D cost pressure for cooperation is frequently reinforced by exponentially increasing unit
cost/price factors and very limited world-wide markets. Additionally, the bygone ability of U.S. firms to exploit their larger
market base and attendant advantages of scale has stumbled against
the rapidly growing industrial nationalism of both developed and
less developed countries. Despite their disadvantages, conationals
are perhaps the only way to achieve the required scale while
guarding national "independence".

Finally the technological explosion in communications and transport
has increasingly forced industries in almost every sector to
regard the world not just their home country as a potential market.
Here again industrial chauvinism or nationalism makes the creation
of conationals increasingly likely, even between purely private
enterprises.

In view of these trends it would seem that more scholarly attention
should be devoted to this class of industrial organization, particularly in view of the limited success enjoyed by conationals to
date.

Figure 1 : A Taxonomy of Conational Organizations

Figure 1 : A Taxonomy of Conational Organizations

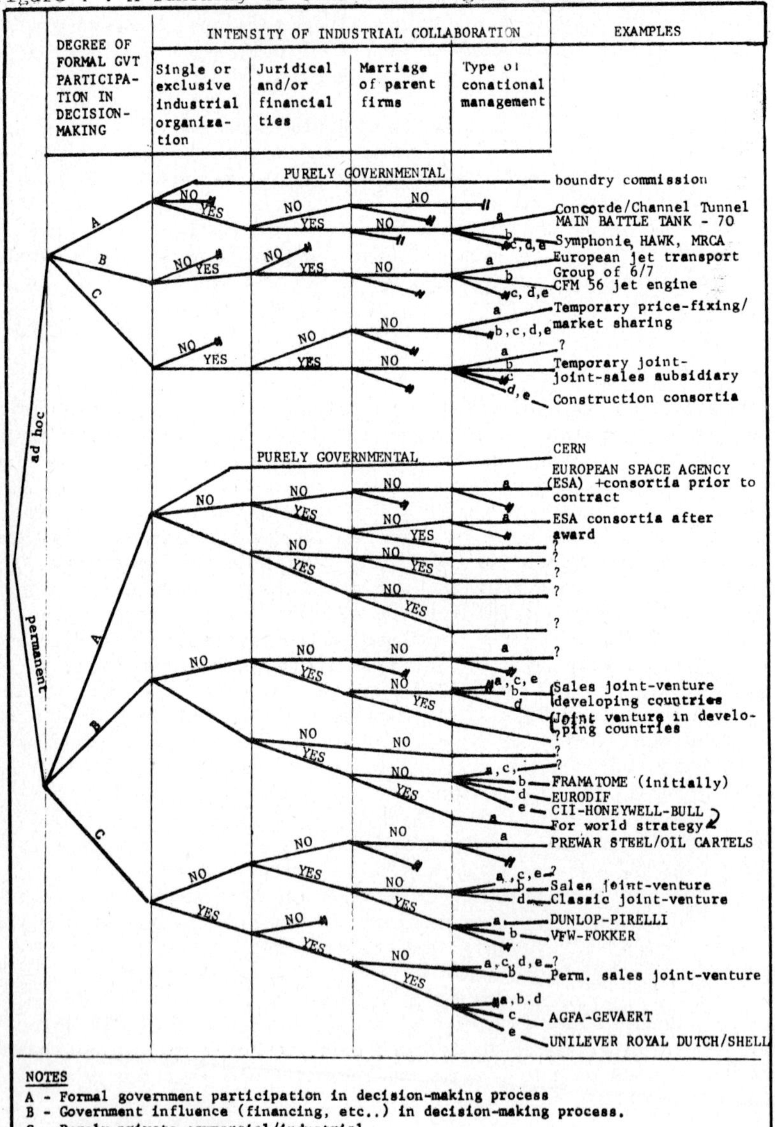

NOTES

A - Formal government participation in decision-making process
B - Government influence (financing, etc.,) in decision-making process.
C - Purely private commercial/industrial.

✗ - Unlikely or impossible
? - No examples identified
a - Some management by joint-committee
b - Formal conational organization without conational means of production
c - Common executives between parent or "married" firms.
d - Formal conational with own or separate means of production
e - Formal conational with common/ integrated/rationalized means of production.

References

(1) United Nations, "Hearings Before the Group of Eminent Persons .... Relations" Report ST/ESA/15 (New-York 1974).

(2) Idem, p. 323.

(3) John H. Dunning, The Multinational Enterprise, George Allen & Unwin (London 1971) pp. 16-17.

(4) United Nations, The Impact of Multinational Corporations on Development and on International Relations, Report of the Group of Eminent Persons, ST/ESA 6 (New-York 1974), P.25,ff.

(5) United Nations Economic and Social Council Resolution 1721 (L III), 28 July 1972.

(6) See for example Donald F. Mulvihill "Terminology in International Business Studies, Order Out of Chaos", Journal of International Business Studies (Spring 1973, p. 87).

(7) See for example Yair Aharoni "On the Definition of a Multinational Corporation", Quarterly Review of Economics and Business (Autumn 1971) p. 27.

(8) United Nations "Multinational Corporations in World Development" Annex II, Selected Definitions (New-York 1973), p.120.

(9) Joseph Nye and Robert Keohane (eds) "Transnational Relations and World Politics, Harvard University Press (Boston, 1972).

(10) Raymond Aron, Paix et Guerre entre les Nations, Calman-Levy (Paris 1962), p. 113 (available in English, Doubleday, 1966).

(11) See : Nye & Keohane, op. cit.
Also : Andrea Rosenberg "International Interaction and the Taxonomy of International Organizations", International Associations, November 1967
Karl Kaiser "Transnationale Politik...." Politische Vierteljahresschrift, 1969 (Special issue n° 1), p. 80 ff.

(12) Nye & Keohane, op. cit., preface.

(13) Harvard Business Review, March-April 1964

(14) Stefan H. Robock and Kenneth Simmonds, International Business and Multinational Enterprise, Irwin (Homewood, Ill. 1973) p. 4

(15) Richard D. Robinson, International Management, Holt Rinehart
     and Winston (New-York 1967) pp. 96-154

(16) See : Sidney Rolfe, Les Sociétés Internationales, Chambre de
     Commerce Internationale (Paris 1969, p.13)
     D.C. Waite, "The Transnational Corporation, Corporate Form of
     the Future", European Business, Summer 1974
     R. Mazzolini, European Transnational Concentrations, Mc Graw
     Hill (London 1974).
     M.S. Hochmuth Organizing the Transnational, Sijthoff (Leiden
     1974).

(17) Nye and Keohane, op.cit. See also Susan Strange "Transnation-
     al Relations" in International Affairs, July 1976, pp. 333 ff.

(18) Philipp Jessup, Transnational Law - Yale University Press,
     (New Haven, 1956) (Yale University School of Law. Storrs
     lectures on jurisprudence).

(19) Columbia University School of Law, New York, N.Y.

(20) See e.g. M. Lutter in "Aktuelle Fragen Multinationaler
     Unternehmen" in Zeitschrift für Betriebswirtschaftliche
     Forschung, Sonderheft 4, 1975, p. 70.

(21) M.S. Hochmuth, The Effect of Structure on Strategy - The
     Government Sponsored Multinational Joint-Venture, unpublished
     DBA dissertation, Harvard Business School, 1972 passim.
     Also Hochmut,Organizing the Transnational, op. cit (17)

(22) See for example : Kenneth Andrews, The Concept of Corporate
     Strategy, Dow Jones - Irwin (Homewood, Ill. 1971)
     H.I. Ansoff, Corporate Strategy,Mc Graw Hill(New-York, 1965).
     Joseph Bower, Managing the Resource Allocation Process,
     Division of Research, Harvard Business School (Boston 1970).

(23) See for example :
     Chester Barnard, The Functions of the Executive, Harvard
     University Press (Cambridge, 1968) passim and chapt XIII
     Peter Drucker, The Practice of Management, Harper and Row
     (New-York, 1954), pp. 351 ff
     Philip Selznick, Leadership in Administration, Harper & Row
     (New-York 1957) passim
     Herbert Simon, Administrative Behavior, The Free Press,
     (New-York,1965) passim
     A. Zaleznik and M. Kets de Vries, Power and the Corporate
     Mind, Houghton Miflin (Boston, 1975) pp. 109 ff.

(24) Hochmuth, The Effect of Structure on Strategy, op. cit.

(25) Idem, pp. 59-95

(26) Op. cit. pp. 16-17

(27) Unpublished research by the author

(28) M.S. Hochmuth, <u>Organizing the Transnational</u>,op. cit.passim ;
     <u>The Effect of Structure on Strategy</u>, op. cit. passim and
     unpublished research.

CYCLICAL INVESTMENT BEHAVIOR OF INDIGENOUS FIRMS AND U.S. FOREIGN AFFILIATES[*]

Robert G. Hawkins

New York University

I. *Introduction*

It is widely accepted that multinational corporations enjoy an advantage over local (national) firms in financing capital expansion. This advantage may provide multinational corporations (MNCs), with superior access to external financing, with the capacity to avoid the restrictive impacts of macroeconomic policy during periods of restraint in host countries[1]. This would permit foreign affiliates (1) to capture higher shares of capital spending during periods of economic boom and credit restriction ; and (2) to magnify cyclical instability of the economy by adding to inflationary pressures when local firms are more susceptible to domestic credit controls.

The second effect implies that the problem of "demand management" is magnified by the presence of foreign direct investment. The first suggests that local enterprise is placed at a disadvantage relative to MNC affiliates in its own local market.

Some investigation of this question has already been carried out. Stobaugh, in an interview survey of 43 MNCs, found that a high percentage indicated that (a) international interest rate differentials were important considerations in arranging the financing for foreign subsidiaries, and (b) the parent companies extended loans to foreign affiliates when local monetary policy made it difficult to secure local funds[2]. While interpretations of interview surveys are always difficult, and although the question of

---

[*]Research on this paper was supported by the New York University project on "The Multinational Firm in the U.S. and World Economy". Computational and other assistance was provided by Donald Macaluso and Roma Koundinga. A part of the results were reported in an earlier paper, Robert G. Hawkins and Donald Macaluso, "The Avoidance of Restructive Monetary Policies in Host Countries by Multinational Firms", Journal of Money, Credit and Banking(1977).

whether this financial behavior of MNCs actually resulted in an advantage for the foreign affiliates over local firms is not addressed, the suggestion is clear that MNCs are aware of and attempt to use the financial advantage of their multinationality. A related study has shown that take-overs of Canadian firms have been negatively related to the liquidity of the domestic corporate sector[3]. This may be interpreted to imply that MNCs use their superior financial ability to acquire local (Canadian) firms during periods of tight money when financial difficulties for local firms are likely to arise[4].

This paper adds to the tentative empirical evidence on this issue. For six major industrial host countries of U.S. affiliates, the evidence for the period 1960-1972 is examined.

Limiting the study to American affiliates in only six host countries is necessitated by data availabilities. The countries included -- Belgium, Canada, France, Germany, Japan and the United Kingdom -- do, however, account for a majority of U.S. foreign investment. Also, data problems forced the use of annual values as the unit of observation, and the interpretation of the results must therefore be correspondingly qualified.

The paper proceeds as follows. The sources of the financial advantages of MNCs will be briefly recited in the following section. Thereafter, section III presents empirical tests as to whether capital spending by U.S. affiliates follows a significantly different time pattern than total capital spending in the host country. If not, then the issues of escape from monetary policy and cyclically destabilizing investment behavior can be laid to rest, irrespective of presumed financial advantages of MNCs. To anticipate the findings in several cases, the patterns do diverge significantly. Finally, Section IV presents evidence on whether U.S. affiliates are able to adjust their financing and their share of total capital formation (relative to local firms) during periods of tight monetary policy in the host country. The final section briefly summarizes the findings.

II. Sources of Financial Advantages of MNCs

The hypothesized financial advantages of MNCs over local firms rest in their flexibility to utilize sources of funds which may be less freely available or on less attractive terms to local firms. These advantages may arise from three sources :

1. Local affiliates of the MNC may receive funds from the MNC network through :

(a) Borrowing from the parent or related affiliates, or receiving new equity funds from the parent ;
(b) Adjustment in transfer prices for the exchange of goods
and services among units in the MNC system so as to lodge
more profits in a local affiliate requiring additional
financing ;
(c) Increasing the profit-retention rate of the affiliate by
reducing remitted profits to the parent, or deferring
interest and fees payable to the parent or related affiliates.

2. MNC affiliates may have superior access to <u>external</u> financial
markets by borrowing with parent-company guarantee, an option
not open to local firms.

3. MNC affiliates may have preferred access to funds from <u>local</u>
financial institutions. This may arise during restrictive
credit conditions because of credit rationing[5]. The foreign
affiliate of a MNC, because of explicit or implicit guarantees
of its debt by the parent, its relatively large size, and the
relative stability of its earnings, all tend to make it a superior credit risk for local financial institutions. Thus, as
funds are rationed, MNC affiliates may be among the last to
have local sources curtailed.

These financial advantages would be translated into the ability
of MNC affiliates to continue real capital spending in the face
of tightening local credit conditions to an extent greater than
is true for local firms. As local interest rates rise, the MNC's
ability to shift to alternative sources of funds would result in
a decline in its average cost of capital relative to that faced
by local firms. In addition, the MNC affiliates could more readily substitute alternative means of financing for sources withdrawn
as credit rationing occurs. As an average tendency, then, the
foreign affiliates would face a favorable situation with respect
to availability and cost of funds as compared to local firms
during periods of restrictive credit.

These relationships are diagrammed in Figure 1. Restrictive credit conditions may lead to an adjustment in the sources of finance
by the foreign affiliates which, in turn, may systain real investment by foreign affiliates relative to that by local firms. Empirical tests of various components of these relationships follow.
The following section examines whether the variables in the extreme right box do actually move in different patterns -- i.e.
whether capital spending patterns by foreign affiliates are different from or similar to the patterns of local firms. The ensuing
section reports evidence for linkages A and C. Data are not available to explore relationship B.

Figure 1.

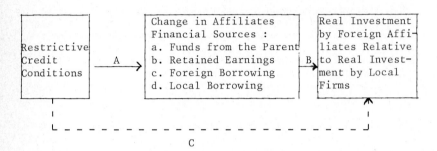

This description of the cyclically destabilizing potential of
foreign affiliates is valid only if two additional assumptions
are substantially true. One is that investment spending by local
firms or MNCs is affected by monetary conditions at all. If
monetary policy has no independent affect on business investment
by local enterprise, MNC affiliates cannot be less affected, and
the entire argument that MNCs erode the effectiveness of monetary
policy is vacuous. Clearly, the concern voiced over this presumed MNC behavior indicates a widespread belief that monetary
policy is effective to some extent. Although there is still much
econometric debate over the responsiveness of business investment
to monetary factors, there is a significant body of literature
which finds observable effects upon business spending decisions
of interest rates, the money stock, or other financial variables[6].
We accept this positive evidence and thus believe that there is a
restrictive effect for MNCs to avoid.

The second assumption is that local firms do not have as ready
or equal access to foreign funds as MNCs. This appears to be a
valid assumption for several reasons. First, the institutional
structure in which monetary policy operates typically brings
local firms more directly under the control of local monetary
authorities. For example, several countries (e.g. France) require
government approval for foreign borrowing by domestic firms. MNC
affiliates, on the other hand, may rely on the foreign borrowing
of the parent system, and receive the funds through various
channels which do not typically require host government approval.
In addition, local firms (aside from host-country based MNCs)
do not typically have the multinational network of banking ties,
or the sophisitication and information to utilize external sources even if allowed to do so by government policy. This may be
the case even if the local firm is as large as or larger than the

foreign affiliate of the MNC. Also, the leverage which the central
bank may exercise through moral suasion is likely to be greater
over local firms, including large locally-based MNCs, than over
foreign affiliates. While foreign affiliates may seek to be "good
local citizens", the share of total earnings of indigenous enterprise under the direct or indirect influence of the local monetary authorities is usually much greater, and the seriousness
given to non-mandatory appeals about capital spending is correspondingly greater.

III. *Coincidence of Movements in Capital Spending by U.S. Affi-liates and Local Firms*

This section reports the results of empirical investigations of
the time pattern of capital spending by foreign affiliates of
American firms as compared with locally-financed capital expenditures, in five industrial countries. Because of data limitations,
the variables refer only to annual plant and equipment (investment) expenditures (inventory or stock changes are excluded) over
the period 1960 to 1971[7].

The rationale of the tests employed is that if capital spending
by MNCs is relatively unconstrained by local credit conditions
in host countries while locally-owned firms have less opportunity
to escape such constraints, there should be observable differences in the variations of the two series through time. There are,
obviously, other factors which may cause the two patterns to
diverge. These factors, however, are not considered directly.

Co-Movements in Aggregate Capital Spending

As an initial step, one should discover whether MNCs have something to avoid. If all countries have simultaneous cycles, the
advantage of shifting financial sources from one country to
another would be minimal.

Under the relatively safe assumption that cyclical movements in
financial variables correspond closely in time with cycles in
capital spending in a country, disparities in credit conditions
among countries can be inferred by observing the disparities
in their capital spending movements. This is the objective of
Table 1 which shows simple correlation coefficients between
domestically-financed (i.e. non-U.S. affiliate) capital spending
between each pair of countries. The correlations were calculated
on annual data (the shortest period for which relatively comparable data are available), and for both levels and year-to-year
first differences. Two degrees of industry coverage are shown
for some of the countries -- one is for all industries, the other
is for manufacturing only.

Table 1 : Simple Correlation Coefficients – Domestically Financed Capital Spending Among Selected Countries (annual data, 1960–1971).

	Canada	Japan	U.K.	France	Germany
			ALL INDUSTRIES		
U.S. : Levels	.984	.920	.980	.965	.337
First Differences	.721	-.165	.399	.189	-.273
Canada : Levels		.867	.961	.935	.310
First Differences		-.279	.875	.247	.193
Japan : Levels			.958	.982	.456
First Differences			.382	.735	-.292
U.K. : Levels				.985	.360
First Differences				.244	-.621
France : Levels					.459
First Differences					-.145
		MANUFACTURING INDUSTRIES ONLY			
U.S. : Levels	.926		.876	.911	
First Differences	.526		.187	-.122	
Canada : Levels			.855	.900	
First Differences			.385	.574	
U.K. : Levels				.921	
First Differences				.432	

Note : For all countries other than the U.S., the variable is defined as Total Fixed Domestic Investment minus Capital Spending by U.S. Affiliates in the country.

The table clearly shows that, aside from Germany, the movements
in the levels of capital spending in the various countries was
very similar, reflecting the dominant upward trend in investment
in all countries. But the more rigorous test of parallel movements over the course of the business cycle, or over a "credit"
cycle, is based upon the first differences in annual values, or
year-to-year changes in capital spending. Aside from the U.S.-
Canada, Canada-U.K., and Japan-France relationships, the countries
demonstrate relatively low positive associations among annual
changes in capital spending, and a negative average relationship
in several cases. These statistics show a strong positive relationship, across country, for changes in the internally generated
capital expenditures in relatively few cases. A strong association was found between Canada and the U.S., for which the coincidence of the business cycles through time is notorious. Others
are between Canada and the U.K., and France and Japan, for which
such straight-forward explanations are not obvious. For the
remainder of the country pairs, however, there is little positive
(or negative) association between movements in local capital
spending. This implies that the MNC, to the extent that it has
access to various national (and international) sources of funds
does not often find the industrial countries at similar phases
of the business cycle simultaneously, and thus credit conditions
may differ substantially among local capital markets[7].

It may also be observed from Table 1 that capital spending in
manufacturing industries is less closely correlated (in almost
every case) among the countries than is total (private) capital
spending. Since the arguments that MNCs may escape from local
policy strictures tends to be focused mainly on manufacturing
affiliates, this observation adds evidence that the opportunity,
if not the practice, exists for MNCs to exercise the financial
advantage in the face of differential national credit conditions.

Foreign Affiliate Spending versus Locally-financed Spending

A convenient means of summarizing the relationship between U.S.
foreign affiliate spending and locally-financed capital spending
is to regress the former on the latter, and examine the resulting
statistics. This technique was used for both the levels of capital
spending and the year-to-year changes in capital spending (first
differences). Since there was a distinct upward trend in both
variables, the "levels" regression included a time-trend factor,
as follows :

$$I_{us} = a + b(I_1) + c(t)$$

where I_{us} is the capital spending of U.S. foreign affiliates, I_1
is the level of capital spending of the locally-owned firms,

t is the trend variable, and "a", "b", and "c" are the regression coefficients.The same regression was run on the first differences of I_{us} and I_1, but omitting the trend term (t).

Taking the regressions for "all industries", the relationship between fixed investment by U.S. affiliates and by local firms based on levels, with the trend term included, is close except for the case of Germany. The R^2s are .93 or above in each case, and aside from Canada, the D-W statistic indicates lack of auto-correlation in the residuals. The major ambiguity in the interpretation is that the trend term and the locally-financed investment term are themselves correlated, thus making it uncertain as to whether the estimated coefficients truly reflect the relative explanatory power of the two variables. For Germany and the United Kingdom, the coefficient relating the two investment variables is not significant at the 90% level of confidence.

The more meaningful test may be that employing the first-difference regressions. Again, the relationship between the investment variables is significant for Canada and France, and insignificant for Germany and the United Kingdom. But even for the countries where a very significant relationship exists between domestic investment spending and capital spending by U.S. affiliates, a large share of the variance in the latter is not accounted for by the former. This suggests that the cyclical pattern of movements in the two series is not a very tight one. A part of this disparity in annual changes in the two investment series might, therefore, be accounted for by MNC financial advantages during restrictive credit periods. It is this possibility which is addressed in the next section.

IV. Capital Spending by U.S. Affiliates and Host-Country Credit Conditions

This section presents evidence as to the extent to which foreign affiliates of U.S. firms adjust their sources of financing to avoid the effects of restrictive local credit conditions. The tests encompass relationships A and C in Figure 1. The variables employed will be described first, followed by the presentation of the results.

The Variables

The ultimate indication of avoidance of tight credit conditions is a systematic change in the capital spending by U.S. affiliates relative to that by local firms associated with changing local financial conditions. For this test, two versions of the dependent variable are defined (see Appendix A for a description of the data):

Table 2 : Regression Results for Capital Spending by U.S. Affiliates Regressed on Locally-Financed Fixed Investment and Time (annual data : 1960-1971)

Country	Regression Coefficients and "t" Values		R^2	D-W Statistic
	Locally Financed Investment	Time		
All industries				
Canada :				
Levels Regression	0.35 (5.29)*	-52.45(-1.28)	.971	1.26
First-Difference Regression	0.35 (5.31)*		.779	2.27
Japan :				
Levels Regression	0.36 (2.56)*	4.54 (1.54)	.962	1.85
First-Difference Regression	NOT AVAILABLE			
United Kingdom :				
Levels Regression	0.78 (1.85)	8.84 (.28)	.956	2.21
First-Difference Regression	0.12 (0.21)		.015	2.50
France :				
Levels Regression	0.33 (2.41)*	-128.8 (-.75)	.933	1.83
First-Difference Regression	0.41 (2.26)*		.391	1.75
Germany :				
Levels Regression	0.57 (.11)	201.95 (3.32)	.666	1.80
First-Difference Regression	0.12 (.27)		.012	1.75
Manufacturing				
Canada :				
Levels Regression	0.66 (2.99)*	0.73 (.23)	.874	1.00
First-Difference Regression	0.50 (3.12)*		.550	1.62
United Kingdom:				
Levels Regression	0.22 (2.41)*	18.38 (2.73)	.937	1.85
First-Difference Regression	0.15 (1.40)		1.98	1.97
France : Levels Regression	0.64 (3.34)*	33.62 (.51)	.956	2.08
First-Difference Regression	0.89 (3.25)*		.570	2.15

Table 2 : continued

Note : Numbers in parantheses following the regression coefficients are "t" values. A description of the data utilized in the regressions may be found in Appendix A.

* Denotes that the regression coefficient is significantly different from zero with 95% probability.

(I_f/I_d) = the annual ratio of fixed capital investment by
                foreign affiliates of U.S. firms to fixed capital
                spending by all other firms (1960-71)

$(I_f/I_d)_{mfg}$ = the identical variable covering manufacturing indus-
                try only.

These series have two serious drawbacks. The first is that they
are available only on an annual basis, thereby severely limiting
examination of the structure of any lag in the relationships.
The second is that investment data for foreign affiliates (and
thus the entire variable) contain only fixed investment, excluding
changes in inventories and other working capital. The fact that
fixed investments have longer gestation periods and are expensive
to propose and plan probably makes them less responsive to credit
conditions than working capital. Unfortunately, no time series
is available for working capital or inventory investment by U.S.
affiliates. Both of these data problems probably produce a bias
(unmeasured) towards <u>not</u> finding evidence of avoidance of monetary controls by foreign affiliates.

Two independent variables denoting the financial structure of
foreign affiliates of U.S. firms were employed. These reflect
an attempt to examine relationship A in Figure 1. An annual unit
of observation for the years 1960 to 1971, covering foreign affiliates in all industries, is the only data available.

RET = Ratio of Retained Earnings to total pre-tax profits of
        U.S. foreign affiliates in the country.

REQI = Retained earnings plus new equity funds as a ratio of
        fixed investment by affiliates.

A positive association of each variable with restrictive local
monetary conditions would imply an increase in the MNC's utilization of foreign sources of funds available from the MNC network
during such periods. But data limitations make it impossible to
cover adjustments in all external sources of funds, such as
altering the <u>level</u> of profits in the affiliate by adjusting transfer prices, or by external borrowing by the affiliate. Thus, even
though there might be no positive indications of avoidance of
tight credit by MNCs indicated by changes in these variables, such
avoidance may still exist through other avenues, and thus be
reflected in the (I_f/I_d) variables.

The selection of an appropriate <u>independent</u> variable as a proxy
for credit conditions was quite frustrating. Interest rate variables, for example, are not always closely correlated with changes
in the money stock, or in the stock of credit. The result was

incompatible indications of credit stringency among potential
proxies, compounded by the fact that the proxies for credit must
be consistent with the annual observations of the dependent variables[8].

Without a strong theoretical basis for deciding that any one
quantitative proxy was most appropriate for a particular country,
it was decided to construct a composite quantitative-qualitative
dummy variable for tight monetary conditions. Thus,

DUM = a 0-1 dummy variable, in which 1 denotes years of restric-
       tive monetary policy and 0 years in which monetary policy
       was not restrictive.

The construction of DUM involved an evaluation of the confluence
of appropriate movements among rates of change in the money
supply, local interest rates, and the credit supply[9]. For several
situations of ambiguity, the appraisal of financial analysts and
journalists was sought[10], with the final decision sometimes involving the subjective weighting of qualitative and quantitative
factors.

The quantitative proxies for credit conditions were defined as
follows :

R = the change in short-term money market interest rates (as
    defined by the Treasury Bill rate, for most countries) from
    the previous year.

M = the percentage change in the money stock (M_1) from the pre-
    vious year, adjusted to remove changes in GNP ; i.e., a
    measure of the change in the nominal income velocity of money.

C = the percentage change in the aggregate supply of credit[11],
    adjusted for GNP change ; i.e., a measure of the "income
    velocity of credit".

The adjustment of the money stock and credit supply variables to
remove GNP changes deserves comment. Restrictive credit conditions are meaningful only when placed in relation to the demand
for money and/or credit. Slow or negative growth in money or credit outstanding does not denote restrictive credit conditions if
the demand is falling, and vice versa. In order to remove approximately the influence of demand changes, the nominal GNP was
used, thereby leaving us with income velocity measures[12]. Interest
rate movements, on the other hand, being movements in a market
price, reflect demand and supply changes, and are presumably valid
indicators of local credit conditions[13].

In addition to these quantitative measures, two "relative" measures of credit conditions were tested.

RTERM = is a variable reflecting the term structure of interest
         rates in the host countries ; the long-term bond rate
         minus the short-term rate.

The variable attempts to capture the "expectations hypothesis" of the yield curve. A low or negative RTERM would typically denote very restrictive credit conditions and the market's expectations that short-term interest rates would decline.

RDIFF = differential between the short-term (Treasury Bill) rates
        in the host country and the same rate in the United States.

This variable reflects the view that the credit conditions in the host country, from the point of view of avoiding restrictive conditions by MNCs, is relevant only with reference to credit conditions elsewhere, but especially in the home country of the MNC.

The Empirical Results

Two groups of empirical tests were conducted to discover indications of escape by MNCs from host country policies. The first deals with the ratio of capital spending by U.S. affiliates to other capital spending, which should reflect the ultimate result of the MNC advantage. The second group is concerned with the adjustments in the sources of funds of affiliates, which are likely to indicate the process of exercising that advantage. For each group of tests, regression analysis was employed, utilizing the same alternative variables for host-country credit conditions (DUMN, R, M, C, RTERM, and RDIFF). Multiple regressions (not reported) were also attempted, but with no improvement in results.

Since there has been a secular rise in the share of U.S. affiliates in the capital formation of each of the countries (except Canada) over the period studied, the elimination of the influence of these trends (which differ from country to country) was attempted in two ways : by inserting a trend term as an independent variable, and by using frist differences rather than levels.
Thus, two forms of each test were employed :

(a) $Z = a+b(C) + c(t)$

(b) $Z = a'+b'(C)$

where Z is the dependent variable (either the capital formation ratio or the financial sources variables), C is the credit

conditions indicator, and t is the time trend. Since there is
some reason to expect that there may be lags in the responsiveness
of the financial or investment variables to credit conditions,
and some possibility that MNCs anticipate changes in credit conditions in structuring their financing, experiments with both lags
and leads in the dependent variables were carried out. These are
only selectively reported below.

MNC Fixed Investment Relative to Other Fixed Investment.

The bivariate analysis for the ratio of U.S. affiliate capital
spending to all other capital spending for the six countries is
reported in Table 3. Since the concern is with the existence of
significant relationships, only the "t" values of the coefficients
for the credit conditions proxies are reported. As noted above,
two regressions, corresponding to equations "a" and "b" are shown.
Although the statistics for the trend term are omitted, the coefficient for time is positive and significant at the 95% confidence level for each country except Canada. For the latter, there
was a significant (but small) upward trend in manufacturing, but
not in the ratio for total capital formation.

Although there is not a consistent pattern of significant relationships across countries, there are some definite significant
relationships for individual countries. It may be noted that
there is no indication at all of a responsiveness of the share of
U.S. affiliates in total capital formation to Belgian credit
conditions.

But there is rather strong (and consistent) evidence that the
ratio does respond positively in Germany, Japan, and the United
Kingdom. In each instance, this response seems to occur with
a lag of one year, perhaps not unexpected since the dependent
variable is fixed investment. The strongest relationships in
each case are those with the lagged DUM. Certain indicators
also show significant relations in each case. For Germany,
(Rt-D) and RDIFF exhibit strong relations with the dependent
variable ; for Japan, the M,C, R(t-1); and RDIFF are each significant ; and for the United Kingdom, R(t-1) and M(t-1) tend to
support the evidence supplied by the regression DUM(t-1). It
should be noted that the results for the two forms of specification (i.e., of the adjustment for the upward trend and first
differences) are generally quite consistent with each other.

The two remaining countries -- Canada and France -- exhibit a
rather mixed picture. For Canada, the composite credit conditions
dummy shows no real indication of MNC escape from tight credit in
Canada. Only one coefficient (for all industries in the "annual
change" regression) is significant at the low 80% confidence level.
Yet the growth-adjusted supply-of-credit variable (C) is signifi-

Table 3 : Regression Results : Ratio of Capital Spending by U.S. Affiliates to other Capital Spending ("t" values for alternative indicators of credit conditions)

Credit Conditions Proxy : Required Sign to Indicate Escape

Host Country	Coverage and Form of Regression	DUM	DUM(t-1)	R	M	C	R(t-1)	M(t-1)	C(t-1)	RTERM	RDIFF
		+	+	+	-	-	-	-	-	-	+
Belgium	All industries										
	-levels trend term	-0.91	-0.36	-1.73	1.34	0.70	0.35	1.44	0.48	0.04	0.43
	-changes	-0.74	0.41	-2.18	2.34	2.44	0.69	0.14	0.06	0.31	0.62
	Manufacturing only										
	-levels trend term	0.93	-0.26	-0.16	1.13	0.40	0.41	1.41	0.50	0.22	0.31*
	-changes	-1.12	0.71	-1.84	2.13	2.32	0.16	0.14	0.22	0.23	0.94*
Canada	All industries										
	-levels trend term	-0.27	0.72	-0.54	0.51	-1.10*	1.45**	-0.95*	0.77	-1.03*	-0.68
	-changes	0.16	0.87*	-0.61	-0.75	-1.36*	1.34*	-1.41**	1.60	-0.86*	0.54
	Manufacturing only										
	-levels trend term	0.04	-1.54	1.15*	-1.12*	-1.10*	-0.29	0.46	-0.44	-1.73**	0.38
	-changes	-0.24	-1.94	0.42	-0.63	-0.44	-1.00	1.30	0.27	0.41	0.04
France	All industries										
	-levels trend term	1.43*	0.76	-0.11	0.04	-0.58	1.53*	-0.44	0.80	1.60	0.15
	-changes	1.80**	0.02	0.15	1.09	1.40	1.31*	-0.34	1.08	-0.10	0.14
	Manufacturing only										
	-levels trend term	0.24	0.08	0.05	-1.07**	-1.41**	0.79*	-0.71	-0.67	0.75	0.69
	-changes	1.19*	0.14	-0.61	0.45	-0.35	1.05*	0.20	0.52	0.33	-0.59

Table 3 continued

Germany										
All industries										
−levels trend term	0.01	1.62**	−0.61	0.70	−0.54	0.82	0.09	1.76	0.87	1.05*
−changes	1.67**	1.21*	0.36	1.31	−0.18	1.41**	−0.79	1.55	−0.66	1.78**
Manufacturing only										
−levels trend term	0.02	1.71**	−0.68	−1.02*	−1.52*	0.67	−0.92*	−1.04*	0.26	2.21***
−changes	1.12*	1.32*	−1.30	−0.03	−0.18	1.50**	0.21	0.45	0.28	0.29
Japan										
United Kingdom										
All industries										
−levels trend term	−1.18	2.04***	−0.96	0.77	0.14	1.08*	−1.90***	−0.47	0.83	0.55
−changes	0.86	2.16***	0.72	0.16	−0.01	0.93*	−1.69**	0.44	−0.34	0.94*
Manufacturing only										
−levels trend term	−1.44	0.23	−0.08	0.19	0.14	0.73	−2.74***	0.01	−0.44	−0.17
−changes	−0.01	1.86***	0.80	−0.86	0.51	0.18	−2.23***	−0.23	−0.59	−0.04

Note : Astericksdenote that the regression coefficient has the appropriate sign for indicating avoidance of credit policies by MNCs and that the coefficient was statistically different from zero at the 80%(*), 90%(**) or 95%(***) level of probability. Since indications of avoidance require a specific sign for each credit condition indicator, the one-tail test of significance is employed.

cant in three equations, and R(t-1) and M(t-1) in two regressions.
Note also that RTERM is significant when it is combined with the
trend term. For France, there is a significant coefficient for
DUM in the current year, for all industries. For manufacturing
only, the coefficient has the right sign but is significant at
a low level of confidence. Other regressions using quantitative
indicators also demonstrated some significance for unlagged
relations.

Adjustments in Sources of Funds of U.S. Affiliates.

As indicated above, observed changes in the ratio of foreign affiliate to other <u>fixed</u> investment as evidence of avoidance of stringent local credit policy has the weakness that changes in working
capital are not reflected in the variable, yet may be as cyclically destabilizing as changes in fixed investment. In addition,
the ability of foreign affiliates to adjust the sources of financing in response to local credit conditions is itself an indication of avoidance of domestic monetary policy, and serves as a
supplement to the evidence from the fixed investment ratios.

Regression tests using RET and REQI were carried out. Since these
variables did not demonstrate a secular trend, only the first
difference form was estimated. With the above tests, both
single indicator regressions and multiple regressions on several
indicators of credit conditions were estimated. Since the conclusions drawn were identical, only the single indicator regressions
are reported. Also, unreported experiments with lags and leads
of the dependent variables were conducted, with greatly inferior
results.

The "t" values for the regressions using annual changes are shown
in Table 4. Systematic association of the finance ratios with
tight local credit appear to exist in three countries : Belgium,
Germany and France.

On the other hand, there was no evidence (in the regressions
reported or those not reported) of systematic adjustment of sources of funds of U.S. affiliates to credit conditions in Japan,
and the United Kingdom, with mixed evidence for Canada. This is
somewhat surprising for Japan and the U.K., since positive indications were found for both countries in the earlier regressions
utilizing foreign affiliate capital spending relative to local
investment (I_f/I_d).

The explanation evidently lies in the fact that only two sources
of funding for foreign affiliates are examined here. Borrowing
from local sources, adjustments in the volume of profits left with
the affiliate (by transfer pricing or leads and lags in payments)
or direct foreign borrowing by the affiliate are not included in

Table 4 : Regression Results : Changes in the Structure of Sources of Funds of U.S. Foreign Affiliates (t values for alternative indicators of credit conditions)

Dependent Variable	DUM	M	C	R	RDIFF	RTERM
Required sign for escape	+	–	–	+	+	–
RET = Change in Retained Earnings/Profits :						
Belgium	-.03	-1.30*	.07	1.25**	-1.26	1.33
Canada	.95	-1.48*	.87	1.71*	1.73**	.22
France	1.52*	-.74	.84	1.37*	.41	-1.82**
Germany	.44	-1.78**	.37	.55	-1.04	-1.00
Japan	-.61	.99	1.26	-.18	.65	-.56
U.K.	.61	-1.53*	-.87	-.22	-.64	.38
REQI= Change in Retained Earnings plus New Equity from Parent/Fixed Investment						
Belgium	1.25*	-4.23***	-1.28*	2.34***	.21	-1.56**
Canada	.56	-1.87**	.56	1.24*	1.01	-1.36*
France	1.58***	-.36	.71	1.22*	.48	-2.30**
Germany	2.36***	-2.22***	-.30	2.02***	.70	-.83
U.K.	-.24	.21	.48	.50	-.08	.37

Notes : See Table 3

the sources of funds examined here, and may well be the means of
financing the observed fluctuations in fixed capital shares during
tight money periods in these countries[14].

V. *Conclusions and Implications*

Despite serious inadequacies in the data, three fairly definite
conclusions can be drawn from the analysis presented. First, at
least during the decade of the 1960's, business and credit cycles
in the major host countries for U.S. foreign direct investment
were not sufficiently synchronous, nor sufficiently parallel to
cyclical swings in the United States to neutralize the advantage
of MNCs over local firms in seeking easier credit markets to avoid
national markets where funds were tight. Second, there was
sufficient departure of the time pattern of capital spending by
U.S. foreign affiliates from the time pattern for local firms to
suggest that U.S. MNCs may have utilized their financial advantages to avoid local credit stringency. Third, there are significant positive indications that U.S. MNCs did adjust the financial
sources of their affiliates, and were able to increase their share
of total capital spending, during restrictive credit periods in
some of the major host countries. On the other hand, for at
least two countries, there was little if any positive evidence to
that effect.

Thus, on average, the fixed capital spending of U.S. affiliates
rose relative to that of local (non-U.S.) firms (appropriately
adjusted for trend) during or after tight credit periods in
Germany, Japan and the United Kingdom. Positive but less persuasive evidence was found for France, and no evidence was found for
Belgium and Canada. An indication that MNCs utilize their superior financial flexibility is the adjustment in their sources of
funds during periods of tight local credit conditions. Indications
of such adjustment were found for Belgium, France, and West
Germany ; a weaker indication exists for Canada ; and no indication was found for Japan and the United Kingdom.

Aside from inadequacy in available data, the variations in the
findings among the countries studied may be a result of differing
financial systems and modes of monetary control, and in different
regulatory structures over foreign firms. Thus, the fact that no
evidence was found that U.S. affiliates adjust their sources of
funds to credit conditions in Japan is more likely an indication
that the Japanese surveillance of credit availabilities and investment extends to MNCs than due to an absence in the desire to
adjust their funds flows.

Yet the evidence is persuasive that MNCs do have a differential
advantage over "local" firms during periods of restrictive credit
policy, which is one, perhaps small, source of the competitive
strength of MNCs.   Furthermore, the evidence suggests that MNC
affiliates may be able to engage in cyclically destabilizing
spending behavior to an extent greater than is possible for local
firms. This generalization must, of course, be tentative in light
of the relatively poor and limited data upon which it is based,
and qualified to reflect the particular characteristics of credit
control of individual countries.

A final implication of this evidence is that MNCs, in utilizing
their financial flexibility, tend to be an integrative force in
international financial markets. They are a vehicle for transferring credit conditions from one country to another, and thus have
increased the need for effective coordination of monetary policies across countries.

References

1. This criticism was implicit in, for example "The Werner
    Report" on the industrial policy of the European communities.
    See, e.g., EEC Information "Release" of 1 April 1970 and
    Testimony of Guido Colonna Di Paliano before the Subcommittee
    on Foreign Economic Policy for the 1970's, July 1970, Part 4,
    pp. 750 ff. Similar concerns have been evidenced in Canada,
    especially in the "Watkins Report", Foreign Ownership and the
    Structure of Canadian Industry, prepared for the Privy Council
    Office, January 1968. The case had been put in somewhat
    different terms by John Helliwell, who argues that "scarce
    liquidity" locally has less of an impact on a subsidiary of a
    foreign firm than on a locally-owned firm. (See Public Poli-
    cies and Private Investment, Clarendon Press, 1968, pp.150ff).
    Indeed, some countries restrict the inflow of foreign funds
    by foreign investors to force them to borrow locally so as to
    avoid the presumed unfair advantage of the MNC in access to
    capital. (See S. Robbins and R. Stobaugh, Money in the Multi-
    national Enterprise, Basic Books, 1973, p.60).

2. Robert Stobaugh, Jr., "Financing Foreign Subsidiaries of U.S.-
    Controlled Multinational Enterprises", Journal of Internation-
    al Business Studies, Summer 1970, pp. 43-64.

3. Grant Reuber and Frank Roseman, "International Capital Flows
    and the Take-Over of Domestic Companies by Foreign Firms :
    Canada 1945-61", in F. Machlup, W.S. Salant, and L.Tarshis
    (eds.), International Movement and Mobility of Capital (New
    York : Columbia University Press, 1972), pp. 465-503.

4. Although this study focuses on MNC behavior in advanced
    industrial countries, where general monetary policy is likely
    to be relatively more important than it is in developing
    countries, the avoidance of credit restrictions should not be
    considered exclusive to advanced countries. One case example
    of MNCs presumably avoiding a very restrictive credit policy
    of a developing country while local firms suffered a severe
    liquidity squeeze (and several bankrupcies) is that of Brazil
    in 1964-66. (F. Morley and G.W. Smith, "Import Substitution
    and Foreign Investment in Brazil", Oxford Economic Papers,
    March, 1971, pp. 120-135.

5. The literature on credit rationing in the United States is
    extensive, but a useful survey of the evidence can be found
    in B.M. Friedman, "Credit Rationing : a Review", Federal
    Reserve System Staff Study, No. 72 (June, 1972). The existence
    of credit rationing in other countries has not been so tho-
    roughly investigated, but clearly depends upon the degree of
    selectivity in monetary policy tools and extent of surveillance

of lending to individual customers exercised by the central
bank. Credit rationing is in fact one of the monetary policy
tools in France and Japan, for example. If it is used as a
central bank tool, there is no expectation that MNC affiliates
will have any advantage in access to local credit. Where credit rationing is the result of private decisions (e.g.,
Canada), such an advantage is more likely to exist.

6. Much of this literature is surveyed in Robert Eisner and
    Robert Strotz, "Determinants of Business Investment", in
    Commission on Money and Credit, Impacts of Monetary Policy
    (Englewood Cliffs, N.J. : Prentice-Hall, 1963), pp.60-337,
    and Dale W. Jorgenson, "Econometric Studies of Investment
    Behavior : A Survey", Journal of Economic Literature, December
    1971, pp. 1111-1147. Perhaps a more persuasive indication
    that monetary variables have an effect is that such variables
    (mainly interest rates) are contained in national econometric
    models of four of the six countries studied here. See R.J.
    Ball (ed.), The International Linkage of National Economic
    Models (Amsterdam : North Holland, 1971).

7. It should be noted that the period covered by the data did
    not include the "world-wide" recession years of 1974-75.
    Had the data been extended forward, the degree of positive
    association among countries would surely have been higher.

8. Assuming that movements in these several monetary aggregates
    have separate and independent effects on "credit conditions"
    two possible approaches were possible. One was to carry out
    a factor analysis on quantitative proxies, an alternative we
    rejected because of the limited number of observations, the
    fact that the factor weightings would vary greatly from
    country to country, and that the additional insight was likely
    not to be worth the effort. The second was to regress the
    dependent variables on one or more quantitative proxies, which
    was in fact done. The results were sufficiently similar to
    those reported here that they are omitted from the tables
    and discussions.

9. For a detailed description of the construction of DUM, see
    Donald Macaluso, "The Financial Advantage of Multinational
    Firms During Tight Credit Periods in Host Countries",
    Unpublished Doctoral Dissertation, New York University, 1975,
    Chapter 4.

10. Basically, two sources were consistently referred to for
    qualitative descriptions of monetary conditions : the OECD,
    Economic Survey (annual country issues), the local press as
    digested in IMF International Financial News Survey.

11. The supply of credit is defined as "credits to the economy" in IMF, International Financial Statistics, and thus includes lending not only by banks but also by non-bank financial institutions and acquisitions of financial assets by the non-financial sector.

12. For evidence that short-run movements in the income velocity of money in the United States is an indicator of monetary policy ease or tightness, see George Garvey and Martin Blyn, The Velocity of Money (New York : Federal Reserve Bank of New York, 1970).

13. This, of course, is true only if interest rates are allowed to vary freely, which was not the case for most of the period covered by this study in France. Interest rate movements are also inadequate as credit-conditions indicators if inflationary expectations change, and are reflected in interest rates. The latter could be removed by adjusting nominal interest rates by movements in an appropriate price index. This procedure was rejected because (a) for most the period in the countries covered, prices (or the rate of inflation) were relatively stable ; (b) when there were bursts of inflation (e.g., France, 1969) these were not rapidly reflected in interest rates ; and (c) adjustment by a price index would have introduced (for the period covered)a considerable amount of "noise" in the variable which was unrelated to credit conditions.

14. In experimenting with regressions utilizing lagged or leading dependent variables, it was found that U.S. affiliates in the United Kingdom apparently adjust their sources of funds in anticipation of tight money in the U.K., yet this hardly seems compatible with the expected lagged response in capital spending shares. The apparently spurious relationships found in the sources of funds variables for the U.K. may well be the result of U.S. firms' adjustments to the recurring exchange crises in the U.K. for that period, rather than to anticipating local credit conditions.

Appendix A : Description and Source of Data

Dependent Variables :

The sources of the data utilized in the empirical analysis is as follows : Capital spending (I_f) and sources of funds (RET and REQI) were all taken from the Department of Commerce, Bureau of Economic Analysis series for foreign affiliates of U.S. firms as reported in the <u>Survey of Current Business</u> (various issues).Fixed capital investment in each of the six host countries (I_d) was compiled from the United Nations, <u>Yearbook of National Account Statistics</u> (various issues).

Dependent Variables : Credit Conditions Indicators

DUM -- A qualitative dummy variable, in which "1" denotes year of stringent credit restriction (tight), and "0" denotes year of credit ease or moderate restriction (non-tight). This variable was developed and described in detail in Macaluso, <u>op.cit</u>. Chapter 4

R   -- Average annual percentage changes in short-term interest rates : derived by averaging quarterly changes over four-quarter intervals. The Treasury bill rate was used for Canada, Belgium, Germany, and the U.K. Since treasury bill rates are unavailable for France and Japan, the call money rate was used for France and the Central Bank discount rate for Japan.
    <u>Source</u> : IMF, <u>International Financial Statistics</u>

M   -- Average annual percentage changes in money supply (M_1), adjusted to remove changes in nominal GNP. Quarterly differences (percent change in M_1 minus percent change in GNP) were averaged over four-quarter intervals. The index of industrial projection was used in lieu of GNP for Germany, Belgium , and France since Quarterly GNP data was unavailable.

    <u>Sources</u> : M: IMF, International Financial Statistics   GNP and Ind. Pr. : United Nations, <u>Yearbook of National Accounts Statistics</u>.

C   -- Average annual percentage changes in credit supply (mainly commercial bank credit), adjusted to remove changes in nominal GNP, following the same procedure as for M.

    <u>Source</u> : Same as M.

RTERM -- A term structure of interest rates variable. Average
annual differential between long-term government bond
rate and short-term Treasury bill rate. Average of semi-
annual differentials.

Sources : Government bonds : OECD, Financial Statistics;
Treasury bills : IMF, International Financial Statistics.

RDIFF -- Average annual interest rate differential between each
host country and the United States. Government bond rates
in each country. Average of semi-annual differentials.

Source : OECD, Financial Statistics.

Multinational Firms Stock Price Behavior :
An Empirical Investigation

Bertrand Jacquillat & Bruno Solnik

Centre d'Enseignement Supérieur des Affaires
Jouy-en-Josas

Introduction

Most empirical studies of stock markets have focused on price
behavior in national markets. In a domestic framework, a so-called
"modern capital market theory" has been developed, and tested
with some success[1]. More recently, international asset pricing
models have been presented. The theory is still in its development stage and early empirical tests are far from conclusive[2].
The models link expected returns on assets to measures of their
international systematic risk. Asset pricing models are hard to
test since they depend on expectations which are not directly
measurable. The route usually taken is to work on realized returns and a good understanding of the stochastic price generating
process is very useful especially in the international context.

The purpose of this paper is not theoretical. It will not deal
with asset pricing but only with an empirical study of the common
factors influencing stock price behavior in an international setting. Many studies have shown that the national market factor
was the major common influence of domestic stocks (Lessard (13),
Solnik (21),...). On all markets, industry or international factors are weak compared to the national market factor[3]. The
question for firms with international activities and subsidiaries
is whether their stock price behaves as an international portfolio
(value additivity). In other words, a multinational corporation
(MNC) might be looked at as a combination of sub-firms of various
nationalities and its stock price might be influenced proportionally by each national factor.

On the contrary, it is often mentioned that the relevant variable
is control (e.g. Vernon (22)) ; therefore, a French controlled
multinational corporation would have a stockhastic price behavior
similar to that of any purely domestic French firm. Others would

se different arguments to support this conclusion. The location
of the primary market listing of the stock might be preponderant;
a stock exchanged mainly on one national market would be more
affected by the general domestic market conditions than by factors
relevant to the particular nature of its (international) activities. Non additivity is all the more likely to occur when market
are segmented and restrictions on capital flows prevent international portfolio investment and arbitrage.

To summarize, our objective is to investigate whether a multinational corporation would behave as an internationally diversified
portfolio from an investment standpoint. While the influence of
domestic factors on stock prices have been shown to be very important[4]), one might expect that foreign influences would be felt
proportionately to the MNC's activities abroad. In a broader
perspective, this empirical study tries to give a better understanding of the relationships among stock markets, the influence
of exchange rate fluctuations on stock prices and the stock price
behavior of multinational firms.

In the first part, we draw on previous work to derive some test-
\able relations. After a brief description of the data, the
empirical results are reported in part III. A preliminary investigation of the influence of exchange rate fluctuations on stock
markets is performed in section III.1.   Section III.2 deals with
the national stockmarkets interrelationships. The stock price
behavior of a selected sample of European and American multinational firms is studied in more detail in section III.3 and results
of cross-sectional tests are given in section III.4.

I. A Priori Models

We will start by accepting the current empirical evidence that the
national market factor is the primary common source of influence
of domestic stock prices. Again it should be emphasized that such
a stochastic price structure which is consistent with market segmentation, is also consistent with international market integration and pricing of risk. It would simply mean that whenever the
return on the French stock index differs (unexpectedly) from its
expected value, the same will be true for all French stocks.
Nothing is being said here about what determines expected returns.

Our empirical interest lies in the assumption of value-additivity
for MNC. To take a small example, value-additivity would mean
that the stock price of a firm equally invested in France and
Germany would behave as the sum of a French and German stock without any synergetic effects. In other words, industrial diversification would be similar to portfolio diversification.

This direct value additivity has been the object of much interest
in the field of financial theory. The market value of a firm is
usually considered to be determined by expectations about future
cash flows. The traditional terminology is that the value of the
firm is the discounted value of future cash flow. Asset pricing
theory has stressed the portfolio approach and value-additivity
has been demonstrated in the context of a perfect and complete
domestic market. Thus Myers (17) and Levy and Sarnat (15) have
shown that the value of a firm should be equal to the sum of the
value of its components. This argument is often developed in the
case of mergers.

Without getting into sophisticated theoretical development, the
same property should hold internationally if we have perfect and
complete international markets with no segmentation in the product
or financial markets. In other words, the value of a multinational firm (MNC) would be determined by the sum of the values of its
activities in the various countries. As was stressed by Hugues,
Logue and Sweeney (9) in the case of fully integrated markets,
there is no advantage to holding shares in a multinational firm
versus holding shares in a number of domestic firms in different
countries.

A few notations are introduced in Table 1. With those notations
we have :

$$V = \sum_{i=1}^{n} V_i^n \qquad\qquad (1)$$

In complete markets, the value of the firm's activities in country
i has to be equal to the <u>local (country i) market value</u> of these
activities, adjusted by the present exchange rate. Otherwise arbitrage would take place. Therefore, even with stochastic exchange
rates, we have :

$$V_i^n = \int_{in} V_i \qquad\qquad (2)$$

and

$$V = \sum_i \int_{in} V_i \qquad\qquad (3)$$

Given the separation-additivity described above, we will argue as
if the firm's activities in country i (or a competitor, or a
close substitute) is quoted on the stock market of country i.

Table 1 : List of Notations.

$i = 1, 2, \ldots, n-1$ represents a foreign country (and currency) i.
n is the index of the country of reference, e.g., the country of the firm's headquarters.
$\int_{in}^{t}$ is the exchange rate between currencies i and n in period t (expected).
V is the total value of the firm in H.C. (home currency).
V_i is the value of the firm's "activities" in country i, expressed in L.C. (local currency).
V_i^n is the value of the firm's "activities" in country i, expressed in H.C.
X_i is the proportion of the firm's "activities" in country i as a % of the total "activities" of the firms.
I_i stock market index of country in L.C. (pure domestic index).

The domestic market model can be specified for national stocks traded on each domestic market i as :

$$\frac{\Delta \tilde{V}_i}{V_i} = \alpha_i + \beta_i \frac{\Delta \tilde{I}_i}{I_i} + \tilde{\varepsilon}_i \tag{4}$$

where $\dfrac{\Delta V_i}{V_i}$ and $\dfrac{\Delta I_i}{I_i}$ are the rates of return on the stock and domestic market index, with the usual assumption of independence and normality. The total return on the firm is equal to :

$$\frac{\tilde{\Delta V}}{V} = \Sigma X_i \frac{\tilde{\Delta V}_i^n}{V_i^n}$$

with :

$$\frac{\Delta \tilde{V}_i^n}{V_i^n} = \frac{\Delta(\int_{in} V_i)}{\int_{in} V_i} = \frac{\Delta \tilde{\int}_{in}}{\int_{in}} + \frac{\Delta \tilde{V}_i}{V_i} + \frac{\Delta \tilde{\int}_{in}}{\int_{in}} \frac{\Delta \tilde{V}_i}{V_i} \tag{5}$$

For short intervals the last term will be negligible compared to the first two. If we were measuring returns by logs of price relatives (instantaneous compounding), this cross-product will drop exactly. By replacing in (3) we get :

$$\frac{\tilde{\Delta V}}{V} = \alpha + \sum_i X_i \frac{\tilde{\Delta f}_{in}}{f_{in}} + \sum_i X_i \beta_i \frac{\tilde{\Delta I}_i}{I_i} + \tilde{\varepsilon} \qquad (6)$$

This is a relation which can be tested directly by regressing rates of returns of international firms on exchange rate fluctuations and stock indices returns.

MNC often claim that they hedge their foreign investment against unexpected foreign currency movements. This might be achieved through foreign financing policy or various forms of exchange risk covering. This would mean that equation (5) would be replaced by (7) :

$$\frac{\tilde{\Delta V}_i^n}{V_i^n} = \rho_{in} \frac{\tilde{\Delta f}_{in}}{f_{in}} + \frac{\tilde{\Delta V}_i}{V_i} \qquad (7)$$

where ρ_{in} = 1 if no hedging is done

ρ_{in} = 0 if full heding is done

and equation (6) becomes :

$$\frac{\tilde{\Delta V}}{V} = \alpha + \sum_i X_i \rho_{in} \frac{\tilde{\Delta f}_{in}}{f_{in}} + \sum_i X_i \beta_i \frac{\tilde{\Delta I}_i}{I_i} + \tilde{\varepsilon} \qquad (8)$$

If the firm manages to be fully covered the first summation sign (exchange rate influence) will just disappear.

As mentioned in the introduction, many international business specialists would disagree with the international additivity implied in relation (8). Strong synergetic effects might exist. Technical advantage, operating or financial economies, captive markets, managerial skills are often mentioned as important advantages to the MNC. These factors which might exist for domestic conglomerate mergers would be magnified on the international scene (Vernon (22)). A MNC might also differ from an internationally diversified portfolio because of the control system applied from the home country which would transform the MNC into a national

firm operating abroad. This would imply a stock price behavior
fairly similar to that of a domestic firm. Another argument in
favor of this thesis is that the MNC stock price will mostly be
affected by the stock market conditions of the country where its
share is mostly traded (the "home" country). The empirical question is then whether a multinational firm stock price behaves as
an internationally diversified portfolio or as a domestic firm.

To attempt to answer this question, equation (8) will be subjected
to empirical scrutiny. It is not an asset pricing model but a
description of the stochastic generating process assuming additivity of the national characteristics of the firm.

II. *The Data*

The initial test period is from April 1, 1966 to May 31, 1974.
Monthly observations have been collected for the major stock
market indices. Given our European and North American focus for
multinational firms, we worked mostly with Belgium, France, Germany,
Italy, the Netherlands, Sweden, Switzerland, the United Kingdom
and the United States.

End-of-the-month exchange rates were also collected for those
countries. For the major currencies forward exchange rates were
added since they might give a fair representation of expected
future spot rates. Continuous series of exchange rates could not
be found for the Italian Lira and the Swedish Krone. The data
were very carefully screened and generally collected from two
independent sources to check for errors. We avoided using stock
indice of the IMF as many authors do since those are monthly
averages and not end-of-the-month observations.

A sample of 40 European multinational firms and 23 American were
used. These were among the top American and European firms ranked
by their percentage of activities abroad (Business International
and Fortune). They were selected on the basis of availability
of sales and accounting data on the geographical breakdown of
their operations. It should be emphasized that any geographical
breakdown data beyond the ratio foreign/domestic seem very confi-
dential and alsmost impossible to obtain. Firms usually argued
that political problems and potential government controls or competition prevented them from disclosing this type of information.

In general, we used sales ratio to measure the proportion of
foreign activities rather than earnings or assets figures. This
was strongly suggested to us by practitioners (given the usual
manipulation on accounting earnings).

A shorter period of time (January 1970 - May 1974) was selected
for the detailed analysis of the relationship between stock price
behavior and foreign activities since percentage of foreign activities varies over time. Sales figures were usually collected for
the middle year of our period (1972).

At the end, detailed geographical breakdown by countries could
only be obtained for half of our sample[5].

III. *Empirical Tests*

Before getting into a complete test of relation (8) for individual
firms, one needs to get a better knowledge of the relationship
between stock market indices and exchange rates.

III.1 *Exchange Rates and Stock Market Indices*

One always wonders what should be the influence of a de(re)valua-
tion on stock market prices[6]. Theories on the exchange rate-
stock price relationship are not very explicit or simply do not
exist. A general equilibrium model would be needed which would
incorporate production, international trade, financial flows
etc. This is a formidable task. Short of this achievement, some
beliefs have been expressed. Many contend that if markets are
perfect and adjustments immediate, there should not exist any
relationship. Others claim that a devaluation of the domestic
currency (e.g. the US dollar) would be parallel to a down movement
in stock prices.

According to the simplified model of the world that one is using
as a reference, it is easy to criticize the existence of either
a positive, negative or null correlation between stock prices and
exchange rate movements. Instead of getting into a sterile theoretical argument, the empirical route will be taken.

Table 2 gives the correlation coefficients between stock index
movements and exchange rate fluctuations for each stock index.
The column U.S. would give the correlation of the U.S. index
$(I_t - I_{t-1})/(I_{t-1})$ with all the (spot) exchange rate fluctuations
relative to the dollar $(S_t - S_{t-1})/(S_{t-1})$. Therefore the first
element in the column U.S. would be the correlation coefficient
of variations of the U.S. index and British Pound relative to the
dollar (e.g., 0.5 £/$). A positive term means that the U.S.
dollar and the U.S. stock market tend to go up (or down) together.

Bertrand Jacquillat and Bruno Solnik

Table 2 : Correlation Coefficients between Stock Index Returns and Exchange Rate Fluctuations or Forward Agios 1966-1974

Exchange rate	Stock index	United Kingdom	Belgium	France	Germany	Netherlands	Switzerland	United States
British Pound	Spot	–	.0142	-.1513	-.0594	-.0270	-.1309	-.0792
	forward	–	-.1156	-.0992	-.1373	-.001	-.0209	-.1332
Belgian France	Spot	.0176	–	-.0829	-.0061	-.0954	-.2757	-.1399
	forward	-.0662	–	-.1294	.1186	.1708	.1618	.0055
French Franc	Spot	-.0233	.0195	–	.0781	-.0394	-.1377	-.0564
	forward	-.0574	.2454	–	.1246	.2122	.1611	.0952
German Mark	Spot	.1150	-.0424	-.0664	–	-.1438	-.2579	-.1113
	forward	-.0461	-.0522	-.2736	–	.0304	.0566	.0659
Dutch Guilder	Spot	.0447	-.0551	-.0227	.0434	–	-.2235	-.1386
	forward	-.0335	-.1541	-.2771	.0386	–	.0476	.0910
Swiss Franc	Spot	.1641	-.0537	-.0110	.1142	.0732	–	.0143
	forward	-.0654	-.0238	-.2371	-.0379	.0597	–	-.1155
U.S. Dollar	Spot	.1336	.1319	-.0448	-.0485	.0667	-.1456	–
	forward	-.0198	.0380	-.1725	.0707	.0748	.1035	–

Note : A column represents a national stock index and a row a currency. A coefficient (e.g.,-.0664) is the correlation between the column stock index return (e.g., French index) and the exchange rate fluctuation of the row currency (e.g., D.M.) expressed in terms of the stock index country currency (D.M. for French Francs).

In the same table we reported correlations of domestic stock index variations with forward agios. The forward agio is equal to : $(F_t - S_t)/S_t$, where F_t is the forward exchange rate quoted in period t for period $t + 1$. To the extent that forward rates represent expectations about future spot rates[7], the forward agio is a proxy for the expected fluctuation in exchange rate. It is interesting to see whether there exists any relation between variations in domestic stock prices and expectations of exchange rate movement.

All correlation coefficients are very small and no significant sign pattern seems to exist. One needs not get into sophisiticated significance test over all countries and currencies correlation coefficients to see that the dependence between the two variables is, at best, very weak -- the same conclusion was reached after performing other statistical tests (non linear, non parametric). We are not rejecting the existence of a global dependence between stock indices and exchange rates but it has to be a fairly subtle and non systematic one[8].

III.2. *Stock Markets Interrelationships*

The interest in international diversification and international pricing of securities comes from the relative independence of stock price movements across countries. As Lessard (13) and Solnik (21) have shown, the influence of domestic factors on stock prices is much larger than that of international or industry factors. This is the reason why a multinational firm is expected to have a different stock price behavior from a purely domestic firm of the same nationality.

This independence of various stock markets has been reported by Grubel (8), Levy and Sarnat (14), Joy et al. (12). Correlation coefficients between two countries stock index returns are given in Table 3 for the period 1966-1974. These figures are slightly higher than those reported in earlier studies. This might be explained by the larger comovements in stock market prices in the mid-seventies due to growing interdependencies of the developed countries economies. However, even in the past two or three years, no pair of markets[9] have had more than 30% (R square) of common movements. The degree of independence between national factors is still quite large. From a price behavior view point, foreign stocks are no substitute to domestic ones. Besides, multicolinearity will not be a serious problem in the fortcoming tests.

One should not confuse two aspects of intercountry correlations:

- one is that all economies and therefore all stock markets are
somewhat dependent. Therefore each firm, even purely domestic,
will have some (usually small) degree of comovement with foreign
stock markets. This can be visualized as the international dependence "through" the domestic index.

- the second one is that, due to its foreign operation in a
specific country, a firm's price will be directly affected by
what is happening there. This is the aspect that will be quantified and investigated.

A preliminary test of whether a MNC is like an internationally
diversified portfolio can be performed by computing the correlation coefficient of each MNC stock returns with foreign indices.
The firms included in our sample were grouped by country of
origin and the average correlation coefficients for each country
group are reported in Table 4. To make these figures comparable
to those of Table 3, an adjustment had to be performed since we
are dealing with individual stocks instead of stock indices.
In Table 4, a row gives the average correlation of the MNC based
in one country (e.g., the 24 U.S. based firms) with all the
foreign stock indices. With very few exceptions, all the coefficients are larger than for the average domestic firm (stock indices of Table 3). It appears that stock prices of firms with
extensive foreign operations are more sensitive to foreign factors
than the typical domestic firm. The next question is whether they
are as sensitive as they ought to be given the geographical breakdown of their activities.

III.3. *Stock Price Behavior of MNC*

a) We first regressed monthly rates of returns for individual
firms on all the national stock indices returns (period 1970-74).
Therefore we estimated the coefficients whose theoretical value
is $X_i \beta_i$. Without a prior knowledge of β_i, its expected value is
1 ; another alternative would have been to use the beta of a
purely domestic firm with similar activities and financial structure. This implies that all coefficients of the regressions
should be equal (or at least related) to X_i the proportion of
"activities" in country i :

$$\frac{\Delta V}{V} = a + \sum_i b_i \frac{\Delta I_i}{I_i} + \varepsilon \qquad (8a)$$

where $b_i = X_i \, \beta_i$ and with the assumption that

$$E(\beta_i) = 1$$

$b_i = X_i$ percentage of activities in country i.

Table 3 : Correlation between Domestic Stock Indices : 1966-1974

	U.S.A.	Netherl.	Belgium	Germany	Italy	Sweden	France	Switz.	U.K.
U.S.A.	1.000								
Netherlands	.525	1.000							
Belgium	.367	.448	1.000						
Germany	.285	.592	.396	1.000					
Italy	.062	.179	.188	.151	1.000				
Sweden	.385	.326	.356	.317	.208	1.000			
France	.272	.353	.502	.432	.281	.279	1.000		
Switzerland	.360	.550	.399	.496	.172	.166	.440	1.000	
Unit.Kingdom	.298	.249	.210	.207	.018	.202	.253	.149	1.000

Table 4 : Average adjusted Correlation Coefficients of MNF and Foreign Indices 1966-1974

	U.S.A.	Netherl.	Belgium	Germany	Italy	Sweden	France	Switzerl	U.K.
U.S.A.	1	.560	.295	.397	.036	.261	.227	.448	.418
Netherlands	.617	1	.622	.723	.153	.240	.434	.481	.350
Belgium	.456	.773	1	.616	.231	.614	.553	.532	.252
Germany	.327	.611	.396	1	.120	.352	.374	.469	.202
Italy	.092	.174	.205	.119	1	.239	.285	.150	.099
Sweden	.432	.375	.467	.363	.192	1	.253	.353	.306
France	.253	.480	.660	.585	.281	.335	1	.568	.301
Switzerland	.493	.587	.507	.465	.316	.256	.464	1	.327
U.K.	.314	.298	.337	.334	-.019	.247	.313	.286	1

While the individual results would take too much space[10]), summary
statistics are presented in Table 5 and 6. Table 5 gives the
average value of the coefficients and R square per country ; the
same statistics obtained on a single domestic index model are also
reported for comparison purposes.

It is easy to see that only the domestic coefficients are systematically significant and on the average close to one. As a
matter of fact, their values are quite close from those estimated
by using a traditional single index model. All the "foreign"
coefficients are usually small and insignificant , although in
some cases they can be quite large, positive or negative. Many
German and Dutch firms prices seem to be influenced by the US
stock market. All the other relations are weaker. To check
whether adding these foreign factors is useful to explain stock
price behavior, the R square of the regression run using only the
domestic index is reported in Table 5 (all R squares are adjusted
for degrees of freedom). The improvement in explanatory power is
small[11]) (.31 compared to .29). The improvement in R^2 is much
better for European MNF which, in general, have a higher proportion of their activities abroad. This is especially true for firms
from small countries such as Switzerland (.75 versus .52).

It is difficult to reach more detailed conclusions on a country
by country analysis because the percentage of activities in each
country is usually small (and therefore the effects are difficult
to observe) and precise foreign activities geographical breakdown
exists only for a few companies.

b) In the second (and most complete) test of international price
behavior, countries were grouped into geographical areas. Similarly, to test equation (8), a few representative currencies were
selected :

- Rates of return for European firms were regressed against movements in the US stock index, a European stock index and the
domestic one, and against the variation of the exchange rate of
the domestic currency (MNF country of origin) with the US dollar,
Deutsch Mark and French Franc[12]).

- Rates of return for US firms were regressed against movements
in the foreign stock index (Europe and Japan) and the domestic
stock index, the variation of the exchange rate of the domestic
currency (dollar) with the British Pound, Deutsch Mark and French
Franc[13]).

Table 5: Average Betas of Portfolios of Country MNF with Selected National Indices

		U.S.	Netherlands	Belgium	Germany	Italy	Sweden	France	Switzerland	U.K.	R^2 adjusted	Single index beta	Single index R^2 adj.
US	MNF	.94	.12	-.05	-.01	-.04	.04	.02	-.01	-.07	.31	1.02	.29
Dutch	MNF	.31	.76	.09	.16	-.02	-.28	.25	-.21	-.06	.63	.98	.50
Belgian	MNF	-.27	.07	1.04	.06	.03	.19	.06	.08	.07	.58	1.03	.45
German	MNF	.24	.03	-.21	1.18	-.02	-.01	.10	-.15	-.11	.74	1.18	.65
Italian	MNF	-.10	.06	.10	.01	.83	.11	-.19	-.16	.20	.51	.91	.47
Swedish	MNF	.06	-.15	-.02	.08	-.10	.96	.01	.15	.02	.50	.92	.42
French	MNF	-.10	.14	.33	.18	.02	-.16	.95	-.22	.03	.62	1.08	.45
Swiss	MNF	-.12	-.23	-.04	-.09	-.02	.16	-.11	1.74	.16	.75	1.39	.52
British	MNF	-.10	-.11	.30	.09	-.04	-.13	-.09	.07	.84	.49	1.06	.44

Note : All R^2 are adjusted for the number of degrees of freedom.

$$\frac{\Delta V}{V} = \alpha + \sum_i b_i \frac{\Delta I_i}{I_i} + \sum_j a_j \frac{\Delta \int jn}{\int_{jn}} + \varepsilon \tag{8b}$$

where according to equation (8) we should have :

- $b_i = X_i \beta_i$ and with the simplifying assumption that

$E(\beta_i) = 1 : b_i = X_i$ percentage of activities in the domestic

country, rest of Europe, US or the world.

- $a_i = X_i$ or at least positive if foreign assets are not
hedged against exchange risk.

The results for each firm are not reported here because of space
limitations, but are available from the authors. These results
are used in the next section on cross-sectional tests. However
we can make the following observations on exchange rate coefficients.

On the exchange rate side, the order of magnitude of the coefficients is acceptable, however their signs seem quite random. For
US firms, the average coefficients are .08 and .03 with the French
Franc and D.M., therefore in the direction postulated by the
theory ; the average coefficient with the British Pound is -.28
which would indicate that US firms have wisely overhedged their
British assets. In other words, US firms have benefited, stock
pricewise, from the dollar depreciation relative to the DM and FF
and its appreciation relative to the pound. While ad hoc explanations can always be found, the message is not very clear for
firms of other countries. In general, it would seem that multinational firms have avoided exposure to exchange risk by hedging
their foreign activities and, with a few exceptions, stock prices
do not reflect any strong and systematic exchange rate influence.

Despite very careful empirical work, few strong and systematic
foreign influences have been demonstrated. More insights can be
gained by looking at the relations between estimated b's (the
regression coefficients) and proxies of proportions of foreign
activities measures (with error) by percentage of sales.

III.4. Cross-Sectional Tests

Table 6 reports the average values of sales ratio and regression coefficient b's for the 23 US firms and 21 European firms for which we had detailed sales breakdown. Given our assumption that $E(\beta) = 1$, we should have $b_i = X_i$. Clearly the domestic coefficients b seem, on the average, too large compared to the domestic sales ratio (.95 and .97 compared to .62 and .41) while foreign coefficients are too small (.15, .12, .06 compared to .38, .35, .13). Cross-sectional results reported in Table 7 give more information[14]. Regressions were run separately for US and European firms since the data available were slightly different.

First, the sum of the b coefficients should be close to one[15] ; this was tested by regressing the domestic coefficients on the sum of the foreign ones (for each firm j) :

$$b^j_{dom} = C_o + C_1\, b^j_{for} + u$$

where we would expect C_o to be equal to one (or slightly less) and C_1 equal to -1. The results are broadly consistent with our expectations. For the US the coefficients C_o, C_1 in table 7 are not significantly different from their predicted values. The point estimates are very close to one and the R^2 is large (0.56). It implies that a firm with a higher foreign b (sensitivity to foreign influence) will tend to be less sensitive to domestic influence (lower domestic b). The sum of these two coefficients being close to one. The conclusion is somewhat similar for European firms but C_1 is significantly lower than one. However, the negative correlation between domestic and foreign β's in both cases quite strong (R-square of .6) and all coefficients statistically different from zero (.01 level).

We then regressed cross-sectionally the various b's on the corresponding sales ratios. For example, the domestic coefficients for American MNC were regressed against the ratio of domestic to total sales :

$$b^j = C_o + C_1\, S.R^j + u$$

where b^j is the estimated domestic (re foreign) coefficient,

$S.R^j$ is the domestic (re foreign) sales ratio for firm j.

Given $E(\beta_j) = 1$, we should have $b_j = X_j = S.R^j$, if sales ratios are good proxies for percentage of activities. We therefore would expect all C_o's to be close to zero and C_1's close to one.

Table 6 : Average Coefficients

	Domestic Sales D.S.	Foreign Sales F.S.	European Sales E.S.	US Sales U.S.S.	Domest. coef. b_{dom}	Foreign coef. b_{for}	Europ. coef. b_{eur}	US Coef. b_{us}
US MNF[*]	.62	.38	–	–	.95	.15	–	–
EUR MNF[***]	.41	–	.35	.13	.97	–	.12	.06

[*]   23 firms
[***] 21 firms

Table 7 : Cross-Sectional Regressions[1]

US MNF	$b_{dom} = 1.12 - 1.13\, b_{for}$ $\quad\;\;(.35)^{*}\;\;(.22)^{*}$	$R^2 = .56$
EUR.MNF	$b_{dom} = 1.09 - .66\,(b_{eur}+ b_{us})$ $\quad\;\;(.22)^{*}\;\;(.12)$	$R^2 = .62$
US. MNF	$b_{dom} = .26 + 1.09\ D.S.$ $\quad\;\;(.14)^{*}\;\;(.88)$ $b_{for} = -.23 + .98\ F.S.$ $\quad\;\;(.22)\;\;\;\;(.57)$	$R^2 = .07$ $R^2 = .12$
EUR. MNF	$b_{dom} = .86 + .31\ D.S.$ $\quad\;\;(.35)^{*}(.35)^{*}$ $b_{eur} = -.31 + 1.16\ E.S.$ $\quad\;(52)\;\;\;(.65)$ $b_{us} = .14 - .60\ U.S.S.$ $\quad\;\;(.36)\;\;\;\;(.91)$	$R^2 = .04$ $R^2 = .15$ $R^2 + .02$

1) Standard deviations in parentheses. A * means a coefficient statistically different from zero at the .05 level. E.S. means European Sales, D.S. means Domestic Sales, US S means US Sales.

The point estimates for C_1 are remarkably close to one for American
firms (standard error are very large). It implies that the domestic betas would vary as (1-FS), i.e. the higher the percentage of
foreign sales the lower the domestic β and the higher the foreign
β (with a coefficient of proportionality of one). While the percentage of variance explained is low, the influence of international activities is clear. The intercept is significantly
positive for domestic betas and negative for foreign betas as one
would expect given the average values of these coefficients
(Table 6). For European firms, point estimates are not so good.
However, given the size of the estimates standard error, little
can be said which would be "statistically significant" except that
in both cases the domestic b's have a positive and significant
bias[16]. This would indicate that MNC share prices behave more
like a domestic share than like an international portfolio as
justified by its foreign investments.

VI. *Conclusion*

In this paper, we conducted an empirical investigation of multinational firm stock price behavior with two purposes :

- One was to give a better understanding of the relationship
between stockmarkets, the influence of exchange rate fluctuations
on stockprices and the stock price behavior of multinational firms
during the period 1966-1974 ;

- The other was to investigate whether a multinational firm would
behave as an internationally diversified portfolio from an investment standpoint.

A simple model for international firms was developed linking individual stock returns to rates of return on several market indices
and exchange rate fluctuations.

A preliminary test at the aggregate level did not indicate any
systematic dependence between stock market indices and exchange
rate fluctuations. The empirical study of individual security
prices started with simple correlation tests which indicated that
stock prices of multinational firms with extensive foreign operations are more sensitive to foreign factors than typical domestic
firms, as suggested by the theory. However, multiple regressions
of rates of return of multinational firms with selected foreign
stock market indices and exchange rates showed that international
firms are less sensitive to foreign factors than they ought to be,

given the geographical breakdown of their activities. As a matter
of fact, only the domestic coefficients are systematically (statistically) significant. Exchange rates fluctuations seem to have
little influence on the value of the firms, possibly because of
hedging policies.

Cross-sectional tests gave weak support to the "additive" international model developed above. The relationship between estimated betas, domestic and foreign, and percentage of activities
measured by sales ratios, domestic and foreign was consistent with
the theory except that domestic betas are significantly too high.
However in all cases the association between the two sets of
variables is quite poor.

This is not a surprising result given our ambitious target and
the poor data. Data limitations are very serious in the estimation of foreign activities and very gross proxies have been used
(sales figures). Many of the effects might be too small to
detect given the size of the measurement errors ; this is especially true for the influence of individual currencies movements.
Given all the model specifications and assumptions that are
tested simultaneously, definitive conclusions are hard to reach.
It seems however that international firms stock prices are more
sensitive to foreign influences than purely domestic firms but
less than one might have expected.

It should be made clear that this study was not intended to and
does not prove or reject market irrationality, or international
market integration, or international pricing of risk. It might
indicate that investors do not correctly appreciate the international dimension of a MNC stock, or that segmentation in the
markets for goods and capital has strong influences on asset
prices. The empirical predominance of domestic factors, even for
a firm with extensive foreign operations, might simply mean that
foreign activities or subsidiaries of a firm are not viewed by
investors as a direct substitute to equivalent firms[17]). It is
often mentioned that multinational firms are controlled from the
home base to maximize profits to the ownership who is mostly
located in the home country. This control over an international
organization allows it to shift activities between countries and
avoid dependence on a single one except the home country. This is
a marked difference with portfolio diversification where the
stockholder does not have "control" of his portfolio. The increasing constraints imposed by governments on capital flows and
acquisitions of local firms by foreign ones might reduce these
differences. From a practical investment standpoint, this study
gives some indications that a multinational firm cannot be regarded as an internationally diversified portfolio.

Further research might provide more answers to the important questions raised ; however data availability and precision will always limit the scope of the analysis.

Footnotes

1)   For a summary of work on the U.S. market see Jensen (11),
     for the other stock markets, see Jacquillat and Solnik (10).

2)   Theoretical models have been developed by Adler and Dumas
     (1), Grauer, Litzenberger and Stehle (7), Solnik (20).
     Tests of the international pricing of risk have been perfor-
     med in Agman (2), Lessard (13), Solnik (21).

3)   This implies that international pricing of stocks (if any)
     would primarily be transmitted through the international
     pricing of national indices.

4)   See Blume (5), Fama (6), Lessard (13), Pogue and Solnik (13),
     Solnik (21), Agmon (3).

5)   We thank Eurofinance for giving us access to their files on
     European firms.

6)   We will call devaluation any downwards movement of a currency,
     either by an official change of parity or by an exchange
     rate fluctuation in the free market.

7)   See Aliber (4), Roll and Solnik (19), Solnik (20).

8)   On the other side, some firms might be more affected, because
     of their international operations, than the average domestic
     firm.

9)   With the exceptions of closely dependent economies such as
     U.S., Canada. Joy et al. (12) have presented a detailed
     analysis of specific structures of dependence ; they have
     also shown that exchange rate movements had little impact
     on the value of the correlation coefficients and studied the
     growing internationalization of the capital markets. This
     internationalization is far from complete and international
     diversification is still advantageous especially because of
     the general increase in price volatility.

10) A full table will be sent to interested readers upon request.
     The sample used is reported in Table 7.

11) The addition of a Japanese index to those regressions for
     U.S. firms only caused the R^2 to increase to .32 with 6
     significative coefficients (out of 23) and a mean coefficient
     of .09.

12) International indices are GNP weighted averages of national stock indices. In all these tables European relates to the rest of Europe, therefore excluding the national index of the firm. The same applies to sales data.
Given the large degree of comovement between many of the currencies, the selection of only a limited number of those in the empirical tests still allows us to capture most of the exchange rate influence phenomenon.

13) Results for individual firms are not given because of space limitations, but are available from the authors.

14) The errors in measurement in cross-sectional tests might create serious estimation problems, especially for the first two regressions.

15) As a matter of fact, it should be slightly less since we did not consider all foreign countries. For European firms, U.S. and total European sales represents 9°% of total sales.

16) Similar tests were performed in the exchange rate coefficients for the few firms where we had detailed geographical break-down. No interesting results could be found.

17) For example, the activities of Ford in Germany might not be considered as comparable to the activities of Volkswagen in its own country, because of organization, management objectives, accounting practices etc.... Although surprising, this result is not irrational. An exporting firm will probably be affected by domestic problems (production,financing availability...) which means that volatility of its stock price will reflect domestic influences as well as (or rather than) foreign influences due to the foreign sales volume or cash flows. Even multinational firms with foreign subsidiaries might shift activities between countries to avoid problems in any single country thereby reducing the dependence on any single foreign economy.

Bibliography

(1)   M. Adler and B. Dumas, "Optimal International Acquisition",
      Journal of Finance, March 1975

(2)   T. Agmon, "The Relationship among Equity Market : A Study of
      Share Price Comovements in the United States, United Kingdom,
      Germany and Japan", Journal of Finance, September 1972.

(3)   T. Agmon, "The Significance of the Country Factor for Share
      Price Movements in the United Kingdom, Germany and Japan",
      Journal of Business, January 1973.

(4)   R.Z. Aliber, "Equilibrium and Desequilibrium in the Inter-
      national Money Market", University of Chicago Working Paper,
      December 1974.

5)   M. Blume, "On the Assessment of Risk", Journal of Finance,
      March 1971.

(6)   G. Fama, "The Behavior of Stock Market Prices", Journal of
      Business, April 1967.

(7)   F. Grauer, R. Litzenberger and R. Stehle, "Sharing Rules
      and Equilibrium in an International Capital Market under
      Uncertainty", Stanford Research Paper, February 1975.

(8)   H. Grubel,"Internationally Diversified Portfolios : Welfare
      Gains and Capital Flows", American Economic Review,
      December 1968.

(9)   J. Hughes, D. Logue and J. Sweeney, "Corporate International
      Diversification and Market Assigned Measures of Risk and
      Diversification", Working Paper, September 1975.

(10) B. Jacquillat and B. Solnik, "Les marchés financiers et la
      gestion de portefeuille", Dunod, Paris 1974.

(11) M. Jensen (ed.), "Studies in the Theory of Capital Markets",
      Praeger Publishers, 1973.

(12) O.M. Joy, D. Panton, F. Reilly and S. Martin "Comovement
      of Major International Equity Markets", University of Kansas
      Working Paper, 1974.

(13) D. Lessard, "World, National and Industry Factor in Equity
      Returns", Journal of Finance, May 1974.

(14) H. Levy and M. Sarnat, "International Diversification of
      Investment Portfolios",American Economic Review,September
      1970.

(15) H. Levy and M. Sarnat, "Diversification, Portfolio Analysis and the Uneasy Case for Mergers", Journal of Finance, September 1970.

(16) J. Lintner, "Inflation and Security Returns", Journal of Finance, May 1975.

(17) S. Myers, "Procedures for Capital Budgeting under Uncertainty", Industrial Management Review, Spring 1968.

(18) G. Pogue and B. Solnik, "The Market Model Applied to European Common Stocks : Some Empirical Results", Journal of Financial and Quantitative Analysis, December 1974.

(19) R. Roll and B. Solnik "A Pure Foreign Exchange Asset Pricing Model", European Institute Working Paper, 1974 revised August 1975.

(20) B. Solnik, "An Equilibrium Model of the International Capital Market", Journal of Economic Theory, August 1974.

(21) B. Solnik, "International Pricing of Risk : An Empirical Investigation of the World Capital Market Structure", Journal of Finance, May 1974.

(22) R. Vernon, Manager in the International Economy (2nd Edition), Prentice-Hall, Inc., Englewood Cliffs, New Jersey, 1972.

PATTERNS IN INTERNATIONAL MARKETS AND MARKET STRATEGY[*]

James Leontiades

Manchester Business School

Corporate strategy is sometimes defined as the adjustment of the firm to its environment. This definition raises a number of questions when the firm in question is a multinational company. What is the relevant environment for such companies ? Is the aforementioned adjustment simply a collection of separate responses to individual national environments or are there international relationships between national markets which may enter into this adjustment ?

The research presented here tests for the existence of such international relationships. The paper is divided into four parts :

Part I. The main hypothesis here is that international markets for specific products fall into one of three categories, depending on their international market penetration considered as a function of per capita GNP. Examples of two such patterns are located and their related properties examines.

Part II. This focuses on variation in consumer characteristics encountered by firms marketing in low income (less developed countries) and high income countries.

Part III. The last two parts are concerned with market positioning. How does the multinational firm position its products in the various countries in which it operates with reference to the main buying groups in those countries ? Does it conform to the national market pattern ?

Part IV. This considers the relationship between market positioning as set out in Part III and market share. Is the positioning of the firm vis à vis major consumer groups related to its market share in its various national markets of operation ?

[*] The survey on which this study is based was made possible by the generous co-operation of marketing personnel in five multinational companies.The assistance of headquarters as well as foreign affiliate personnel proved invaluable.My thanks also to the European Institute for Advanced Studies in Management,where much of the research was carried out.

Empirical Basis

The mechanism for collecting this information was a questionnaire
survey sent to the marketing directors of cooperating multinational firms. Each questionnaire was completed with reference to a
carefully specified consumer product and national territory. Their
views were solicited only on the national market where they
were employed at the time of the survey and relative only to a
product which they were actively engaged in marketing in that
national territory. In effect, the project collected and coordinated the views of these national experts on the same product on
an international scale.

Cooperation from the parent company, secured beforehand, contributed to a response rate of over 85%. Headquarters was also
helpful in dealing with the problem, faced by all such research,
of arriving at internationally consistent definitions of the
products surveyed. The fact that internal reporting systems
within such firms typically require managers in the various international markets to utilize common product definitions was a major
consideration.

Theoretical Basis

The conceptual roots of this research may be traced to the writings of the economist Ernst Engels (no relation to Friedrich
Engels) regarding the existence of systematic relationships
between personal income and consumer expenditure. Income based
relationships are, of course, widely used within national markets.
Internationally, their use has been of the type indicated in Chart
I. Some measure of average national income is used to "explain"
international consumption of durable goods, energy, etc. Despite
the considerable complications posed by different national currencies and government initiated measures effecting demand, this
"cross sectional" approach, considering the dependent and independent variables simultaneously in a number of different national
markets, has proved useful and has been widely employed by international agencies as well as multinational firms. In this paper
we will use this method to consider international changes in
consumer behavior and other variables.

Chart I : Car Ownership and GNP per Capita

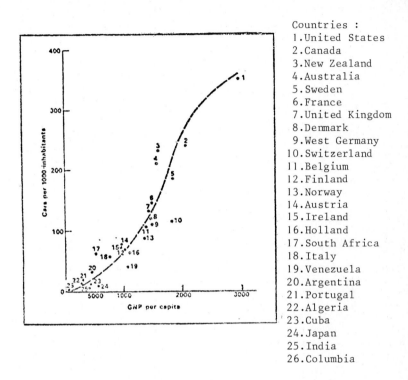

Countries :
1. United States
2. Canada
3. New Zealand
4. Australia
5. Sweden
6. France
7. United Kingdom
8. Denmark
9. West Germany
10. Switzerland
11. Belgium
12. Finland
13. Norway
14. Austria
15. Ireland
16. Holland
17. South Africa
18. Italy
19. Venezuela
20. Argentina
21. Portugal
22. Algeria
23. Cuba
24. Japan
25. India
26. Columbia

Part I : National Product/markets

Engel's notion that the consumption of some goods was positively
related to income while others were negatively related, points
to a possible two category classification. Our hypothesis here
is that international markets fall into one of the following
three categories :

Type A products (income positive)
The national market penetration of these products increases with
higher income (Most of the consumer products of multinational
firms would probably fall into this category).

Type B products (income neutral)
National market penetration of these products is largely independent of national income.

Type C products (income negative)
National market penetration decreases with increases in national
income.

Chart II provides a schematic representation of these three categories.

Chart II : International Penetration Patterns

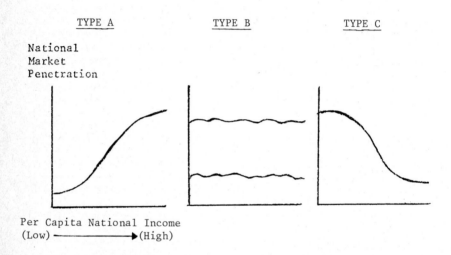

Note : Horizontal axis measures average per capita national income
of various countries in dollars ; vertical axis the percent of
households in each country using the product in question (the
vertical axis here should not be confused with that in Chart I).

In the sections below we will examine examples of type A and Type
B penetration patterns. No examples have been discovered by this
research for Type C. Though there is little doubt that products
negatively income related exist, by definition they would only
appeal to a small segment of the population in high income countries, where most multinational firms originate. This may help
to explain why they are difficult to uncover with the particular
data gathering method employed here but there is no implication
that they are either unimportant or uninteresting.

Type A example : This is a discretionary food product. Results shown here are based on returns from 8 (sometimes 7) countries.

Chart IIIa shows actual product penetration of this type of product (as sold by all sources and not just the reporting firm) in each of 7 countries.

Chart IIIb shows the income group in the various countries contributing most to industry sales of this product. Respondents were asked to indicate which of 5 relative income categories in that country, e.g. top 20%, second 20%... bottom 20% were the most important in terms of retail sales (No 1 on the vertical axis represents the top 20%, etc.).

Chart IIIc shows the occupational categories in the various countries contributing most to industry sales of this product (respondents were asked to choose from a standard listing of 6 occupational categories). Category "A" at the top of the chart represents those in "higher managerial administrative or professional (non manual) occupations, "semi skilled and unskilled workers" and "those existing on state pensions" comprise the last two groups.

Summary of Type A example : The international change here is from an elite market covering only a small percentage of the total national households in the poorer countries to a mass market in the richer countries. Considered internationally, the market experiences a distinct downward trend in its centre of gravity. In moving from poor to rich countries there is a shift in the most important buying groups from higher to lower income categories and from the higher to lower occupational categories.

Type B example : This is a staple food product used in the daily diet. Results here are based on returns from 20 countries.

Charts IVa, b, c respectively show national market penetration, most important relative income and occupational groups for retail sales of this product in each country.

Chart III - Type A - Candy   (7 observations)

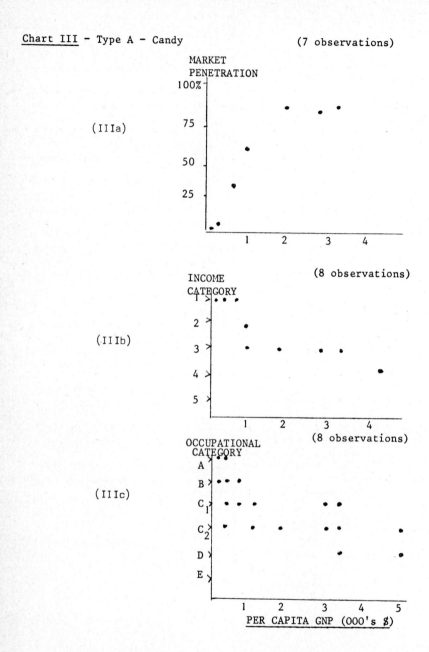

Chart IV - Type B -
        Edible Fat
    (20 observations)

MARKET
PENETRATION

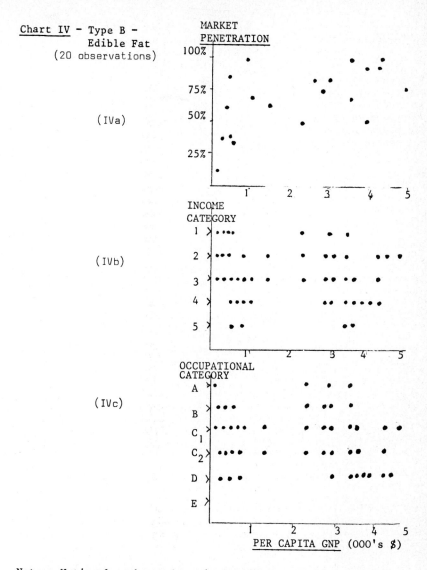

(IVa)

(IVb)

(IVc)

PER CAPITA GNP (OOO's $)

Note : National markets shown include Asian, African, South American, Caribbean and European countries. (Since respondents were allowed to mark more than one category, each vertical column here represents a single national market).

Summary of type B example : This type of product can achieve high
penetration and a mass market situation even in countries with
very low levels of per capita GNP. Moreover, it does not display
the distinct shift we saw in type A in terms of the relative income and occupational categories which comprise its major consu-
ming groups. Also, sales of this product appear to be more diffuse and less concentrated among income and occupational categories
as evidenced by the number of verticle columns in charts IVb and
IVc indicating categories of equal importance within a given
national market.

Summary of Product Examples

International Change areas	Type A	Type B	(Type C?)
1. Market Penetration	Low penetration in low income countries, High in high income countries	High market penetration possible in high and low income countries.	
2. Main consumer - income groups	Higher income groups, only, in low income countries, trending lower in high income	Broadly distri- buted, no definite trend.	
3. Main consumer groups- occupation	Higher occupa- tional groups in low income countries tren- ding lower in high income	Broadly distri- buted, no defi- nite trend.	

Part II : Changes in the Firm's International Markets

This part will consider how the consumer segments serviced by the firm in its various countries of operation change in response to the national differences indicated in the previous section. The difficulty of locating consumer characteristics which could be defined and in some sense measured internationally, necessarily limited the characteristics employed in our questionnaire to a few relatively standard and easily recognisable categories.

In Part I we noted that at the national level our Type A product appeared to find an elite market in the poorer countries changing to a mass market profile in the wealthier countries. In Chart V we see that the consumers serviced by this company in the low income countries are characterized by high car ownership, super-market shopping and a high level of education. There appears to be little difference in certain of these categories as between the characteristics of the company's consumers in the low income countries compared to those it finds buying its product in the high income countries. In fact, in terms of formal education, the comparison between poor and rich countries is the opposite of what one might otherwise expect, the companies customers in the poor countries are characterised by a significantly higher educational attainment than those in the rich. The elite nature of the companies consumer markets with this product in the poor countries becomes even more evident when compared to company experience with our type B product (Chart VI).

Looking at the same comparison with reference to the experience of the company marketing, our type B product we note considerable differences between the company's consumers in low income and high income countries. The lower national income is clearly reflected here in consumer car ownership, shopping outlets, level of formal education, etc. This is in line with the firms high penetration. The fact that it reaches a mass market in the great majority of countries, those with low income as well as those with high, would indicate that the consumer segments serviced by the firm selling this product more closely approximate the national average.

Chart V : Type A Product Example

Consumer Characteristics in High Income and Low Income Countries

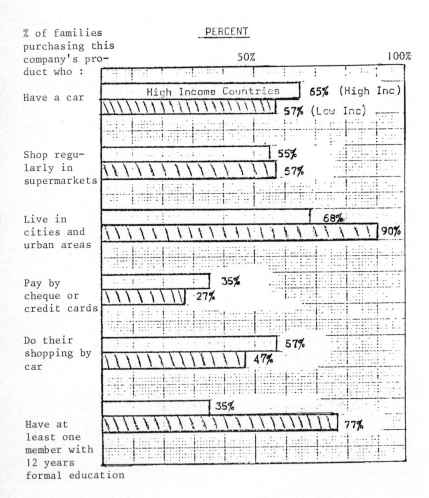

% of families purchasing this company's product who :

PERCENT

Note : High income countries are those with per capita annual GNP above 1,000 dollars ; low income countries are thos below that figure.

Marketing managers in the various countries were asked : What percent of the families who purchase your product in product group (A) in this country would you estimate (circle most appropriate for each line across).

Chart VI : Comparison of Type A and Type B
Consumer Characteristics in High Income and Low Income Countries
% of families purchasing this
company's
product who:

Type A   (%)   Type B   (%)

	Type A	Type B
Have a car	65% (High Inc) / 57% (Low Inc)	63% / 17%
Shop regularly in super-markets	55% / 57%	46% / 19%
Live in cities and urban areas	68% / 90%	61% / 64%
Pay by cheque or credit cards	35% / 27%	13% / 4%
Do their shopping by car	57% / 47%	26% / 13%
Have at least one member with 12 years formal education	35% / 77%	32% / 21%

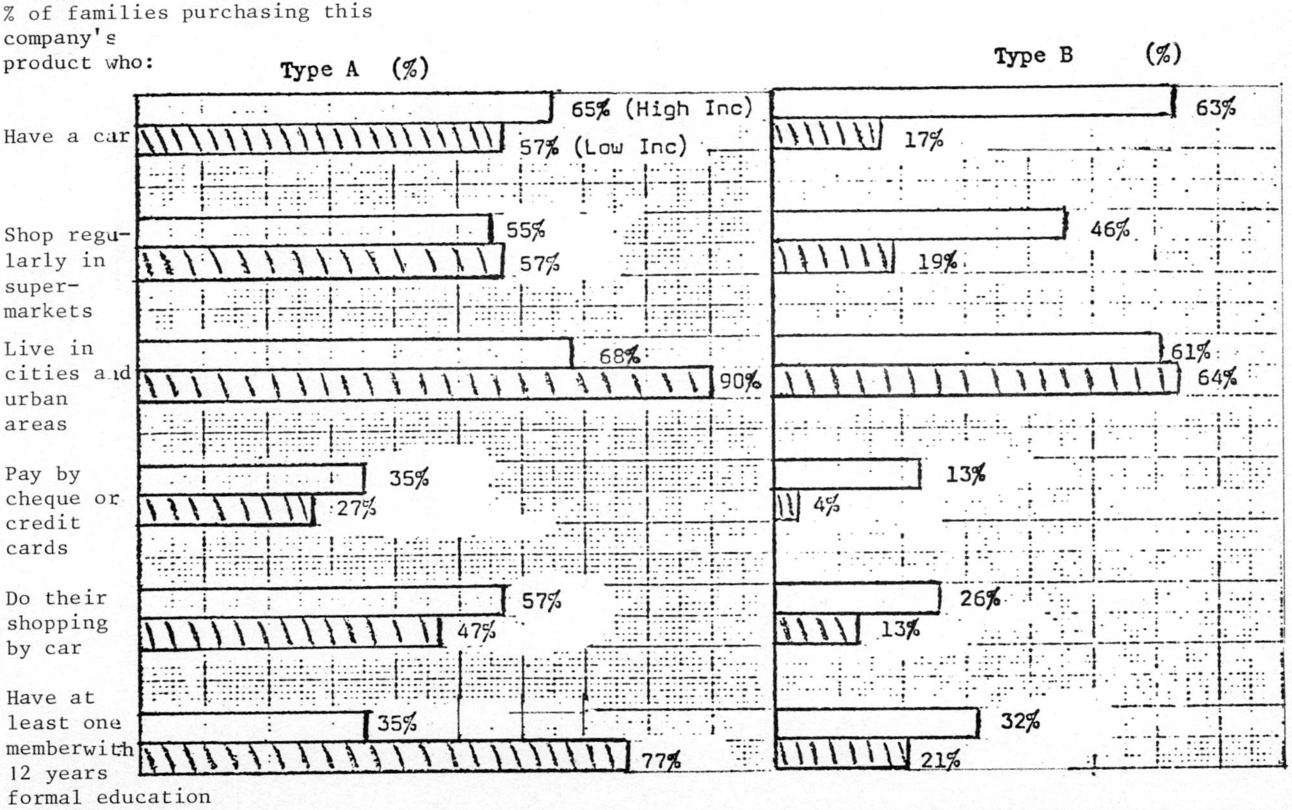

Summary Parts I & II

The firm selling the type A product experiences international
change of a fundamentally different order than the company marketing type B. For example, a manager with the former, on being
transferred from a high income country (e.g. the country of the
parent firm) to a low income market would find himself dealing
with a much narrower, more elite market whose members were often
more affluent than those he had been accustomed to previously.
The reverse would be true with reference to a similar transfer for
a marketing manager with the firm selling type B.

Both would encounter similarities and differences relative to their
original national market. The type A manager, while finding that
the affluence of his consumers made for certain similarities, e.g.
emphasis on supermarkets and shopping by car, would also find the
narrow nature of the market in his new country and its different
position relative to the rest of the population called for substantial changes in his products image and other promotion related factors. The type B manager, would find his consumers and
their standard of living substantially changed, while the fact that
he was still dealing with a mass market indicates certain essential similarities of approach, e.g. mass media. In both cases, the
changes noted at the level of the firm are consistent with those
noted earlier in Part I. There we looked at penetration, income
and occupational groups relative to total industry sales of these
products in various national markets. In this section we noted
that international differences with reference to the firms own
consumers were in line with the national patterns. The following
section will consider the connection between national and corporate markets in greater detail.

Part III : Relation between National and Corporate Market Posi-
tioning.

In the first part of this study we discussed the main consumer
groups and their pattern of variation at the national level.
Respondents there were asked to indicate which income and occupational categories within each national market were most important
(account for highest total industry sales volumes) for the product in question. We noted that these vary widely from one national market to another (Charts IIIb, IIIc, IVb, IVc).

In part III we consider these same "main consumer groups", or
"main market segments" in the various national markets relative
to those most important for the firms own sales. We are especially
interested to note the positioning between the two i.e. the relationship between the main market segments for the firm and those
for the market as a whole. Do international firms respond to the

various shifts which we have already noted in these main consumer groups at the national level from market to market with corresponding shifts in the direction of their own sales ? The answer appears to be in the affirmative.

Table 1 relates the major income and consumer groups for each national market of observation to those of the respondent firm within that same national market. Responses in the "Identical" column refer to those situations where the main market segment for the national market as a whole exactly matched those indicated as most important for the firms own sales in that market, e.g. in India income group number 1 (the top fifth of the income distribution) is the most important income segment for the industry as well as for the respondent multinational affiliate in that country.

Responses in the "Overlap" column indicate a lower level of congruence between national industry and multinational affiliate groups, e.g. income groups 1 and 2 are the most important in the Brazilian market nationally while the respondent multinational affiliate finds that the income group(s) most important for its own sales in that national market are 2 and 3.

Response in the "Completely Different" column indicate non-congruence between consumer groups nationally and those for the respondent firm, e.g. Occupational groups 1 and 2 nationally and 3, 4 for the respondent.

Table 1 shows that in the great majority of cases, the sales of these firms in the various national markets of the world are concentrated in those income and occupational consumer segments which are most important within each national market of operation. The variation previously noted between different national markets is largely matched by variation in the companies own sales orientation from market to market.

These findings are further developed in a mailshot questionnaire sent at random to 500 affiliates of U.S. multinational consumer goods companies. The aim here was to supplement the cross sectional approach of Table 1, focusing as it does on a few products viewed cross nationally, with a much larger product selection. In response to precisely the same questions on income and occupational groups we received the results set out in Table II.

Table 1 : Relationship between National and Corporate Main Market Segments*

National and Corporate Segments are :

Segment Type	Identical	Overlap	Completely different	Total replies
** Income (No.)	35	15	5	55
Income (%)	64%	27%	9%	100%
*** Occupation (No.)	32	13	6	51
Occupation (%)	63%	25%	12%	100%

*   Based on 55 returns from affiliates (including 5 parent company operations in the "home market") of 5 multinational companies from 36 national markets in Europe, North America, Asia, the Caribbean and South America. INC

** Chi-square test indicates less than 1% probability that results due to chance (by chance alone we would expect 6% of responses to fall under the "Identical" heading, 76% under "Overlap" and 18% under "Completely Different").

*** Chi-square test indicates less than 1% probability that results due to chance (by chance alone we would expect 3% of responses to fall under the "Identical" heading, 82% under "Overlap" and 15% under "Completely Different").

Table II : Relationship between National and Corporate Main Market Segments (Mailshot Questionnaire)

National and Corporate Segments are:

Type of Segment	Identical	Overlap	Completely Different	Total Replies
* Income (No.)	29	15	5	49
Income (%)	59%	31%	10%	100%
* Occupation (No.)	28	16	6	50
Occupation (%)	56%	32%	12%	100%

* Chi-square test indicates less than 1% probability that results due to chance (for random distribution see table I).

Note (1) Returns in Table II were based on completed questionnaires from marketing managers in the following countries : Nigeria, Indonesia, Mexico, India, Chile, Philippines, Brazil, Panama, Columbia, Guetemala, Argentina, Cameroon, Kenya, Singapore, Uruguay, Hong Kong, Malaysia, Venezuela, Greece, Spain, Finland, United Kingdom, Australia, Italy, Denmark, Portugal, Germany, Sweden, Switzerland, New Zealand.

(2) The above returns refer to the following products : Cosmetics, Biscuits, Cars, Deodorants, Soft Drinks, Dental Cream, Photographic Equipment, Power Tools, Hair Rinse, Cabinets, Writing Instruments, Potato Crisps, Soups, Cheese, Washing Machines, Perfume, Ladies Slacks, Sewing Machines, Powdered Milk, Toilet Tissue, Pharmaceuticals, Detergent, Irons, Jeans, Sanitary Napkins, Corn Syrup, Chewing Gum.

(3) The rather low response rate here (10%) was anticipated. This mailshot questionnaire was intended as a supplement and test of our main sample which had a very high response rate, but on only a relatively few products. Besides the usual problems, the international charac- ter of the mailshot sample meant additional complications with language, many different national postal systems and use of address list several years old. Over 10% of mailings were returned as non-deliverable.

Returns for both survey samples shown in Tables I and II are
brought together in Tables III and IV. Sample I refers to Table I
and Sample II to the mailshot questionnaire shown in Table II.

The evidence presented above supports the hypothesis that the
multinational firm adjusts its sales positioning from one national
market to another in line with the particular income and occupational groups which are most important for the sales of its product in that national market.

Admittedly, this is a rather limited view of "adjustment". However,
some such constraint is necessary if we are to attempt measurement
even in this crude fashion.

Limited as it is, the data goes beyond simply supporting the statement that multinational firms do adjust to foreign markets (not
as obvious a point as might first appear if one refers to recent
research of authors who find considerable evidence of standardisation in the multinational firms approach to world markets)[2].
It also indicates something of the nature of that adjustment.
The adjustment is one which orients the firm toward the mainstream
of sales (as previously defined in terms of our consumer groups)
in each particular country. This research points to a high degree
of congruence between the most important market segments nationally and those which the multinational firm chooses to make the
focus of its own sales.

This need not have been the case. A number of alternative adjustment patterns suggest themselves. Multinational firms, origina-
ting typically from industrial, high income countries might conceivably have chosen to market their products in such a way as to
emphasize sales to the same consumer groups as they were familiar
with in their home markets. Or, they could have chosen to aim
consistently "upmarket" or "downmarket" from the market mainstream
of whatever country they were operating in. Given the variation
from one national market to another already observed in Part I,
we could reasonably have expected to find, under such circumstances, a lower degree of congruence between main consumer groups
serviced by the multinational firm and those for the industry at
large. A higher proportion of our results would have appeared
in the "Overlap" and "Completely Different" columns.

Market Positioning Related to Market Share

In this section the same market positioning relationships (Identical, Overlap, Completely Different) of the firm vis à vis its
national market of operation will be matched against market share
performance.

Table III : Relationship between National and Corporate Main Income Segments (Combined Results - 104 Returns)*

National and Corporate Income Segments are:

	Identical	Overlap	Completely Different	Total Replies
** Sample I				
Number	35	15	5	55
% of total ...	64%	27%	9%	100%
** Sample II				
Number	29	15	5	49
% of total ...	59%	31%	10%	100%
Total number	64	30	10	104
% of total	61%	29%	10%	100%

* The combined samples include returns from 40 countries on 34 different consumer products from 104 multinational affiliates (including 5 parent company operations).

** Chi-square test indicates results in samples I and II of the survey do not differ significantly. (80%-90% probability that differences here are due to chance).

Table IV : Relationship between National and Corporate Main Occupation Segments (Combined Results – 101 Returns)

National and Corporate Occupation Segments are:

	Identical	Overlap	Completely Different	Total Replies
* Sample I				
Number	32	13	6	51
% of total...	63%	25%	12%	100%
* Sample II				
Number	28	16	6	50
% of total....	56%	32%	12%	100%
Total......	60	29	12	101
% of total	59%	29%	12%	100

* Chi-square test indicates results in samples I and II of the survey do not differ significantly (75%–80% probability that differences here are du to chance).

Table V. National-Corporate Market Positioning and Market Share[*]
         (By Income and Occupational Segments)

National and Corporate Segments :

Type of Segment	Identical	Overlap	Completely Different
Income			
No of firms	35	15	4
** Average Market Share	56%	34%	9%
Occupation			
No of firms	32	12	6
** Average Market Share	58%	32%	23%

---

* Results in the above and subsequent tables refer only to
  Sample I of the survey. They do not reflect any returns from
  the mailshot questionnaire. Market share information was not
  requested in the latter.

** F test indicates variation of market share between columns
   (Identical, Overlap, Completely Different) is significant at
   the 1% level.

The above table tells us two things. Not only do the affiliates of
multinational firms adjust their market positioning from country
to country, bringing it into line with the mainstream of that
markets buying public, as indicated in Part III, but market share
tends to be higher where adjustment is most complete. In terms of
both income and occupational segments, there is substantial difference between average market share in the "Identical" and
"Completely different" positionings. Average market share more
than doubles between these two extremes. This discrepancy is
further underlined by Table VI which shows the distribution of
respondent firms cross classified by market share category as
well as national-corporate positioning.

Table VI. Distribution of Respondents by National-Corporate Posi-
          tioning and Market Share Category.

National and Corporate Segments are :

Market Share is	Identical		Overlap		Completely Different	
	*(Inc)	(Occup)	(Inc)	(Occup)	(Inc)	(Occup)
Over 80%	9	8	0	0	0	0
Over 70%	13	13	1	0	0	1
Over 50%	22	21	3	2	0	1
Over 10%	34	32	14	11	11	3
Less than 10%	1	0	1	1	3	3

* (Inc) = Income ; (Occup) = Occupation

Towards the top of the above table (upper left) in the highest
market share category there is close identity between main consumer segments nationally and those serviced by the company in these
countries.

The situation is reversed toward the bottom of the table (lower
right), where the number of respondents showing a divergence between the national and corporate concentration of sales is in the
majority. In these latter instances, particularly, the firm may
be said to be following a specialist strategy, i.e. avoiding the
mainstream of that particular national market.

It is important to note also what the above presentation does not
say. There is no implication here either that what we have
referred to as a specialist strategy is not optimal or that one of
identity between corporate and national segments is desirable.
Particularly, there is no implication that such identity assures
a high market share. The above data only pretends to document the
point that this identity between corporate and national markets
is associated with high market share.

Of course, if a firm has 100% of a national market the statement
is spurious ; since corporate and national markets are here one
and the same. But there is no such necessary connection over a
wide range of other possibilities below the 100% limit. A firm
may enjoy a very large market share even when the most important
segments for its own products are completely different from those
nationally[3].

Numerous possible combinations of this sort exist in the context
of the framework presented in this study. Indeed, one might specu-
late that multinationals, with their different, technical, customer
and market backgrounds might have been expected to exhibit non-
conformity with national patterns. This was not found to be the
case.

Even removing those extreme situations from Table VI in which
respondent affiliates enjoyed a market share of over 80% does not
change the basic relationship between market share and national-
corporate congruence shown in that table (removal of the over 80%
situations from Table V would change the average market share
figures in the "Identical" column from 56% to 43% for the income
classification and from 58% to 44% in terms of "Occupation", all
other market share figures remaining the same).

Market Adjustment or Determination ?

A possible criticism may be directed against our conclusion that
companies adjust their marketing to local national patterns. This
depends on the direction of causation. Does the corporation determine the nature and emphasis of the national market or must it
adjust to that national market. Our conclusions in this section
assume that latter - the firm adjusts to the national market ; or
at least this is largely the case since it is not necessary here
to deny some degree of interaction. However, the view has been
advanced elsewhere that the truth is more nearly the other way
round. Galbraith, for one, feels that the firm determines the
market. In such a case, the closeness between large market share
and company positioning would supply very little guidance since
presumably the firm has only to consider its own programme and
the national market follows from that. There is no question of
the firm adjusting to the national market since the latter is also
determined by the firm.

As noted earlier, our view is that the national market purchase
patterns are the independent variable, the firm adjusting its own
market activities towards the market centre of gravity in its
country of operation.

The following points can be mentioned in support of this :

1. Substantial congruence between corporate and national segments
   is also found in situations where the respondent firm enjoys
   between 10% - 50% of the market (see Table VI). It is difficult to hold that firms in this situation can control the
   character of not only one, but a large number of national
   markets. This is especially true if we consider that there are
   substitute products which erode market control even in high
   share situations.

2. Corporate determination implies that either low income or high
   income groups can comprise the main market segments within a
   given national market if a company so wills it. It is difficult
   to support this view, particularly in the case of the many
   discretionary and durable goods included in this survey which
   were marketed in countries with a very low per capita GNP.
   Generally, low income levels (in some cases the price of the
   product approaches average annual per capita GNP) would place
   severe constraints on which income segments could purchase
   such products in any volume.

3. Assuming the company could determine which national market
   segments were the heavy buyers of the products in question,
   one would tend to think,a priori, that it would attempt to
   duplicate its own domestic market situation, with which it
   is more familiar and which presumably was the basis of its
   original success. This does not appear to be the case, as
   already indicated.

We conclude that the firm positions itself relative to its national market of operation and not the other way round. A close
adjustment to the market mainstreams, i.e. its centre of gravity,
appears to be a precondition of high market share.

Implications

The research presented here has stressed the variability of local
national markets and the importance of adjustment to these conditions on the part of multinational firms. This supports the
emphasis placed by such companies on local marketing managers.
Living and working on the scene, they are best placed to assess
and respond to these conditions and their requirements.

At the same time, it is useful to consider that the products
marketed by international subsidiaries in their markets of operation were for the most part developed elsewhere (this is verified
in the returns from subsidiaries participating in Sample I of
this survey). In that respect the local marketing manager is

typically involved with both local and non-local marketing elements.   The marketing adjustment he is faced with requires a
blend of external (e.g. imported) and internal factors which is
highly variable from one market to another.

There are signs that in the future, the role of the parent company
may also require skills of this nature. It cannot be assumed that
new products will continue to originate predominately in the
"home" market. In conversations with managers of multinational
firms taking part in this survey it became evident that in some
instances foreign subsidiaries were innovating products within
their own national markets, some of which were occasionally
marketed by other units of the company, including the parent
company operations. There is every indication that this trend will
grow, placing even the parent company staff in the position of
using "foreign" products to penetrate local markets.

The debate over standardization or differentiation of the international marketing mix turns about this point. This latter issue
represents one of the few attempts to consider the marketing
adjustment of the multinational firm from a global perspective.
There is surprisingly little in the way of data on the total
marketing adjustment of such companies across the great diversity
of national markets which actually comprise their market place.
Much of the work presented under the "international marketing"
rubric deals with ad hoc adjustments on a country by country basis
and is predominately descriptive in character. The development
of normative or prescriptive models dealing with the overall
adjustment of the multinational firm to the global market place
has been hampered by the difficulty of gathering data from a
large number of national markets. This survey, bringing together
the perception of marketing managers in many countries, is
intended as a step in that direction.

References

1. Respondents were asked to indicate that category (or categories) which represented the most important group (accounts for highest sales volume for the specific product names) in their country of operation from the following list :

   - Higher managerial administrative or professional (non-manual)
   - Intermediate managerial/administrative/professional or clerical (non-manual)
   - Junior managerial administrative or professional (non-manual)
   - Skilled manual workers (manual)
   - Semi-skilled and unskilled manual workers (manual)
   - Those existing on state pensions without other income.

2. Recent research indicates a substantial element of standardisation, or non-adjustment, of the multinational marketing programme to foreign markets. See : R.D. Buzzell, "Can you Standardize Multinational Marketing?", Harvard Business Review, November-December, 1968 ; R.Z. Sorenson and U.E. Wiechmann, "How Multinationals View Marketing Standarization", Harvard Business Review, May-June 1975. J. Leontiades, "Planning Strategy for World Markets", Long Range Planning, December, 1970.

3. For example, in terms of the 5 income groups referred to in our questionnaire, it is possible that the main consumer segment for the industry as a whole accounts for 24% of the national market and that our respondent firm accounts for half that segment and all of the remaining 4 income segments of 19% each. In that case, the positioning of the respondent firm would fall into the "Completely Different" category, though it enjoys a market share of 88% of the national market.

CROSS-NATIONAL COMPARISONS AND CONSUMER STEREOTYPES -

A case study of working and non-working wives in the U.S. and in France

Susan P. Douglas

Centre d'Enseignement Supérieur des Affaires
Jouy-en-Josas

Introduction

Cross-national comparisons of purchase and consumption behavior often focus on examining overall differences and similarities between countries. In many cases these result in the perpetuation of stereotypes such as those proposed by Dichter (1962) :

"one out of every three Frenchmen brushes his teeth, four out of five Germans change their shirts but once a week".

These generalizations not only tend to emphasize differences rather than similarities <u>between</u> countries but also to a large extent ignore the importance of differences in behavior patterns <u>within</u> a country.

Such a limited approach appears to be little justified from either a theoretical or management standpoint. In the first place,the findings of various sociological and marketing studies (Frank, Massy & Wind, 1972 ; Engel, Kollat & Blackwell, 1968) reveal the existence of considerable heterogeneity in response patterns within countries ; these variations are evident in social class, life-style and geographic location, as well as in personality, interests and purchase behavior. Thus membership in a common culture or society does not necessarily imply similar response patterns, and consequently "national" consumer stereotypes are unlikely to be particularly meaningful or useful.

In addition, management is typically more interested in finding similarities with other countries rather than differences. Often a primary objective in investigating markets overseas is to assess whether production skills or marketing expertise developed in one country can be exploited on a wider scale, by marketing similar products or to similar market segments in other countries

Reprinted by permission of the publisher from the Journal of Marketing Research

(Wind, 1967). With the growth of cross-national communication and of travel between countries, opportunities for pursuing such strategies appear increasingly likely to occur. Thus, rather than segmenting international markets on a country by country basis and developing different strategies for each country, management may be able to identify similar customer groups such as teenagers, senior citizens, status conscious consumers in different countries and, cutting across national boundaries, use uniform strategies throughout the world for each of these groups.

According to the underlying rationale in segmentation, members of a segment should have response patterns which are closer to each other, than to those of members of other segments. Transposing this to the international context the feasibility of utilizing cross-national bases of segmentation depends on whether the behavior patterns of a customer sub-group in one country are more similar to those of the same group in another country than to other customers in their own country. This requires examination of the relative importance of between as opposed to within country differences in consumer behavior. The pilot study described in this paper was intended to provide an illustrative example examining this issue based on a comparison of purchase behavior for grocery products and women's clothing of working and non-working wives in the U.S. and France.

The primary objective of the study was thus to assess :

1) whether working wives in the two countries facing similar problems such as constraints on the time available for shopping would tend to adopt similar purchasing strategies, different from those of their non-working counterparts, or whether differences in behavior patterns between the two countries would tend to be greater. If in fact working wives did have similar behavior patterns further investigation of the feasibility of using a cross national segmentation strategy to working wives would seem appropriate. Such a finding would also suggest that management should treat generalizations about national behavior patterns and about differences between countries with extreme caution.

In addition two other questions were considered :

2) whether behavior patterns would be similar across product classes. Would, for example, working and non-working wives tend to have different behavior patterns for grocery products, but similar patterns for purchasing clothing, or vice versa ?

3) whether differences and similarities in attitudes would be more significant than in relation to behavioral patterns. Would, for example, working wives in the two countries have similar and perhaps more liberated attitudes towards female roles than non-

working wives, or would differences in role perceptions between the two national samples tend to be greater ?

First, the data base for the study and the research methodology are presented. The findings concerning shopping behavior for grocery products and women's clothing and in relation to attitudes towards women's roles are then discussed. Finally, a number of conclusions are drawn concerning the three research questions as well as the implications for future research in the area.

The data base and research methodology

The data base

The data base for the study consisted of a questionnaire administered by personal interview to 98 wives in France and in the U.S.A.[1] All the respondents had been married for at least two years and were between the ages of 25 and 50. Half had held full-time jobs for at least eighteen months, while the other half were not gainfully employed outside the home. The jobs held by the working wives covered a wide range of occupations including lawyers, doctors and researchers as well as secretaries, waitresses and sales clerks. In each country the sample was selected by a quota procedure, and both working and non-working groups were stratified by age, income and number of children. As far as possible the working wives were drawn from similar occupational categories in each country and the non-working wives from families of similar socio-economic status based on husband's occupation and family income. The objective was thus to obtain four groups which were "matched" in terms of background characteristics rather than groups representative of the working and non-working wife populations in each country. Although this structure and the small sample size restricts the extent to which the results can be generalized on a wider basis, it helps to isolate the effect of the wife's employment and to control for the impact of differences in other background characteristics between the working and non-working wife groups or between countries, on behavior and attitudes, which might otherwise obscure the analysis.

The questionnaire covered four key areas : grocery purchase behavior ; women's clothing purchases ; attitudes to various female roles ; and family background characteristics. In relation to grocery purchases respondents were asked to indicate the frequency of purchasing 10 convenience or time saving products and services [2]; and were also questioned on shopping patterns such as store choice and loyalty, and husband involvement in shopping activities. Similarly, in relation to women's clothing purchases, respondents were asked various questions concerning the type of store visited, the role of the husband in selecting clothes, as

well as the relative importance of seven sources of information
for new clothing styles. Attitudes towards four aspects of a
women's role were also examined : a) involvement in home and
family, b) cooking, shopping and other household tasks, c) self-
perceptions and concepts, and d) social interaction. The background characteristics included some describing the home, as well
as various standard family socio-economic and demographic characteristics such as income, age and education of husband and wife.

Research analysis

The principal analytic technique was multivariate analysis of
covariance (Cooley and Lohnes 1971, Green and Tull 1974), a generalization of the classical ANOVA model to cases involving more
than one criterion variable. This explicitly takes into account
intercorrelation among the criterion variables. Thus differences
which are significant in a univariate analysis may disappear in
the overall multivariate analysis ; and conversely, differences
which do not appear in a univariate analysis may emerge in a
multivariate analysis. The rationale and procedure underlying
this technique have been discussed in detail elsewhere, and are
not further elaborated here (Wind and Denny 1974). In this
study a 2 x 2 factorial design (country x working/non-working)
was used to examine variance due to country, the wife's employment, and the interaction between the two variables.

Five sets of criterion variables were examined by means of separate Manova analyses ; four of these sets related to purchases
of grocery products and women's clothing, and the fifth consisted
of ten attitudinal scales (Table 2). These scales were developed
from a series of factor analyses of the attitudinal variables
(Figure 2)[3]. The use of the multivariate procedure took into
consideration possible intercorrelation between variables within
each criterion set, such as the use of different convenience
products, or shopping in different types of stores. Each criterion set was first adjusted for a number of socio-economic and
demographic covariates. This step ensured that significant
differences in the criterion variables observed between the two
national samples or between the employed and non-employed women
would not merely reflect differences in their background characteristics. The four sets of purchase variables were then adjusted
for the ten attitudinal variables, to assess whether these might
account for the observed differences in purchase behavior.

Table 1 : The Statements comprising the ten Attitude Scales
(factor loadings for statements from the joint factor analysis).

Female role perceptions		Price consciousness	
. A woman's place is in the home	.88	. I find myself checking prices even for small items	.90
. Politics are a man's affair	.82	. I am very careful about the amount of money I spend	.71
. I do not think women with young children should work	.65	. I shop a lot for specials	.63
Pride in home		**Opinion leadership**	
. I am unconfortable when my house is not complete-ly clean	.76	. I am more interested in food products than most people	.73
. A house should be cleaned and dusted at least twice a week	.66	. I am generally the first of my friends to buy a new product	.68
. I take a great deal of pride in my home	.53	. People often ask me for my advice about products and brands	.64
Cooking		**Personal shopper**	
. I collect cooking recipes	.81	. I prefer to shop in stores where sales people are friendly	.74
. I love to bake cakes and frequently do	.65	. I like to shop in a store where I feel at home	.69
. The kitchen is my favo-rite room	.62	. One should support local shop-keepers	.64
News and reading interest		**Fashion interest**	
. I spend a lot of time reading	.85	. I keep up-to-date with the latest changes in fashion	.83
. I keep up-to-date on latest news	.54	. I invariably buy the latest fashion	.79
		. An important part of my life is dressing smartly	.65
Personal influence		**Optimism**	
. I often listen to friend's advice about where to shop	.67	. In spite of all my efforts, I don't seem to be getting anywhere	.81
. Before I do something, I often consider how my friends would react to it	.60	. I wish I knew how to relax	.72
. I like to wait and see how other people like new brands before I try them	.59	. What I am doing with my life will not make a last-ing contribution to the world	.63

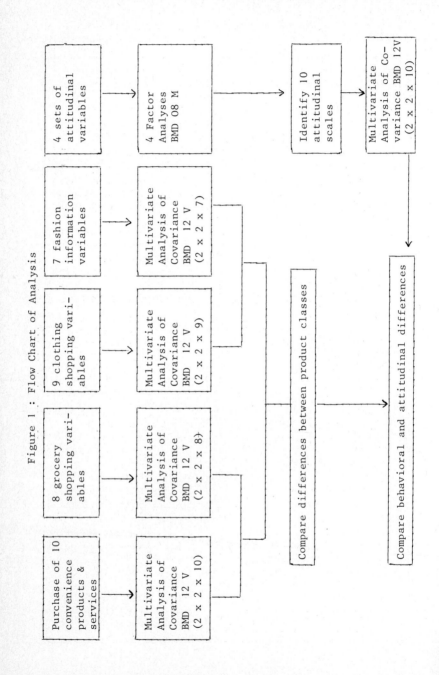

Figure 1 : Flow Chart of Analysis

Research results

1. *Purchasing behavior patterns*

Examination of the purchasing behavior patterns of U.S. and
French working and non-working wives shows that differences between the two national samples are more significant than between
working and non-working wives for all four sets of variables
(Table 2), even after adjustment for the socio-economic and
demographic variables. Thus at first glance the results appear
to confirm traditional views about cultural stereotypes and the
importance of differences in purchasing patterns between countries.
A closer examination of the results via the univariate Anova
reveals, however, that these differences are largely due to the
retail environment.

a) *Grocery purchase behavior*

The main differences between the two national samples in grocery
shopping occur in the type of store in which they shop (Table 3).
U.S. wives tend to shop more in large supermarkets and less in
neighborhood supermarkets and corner store than French housewives,
but then large supermarkets are more common in the U.S. and
equally, small traditional stores less common, than in France.
U.S. husbands also seem more likely to purchase occasional grocery
items than French husbands, though not necessarily to do major
grocery shopping.

As far as the use of convenience products and services is concerned, as one might expect, U.S. housewives tend in general to be
heavier users than French wives (Table 3). However, the differences are most marked in relation to products and services such
as take-out dinners, packaged cold-cuts, paper plates and cups,
which are typically widely available in the U.S. though not in
France. Not all French grocery outlets, particularly small
neighborhood stores, stock such items. On the other hand, the
more common convenience products, such as instant desserts and
canned main dishes, which are found in most stores in both France
and the U.S. appear to be used with similar frequency in both
countries.

The univariate analysis thus suggests that the differences observed are predominantly a reflection of differences in the retail
environment in the two countries rather than in consumer preferences. The high proportion of small independent grocery retailers in France perpetuates the typical pattern of fragmented
purchasing, and is an important factor contributing to the lag
between France and the U.S., in the adoption of new products and
services. It is, however, also possible to argue in the reverse

Table 2 : Summary Table of the Multivariate Analyses of Covariance for the Purchasing and Attitudinal Variables (with 10 Socioeconomic and Demographic Covariates)

(Approximate F. Statistics)

Source of variance	Purchase Variables				Attitudinal
	8 grocery shopping characteristics	10 convenience product services	9 clothing shopping characteristics	rating of 7 fashion info sources	ratings on 10 attitudinal scales
U.S.vs. France	18.94^x	11.52^x	5.36^x	6.51^x	3.38^x
Working vs. non-working wives	2.20^x	1.35	1.57	1.19	2.06^x
Interaction	2.87^x	1.36	1.28	0.53	0.92
Covariates					
No. of children	4.61^x	0.66	3.28^x	2.25^x	0.94
Wife's age	0.83	1.88	2.57^x	1.43	1.22
Daily help	1.01	0.68	0.52	1.78	2.66^x
Wife's education	1.44	2.65^x	0.63	0.78	4.25^x
No of cars	1.63	0.95	1.41	0.96	1.23
Husband's occupation	1.07	2.47^x	0.68	1.90	0.99
Husband's education	0.23	0.65	0.50	2.03	2.63^x
Income	1.23	2.27^x	2.68^x	2.17	2.18^x
No.of rooms in home	1.86	1.20	1.79	0.44	1.20
Live in apartment	1.13	0.95	1.12	0.18	1.01

x significant at the .05 level

Table 3 : Summary Univariate Analysis of Variance for Grocery Variables.

Grocery Variables	U.S. vs. France[1]	Working vs.non-working[2]	Interaction
Frequency of shopping market	72.93^x	7.29^x	15.18^x
Frequency of shopping in large supermarket	$\underline{67.90}^x$	$\underline{0.24}$	0.00
Frequency of shopping in neighborhood supermarket	12.67^x	4.83^x	0.99
Husband shops for occasional items	$\underline{6.08}^x$	0.35	0.98
Frequency of shopping in corner grocery store	5.78^x	1.66	1.74
Husband accompanies grocery shopping	$\underline{1.91}$	$\underline{2.36}$	1.53
Frequency of grocery shopping	1.63	2.63	4.29^x
Husband does major grocery shopping	0.03	$\underline{4.58}^x$	1.00
Convenience products			
Cold cuts	$\underline{34.29}^x$	0.25	1.38
Laundry services	24.74^x	$\underline{1.09}$	1.66
Paper plates and cups	21.90^x	0.15	1.00
Aerosol carpet cleaner	9.21^x	$\underline{3.30}$	8.27^x
Takeout dinner	$\underline{7.57}^x$	3.21	0.13
Baked goods	$\underline{7.06}^x$	0.57	0.14
Instant dusting spray	$\underline{4.07}^x$	0.02	6.34^x
Canned main dishes	0.91	$\underline{1.69}$	0.06
Frozen main dishes	0.50	$\underline{0.97}$	0.15
Instant ready-to-serve desserts	0.23	0.02	0.03

x Statistically significant at the .05 level

1 Figures (underlined) indicate that the mean for the U.S. samp was higher than for the French sample.

2 Figures (underlined) indicate that the mean for working wives was higher than for non-working wives.

sense, that the differences in the retail environment reflect underlying differences in consumer attitudes and preferences in the two countries.

Contrary to expectations, working and non-working wives did not have substantially different purchasing behavior. Since working wives typically have more limited time available for shopping and other household chores and have to perform these tasks at specific times, such as in the evening or at the weekend, it seems reasonable to anticipate that they will organize shopping activities differently from non-working wives, and look for products and services which will enable them to save time in household tasks. In this respect the findings confirm those of other studies which indicate that working wives tend to shop less frequently, and make greater use of husbands in shopping activities than non-working wives (Andersen, 1972). However, working wives do not appear to make greater use of convenience products and services than non-working wives. No significant differences were observed in relation to any of the ten products.

The results of the covariance analysis shown in Table 3 suggest that differences between countries and between working and non-working wives are not substantially affected by socio-economic and demographic differences. Grocery shopping, particularly the frequency of shopping is related to the number of children. Equally the heavier use of convenience products and services in the U.S. appears in part to be a reflection of higher socio-economic status. However the covariate adjustment is minor, and does not affect the main conclusions.

b) Women's clothing

Similar patterns, though less marked, emerge in relation to women's clothing purchases, where again there were significant differences between the two countries though not between working and non-working wives. As in the case of grocery shopping the major differences occur in the type of store where they shop, and again appear to reflect the greater prevalence of small specialty stores in France (Table 4). U.S. wives tend to shop more frequently in department and discount stores as opposed to the boutiques typically frequented by French women. Differences in the importance attached to sources of information about fashion are minor and hence not discussed in detail here, though U.S. women placed greater reliance than French women on almost all sources of information about fashion except magazines and particularly on newspaper advertising, T.V. and radio.

Since a working wife has a dual role as a worker and as a mother and housewife, one might anticipate that she will spend more on

clothes, buying one wardrobe for "work" and as well as one for
"home and social" activities. Contribution to the family income
may also alleviate guilt feelings about expenditure on personal
clothing items (Ryans 1966). Also as in the case of grocery
shopping, time constraints are likely to affect the frequency of
shopping, as well as reliance on print and personal as opposed
to instore sources of information on fashion (Katz and Lazarsfeld
1955). However, once adjustment had been made for differences in
income and stage in life-cycle, no significant differences emerged between working and non-working wives in clothing purchase
in either the univariate or the multivariate analyses. Equally
the only significant differences in fashion information sources
was, as hypothesized, a somewhat greater reliance by working wives
on instore sources of information.

Thus, in all cases differences between countries appear to dominate differences between working and non-working wives. Consequently there is little indication to suggest that a strategy
of cross-national segmentation focusing on working vs. non-
working wife families is likely to be appropriate either for
grocery products or women's clothing. This conclusion does,
however, appear in many respect to result from the lack of differences between working and non-working wives in both countries
and hence does not necessarily imply that national differences
will automatically be more important in relation to other customer
sub-groups, especially if marked differences are observed between
groups within countries.

2. Role perceptions and attitudes

Examination of attitudes towards female roles again reveals greater differences between countries than between working and non-
working wives, though this time the gap between the significance
of the U.S. vs. France and working vs. non-working results is
considerably smaller.

A more detailed analysis of the ten attitudinal scales for the
American and French samples (Table 5) suggests that traditional
attitudes towards a woman's role in society are not necessarily
associated with traditional attitudes towards home-making roles.
As might be expected, differences in cultural norms prevalent in
the U.S. and in French society lead U.S. wives to hold more liberated attitudes. Somewhat surprisingly, however, these views do
not seem to carry over in relation to attitudes to other female
and home-maker roles. One might expect liberated views to be
associated with less interest in traditional home-making activities such as cooking and shopping. Yet, despite their more liberated role perceptions, U.S. wives appear to be more price conscious, more interested in cooking and are more inclined to be
personalizing shoppers than French wives.

Table 4: Summary univariate analysis of co-variance for clothing variables.

	US vs France[1]	Working vs non-working[2]	Interaction
Buys in dept.stores	16.27^x	2.03	1.42
Buys in specialty stores	14.17^x	0.97	0.41
Buys in discount stores	12.18^x	0.00	0.26
Husband helps to choose clothes	1.37	0.04	0.01
Store loyalty	1.12	2.10	4.40^x
Accompanied by husband	0.21	2.19	1.25
Frequency of buying clothing	0.19	0.94	0.20
Buys in general & chain stores	0.03	2.27	0.43
Amt spent on clothes this fall	0.00	1.53	0.00

x   Statistically significant at the .05 level

1   Figures (underlined) indicate that the mean for the U.S. sample was higher than for the French sample.

2   Figures (underlined) indicate that the mean for working wives was higher than for non-working wives.

Table 5: Summary of the univariate analysis of covariance for the attitude scales.

	U.S. vs France[1]	Working vs. non-working[2]	Interaction
Female role perceptions	14.1^x	19.1^x	1.7
Opinion leadership	$\underline{14.0}^x$	$\underline{0.0}$	0.0
Personalizing shopping	$\underline{7.6}^x$	0.7	0.6
Price consciousness	$\underline{7.5}^x$	3.0	0.2
Cooking interest	$\underline{7.4}^x$	3.4	4.4^x
Optimism	5.4^x	1.5	0.3
New & reading interest	$\underline{2.7}$	$\underline{0.2}$	0.9
Fashion interest	$\underline{2.2}$	1.1	0.3
Personal influence	$\underline{2.0}$	0.0	2.0
Pride in home	$\underline{0.4}$	8.9^x	0.2

x Statistically significant at the .05 level

1 Figures (underlined) indicate that the mean for the U.S. sample was higher than for the French sample.

2 Figures (underlined) indicate that the mean for working wives was higher than for non-working wives.

In comparing attitudes of working and non-working wives, the most
important differences also occur in relation to female role perceptions where it comes as little surprise to find that working
wives have more liberated attitudes than non-working wives. Consistently, working wives also appear to be less house-proud.
French working wives are also less interested in cooking than
non-working wives, though the reverse is true in the U.S. case.

Examination of the multivariate analysis of covariance using the
attitudinal scales as covariates suggests that these attitudes
have little effect on grocery purchase behavior (Table 6),but do,
on the other hand, influence clothing purchases, and interest in
various sources of information on fashion. In relation to the
use of convenience products and grocery shopping, only one attitudinal covariate - optimism, is significant, and chiefly affects
the tendency to shop in large or neighborhood supermarkets. In
relation to shopping for clothes, however, interest in fashion
results in a higher frequency of shopping for clothes, coupled
with higher expenditure on clothes, and a greater tendency to
shop in specialty stores. Fashion interest also appears to be
associated with a tendency to rely on personal sources of information, particularly friends. Opinion leadership, susceptibility
to personal influence and personalizing shopping attitudes also
affect sources of fashion information.

Some caution should, however,be exercised in interpreting these
findings, particularly in relation to differences between countries. The same attitude statements, translated into the appropriate language, were used in each country, but no prior analysis
was undertaken to validate the attitudinal scales and the underlying constructs identified from the factor analyses in each
national context. This procedure may bias towards similarity in
attitudes since each construct may not be equally relevant in
each country, nor appropriately measured by the same scale.[4]

Conclusions

Although clearly the illustrative character of the study and the
small sample size do not permit any definitive conclusions, the
findings nonetheless suggest a number of tentative observations
and guidelines for further research :

1) Differences between the two countries overwhelmingly dominate
differences between working and non-working wives. In some cases
similar tendencies are observed between working and non-working
wives in each country, such as increased participation by husbands
in shopping activities, but these traits are not sufficient to
provide a basis for developing cross-national segmentation strategies.

Table 6 : Summary Table of the Multivariate Analyses of Covariance for the Purchasing Variables (with 10 attitudinal scale covariates)

(Approximate F Statistics)

	Purchasing variables			
	10 convenience products services	8 grocery shopping characteristics	9 clothing shopping characteristics	rating of 7 fashion info sources
Source of variance				
U.S. vs. France	13.4^x	34.5^x	8.4^x	6.8^x
Working vs. non-working wives	1.7	3.2^x	1.3	1.2
Interaction	0.9	3.2^x	1.4	0.5
Covariates				
Female Role Perceptions	0.7	0.4	0.6	1.0
Pride in Home	1.0	1.5	1.6	1.7
Cooking Interest	0.8	0.5	1.5	0.9
News and reading interest	1.2	1.4	1.1	1.2
Personal influence	0.8	1.7	0.5	3.2^x
Price consciousness	1.4	1.4	2.1^x	1.3
Opinion leadership	2.1^x	0.8	0.4	2.7^x
Personal shopper	0.8	1.7	1.2	3.2^x
Fashion interest	1.0	0.5	7.7^x	8.5^x
Optimism	1.5	2.5^x	0.6	0.8

x Significant at the .05 level

2) The significance of differences observed both between countries and between the two sub-groups varies with the product
class, and is greater in relation to grocery products than clothing. This implies that the relative importance of national and
sub-group differences is likely to vary from one product group
to another.

3) Behavior patterns appear to differ more in the two countries
than attitudes. This finding may reflect the measurement procedure used in the study, and should be viewed as highly tentative.
Attitudes do, however, appear to be more helpful in understanding
clothing than grocery shopping behavior.

4) Retail environmental factors seem to play a key role in shaping
and conditioning behavior patterns. Consequently, apparent differences in behavior patterns between countries may in many respects
merely reflect current market conditions such as, the availability of different products and services or the number of supermarkets or small traditional retailers. Consequently, low usage
frequency, for example, of convenience products or services does
not necessarily imply absence of a market. If widespread distribution of such products or services is obtained, behavior patterns
may well change accordingly.

In brief, while cross-national differences are on the surface
greater than within country differences between working and non-
working wives, a closer examination shows that observed differences probably reflect differences in the retail environment
rather than in underlying attitudes and preferences. Consequently, focus on apparent differences in behavior between national
samples may tend to be misleading, especially where this leads
to negative conclusions concerning the feasibility of influencing
or changing these patterns. Since, however the impact of retail
environmental factors was not explicitly examined, such conclusions can only be regarded as tentative.

In conducting further research in this area, a number of recommendations emerge from the experience of this pilot study.

1) In the first place, further investigation of the role of retail
environmental factors in influencing customer response patterns
seems desirable. This might, for example, examine whether differences in the availability of various products, or in retail
structure, are a root cause of variance in purchase behavior between countries. For example, a comparison of behavior patterns
of shoppers frequenting various types of stores, for example,
supermarkets, specialty stores, neighborhood stores, in the two
countries, or a comparison of behavior relating to products which
are equally available as opposed to those which differ in availability in the two countries would seem appropriate. Attention

should, however, be focused on comparisons relative to specific product classes, or groups of products.

2) Secondly, examination of appropriate research procedures in making cross-national comparisons of attitudinal variables is needed. Although relatively little bias appears to be introduced by using equivalent measurement instruments and procedures to examine behavioral variables, it is not clear that such an assumption can be made in relation to attitudes. A more detailed investigation of the effect of using different measurement and analytic procedures on research findings is therefore needed. In particular, attention should be directed at assessing how adequately equivalent concepts such as innovativeness or opinion-leadership are measured by the same measurement instrument in different national contexts ; how far the exclusive use of concepts and measures for which equivalents are available in each country tends to bias findings ; and to what extent country-specific concepts should be included, and if so, how they should be integrated into the comparison.

3) Thirdly, the approach based on the use of "matched" groups in each country seems a promising one. In this particular case, the conclusions concerning the relative importance of cross-national differences appear largely to result from the lack of differences between working and non-working wives. Use of a similar procedure investigating other customer groupings where more marked differences are observed within countries could prove highly illuminating. In any event whether in relation specifically to marketing or other aspects of social behavior comparisons of similar groups in different countries appears to provide an instructive way of examining the role of national environmental factors influencing behavior patterns, and isolating their impact and interaction with other variables such as socio-economic, demographic and attitudinal characteristics.

Footnotes

1. Initially 106 wives were interviewed in the U.S., and 102 in
   France. However the Manova analysis required equal cell sizes,
   and hence the sample size was reduced to 49 working and 49
   non-working wives in each country.

2. Products and services were defined as "convenience" insofar
   as they enabled women to economize on time devoted to the
   performance of meal preparation and other household tasks.

3. The attitudinal data, which consisted of 70 statements rated
   on a 6 point Likert scale, was divided into four subsets,
   relating to the four aspects of a woman's role. Each subset
   was first factor-analyzed separately for each national sample.
   Highly similar underlying factor structures were identified
   in both cases. Consequently, joint analyses (across countries)
   were conducted for each of the four attitudinal subsets. Ten
   attitude scales were then constructed, using for each scale
   the three statements with the highest loadings on the first
   two or three factors identified in each of the four analyses.
   In each case the two or three factors accounted for the 60-80%
   of the variance. For further discussion of the rationale
   underlying this procedure see Douglas and Le Maire (1974).

4. Some safeguard was taken against this problem since separate
   factor analyses were first conducted for each sample, and
   similar factor structures were identified in each case. However
   the initial battery of questions was the same, and hence did
   not allow for "decentring", i.e. the inclusion of items relevant in one country but not the other (Triandis 1972).

FACTORS AFFECTING THE PRE-EXPORT BEHAVIOUR OF NON-EXPORTING FIRMS*

Hans Christer Olson & Finn Wiedersheim-Paul

University of Uppsala

Introduction

Since the early sixties, increasing attention has been paid to
problems connected with exports and direct investments. A considerable amount of research has been done in this area, both on
the macro and micro level. But the vast majority of these studies,
on both levels, have used the large American enterprises and their
export and direct investment behaviour as the object of research.
The large American firms, to a great extent of a multinational
character, usually made their export debut a long time ago,
already well established in their large domestic market. Most of
the models and theories developed on this ground have limited interest and applicability for those, who try to describe and explain
the export behaviour of small and medium-sized firms, of which
many have not yet become exporters.

In a research project, of which this article is a first report, we
are interested in answering questions like the following :

- What kinds of firms become exporters ?
- Under what circumstances are they making their export debut ?
- To what extent are they continuing as exporters ?

A widened knowledge in this field would not only cover a gap in
the knowledge of firms' behaviour, but could also have policy
implications for the choice of methods employed in order to
increase a nation's export volume[1].

---

* This study has been financially supported by the Swedish Council
for Social Science Research, Svenska Handelsbanken Foundation for
Social Science Research and the Department of Industry, Stockholm.

A rather limited number of studies have been published in this problem area[2]. Most of these studies may be criticized on the ground that they usually considered only firms that already were exporting[3]. This simplification is hardly defensible, if one aims to understand why a firm starts its internationalization process. It must then be very important to investigate the behaviour of exporting firms before their export debut, as well as the behaviour of firms which have not yet started exporting – and perhaps never will– and firms which have been exporters but ceased for one reason or another.

Our aim in this article is to discuss

- an outline of a dynamic model trying to describe and explain the first steps in the internationalization process of the firm, i.e. the transition from a non-exporting to exporting state ;

- possible conclusions for export promotion activities.

The model will be illustrated by empirical data, but we do not aim at rigorous tests of our propositions at this stage of research.

Export-propensity – A Model

As a point of departure we make the assumption that all industrial firms, when they start, are non-exporters[4]. Looking at a single firm in this situation, the question we raise is : Will it become an exporter, and if so, why and when ? In order to give an answer to this question, or at least to contribute to its solution, a model is needed which summarizes important factors behind the first step in the internationalization process of the firm. As has been said before, realistic and comprenhensive models or theories in this field are rare[5]. We will therefore take results from the earlier research, as well as our own, and combine it into a model. An outline of a model of the firm's pre-export behaviour is illustrated in figure 1.

The firm's export behaviour can be split up into different phases, where the first phase, pre-export behaviour, covers the period until the firm realizes its first export sale[6].

The pre-export behaviour is the object of our main interest in this article. This focus, on the period directly preceding the first export sale, may have many disadvantages. This first export order may be important for some types of firms, for others not. It is perhaps not at all possible to identify a certain moment in time when a firm becomes an exporter. It might in several cases be an extended process of many small steps. The first export order might therefore be called an important – but not a decisive

Figure 1 : Factors Affecting the Pre-export Behaviour of the Firm.

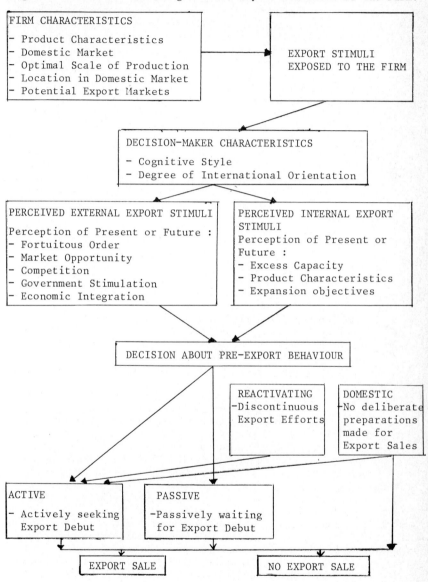

factor - in the internationalization process. From the point of view of the empirical researcher, it is easy to identify and remember. We will therefore consider it as a central component in this study. It will further be assumed that the majority of firms during the period after their first export order, will undergo a gradual increase in their business with foreign customers and/or carry out efforts in order to obtain such business. These firms will be considered as established exporters and will not be dealt with in our model. Firms, which cease to export are looked upon as an exception and are explicitly considered a special case in our model of the pre-export behaviour.

In our model, certain aspects of the decision-maker play a central role. In many smaller firms there is perhaps only one decision-maker making all important, strategic decisions - a true entrepreneur. This was found to be the case in a Swedish study of small and medium-sized firms' export behaviour[7]. In other firms, a group of individuals participate in important decision-processes, e.g. when considering the alternative to sell abroad. We assume here that one individual, the managing director, will dominate the decision-making process. Subsequently, we will refer to him as the decision-maker, although we are aware of the fact that he is interacting with other people, whom we assume he has chosen to get a combination of assistants who give him support.

Our view is supported by other studies which indicate that the firm's managing director has decisive importance in decision-making. Mintzberg has concluded :

"The manager is nerve center of both internal and external information".

Mintzberg (1970), p 21

"The nerve center role suggests that only he can fully understand complex decisions, particularly those involving difficult value tradeoffs. As a result, the manager emerges as the key figure in the making and interrelating of all significant decisions in his organization, a process that can be referred to as strategy-making".

Ibid. (1970), p 23.

Our model suggests that different kinds of stimuli factors which are latent in the firm's internal and external environment (2) are exposed to the decision-maker. The likelihood that a decision-maker is exposed to certain stimuli factors depends to some extent on the individual characteristics of the firm (1). The likelihood that the decision-maker shall perceive such stimuli factors and the interpretation of these, is dependent upon the decision-maker's characteristics (3). Further, we distinguish between the decision-maker's perception of stimuli external (4) and internal (5) to the

firm. The decision-maker's perception of and conclusions drawn
from stimuli exposed to him will influence his decision about the
firm's pre-export behaviour (6). Here we make a distinction
between four different kinds of such behaviour, namely active,
passive, domestic and reactivating. Below we will discuss the
model in greater detail.

Export Stimuli

The stimuli factors are the most dynamic elements in the model
and we therefore prefer to begin by explaining them further. To
be more specific, it is the stimuli in the firm's environment
which provide the real input in the model (2). However, these
stimuli are interesting only to the extent that they are perceived
by the decision-maker, and we will therefore discuss in more
detail the most important categories of stimuli in this respect.
Among perceived stimuli, the main distinction is between internal
(5) and external export stimuli (4).

The internal export stimuli are related to the goals of the firm
and the extent to which they have been or are expected to become
realized in the present environment of the firm. Deficient goal-
fulfilment in the present environment of the firm, and/or expectations of such deficiencies, can create stimuli for widening the
environment through export[8].

The internal stimuli factors can be specified in different ways
depending upon the choice of description-level. We have chosen
to identify three such factors, namely

- excess capacity in resources of management[9], marketing, production and/or finance
- product characteristics
- expansion goals.

These three groups of factors are to some extent dependent upon
each other. Present or anticipated free capacity in the firm's
resources is a factor that has earlier been mentioned as an
export stimulating factor[10]. But it is important to stress that we
do not only refer to production capacity, but to excess capacity
in all kinds of company resources.

Recruitment by a firm of a sales executive with considerable
export capacity can serve as a stimulus, as well as a feeling of
tediousness[11] and a desire in existing management for new excit-
ment. The second class of stimuli - product characteristics -
can be seen as a special case of the first class. These have
been classed separately because of the observation that unique
product characteristics probably have a greater attractive power

on the environment, presumably because they are more easily iden-
tifiable.

Expansion goals could be a consequence of excess capacity, e.g.
through the economics-of-scale mechanism which forces a firm to
expand, to be able to strengthen its competitive power. But
expansion goals could also be the consequences of a change of
owners or a high profitability demand among the existing ones.

In the group of external export stimuli, we will identify the
following five factors :

- fortuitous orders from foreign customers
- market opportunities
- competition
- economic integration
- government export stimulation measures.

The first group - fortuitous orders - has in several different
studies been mentioned as the most important factor behind export
debuts[12]. However, it is important to note that the probability
of acquiring such an order could be dependent upon the pre-export
behaviour of the firm, i.e. the way it has acted before it realizes its first export sale. This factor will be discussed later
in this paper.

Market opportunities abroad are usually assumed to exert a strong
influence upon a firm's willingness to export. Empirical evidence
from our own experience shows that market opportunities cannot be
ignored as stimuli factors, even though they, like most other
stimuli, are not a sufficient condition for the creation of new
exporters.

Competitive stimuli can arise either from a tendency among domestic competitors to go abroad[13] or from stronger competition in
the domestic market caused by domestic or foreign competitors.
Such tendencies are, of course, not independent of excess capacity considerations[14].

Economic integration, which can lead to decreasing tariffs but
also to a reduction of non-tariff barriers and of psychic - or
cultural- distances[15] between the countries involved, can serve
as a stimulus factor[16]. Finally, it is at least assumed that
government export stimulation measures have in fact a stimulating
effect, an assumption that is not to any great extent based upon
empirical evidence[17].

It is important to note that it is not the stimuli factors per se,
which are important as explanatory factors behind the pre-export
behaviour of the firm, but the decision-makers' perception of

these factors. On this point we advocate a view which has not
been usual in models of corporate export behaviour. Whereas in
traditional models only present states have been recognized as
stimuli factors, we would like to stress also the importance of
future expectations[18]. Perhaps such factors play an even more
important role as export stimuli than existing states. We will
return to this question later.

It is quite natural that the stimuli factors cannot be seen as
isolated from the firm itself and its characteristics. Especially
the external stimuli will probably be significantly dependent
upon certain firm characteristics (identified in box 1, figure 1):
namely product characteristics, domestic market, optimal scale
of production, location in domestic market, and potential export
markets. It is assumed that the form and strength of stimuli exposed to the firm can vary in relation to differences in these
characteristics.

The first mentioned property is product characteristics. The
product-line of different firms varies according to the degree of
standardization and complexity and contains different proportions
of hardware and software[19]. Differences in these properties of
products will probably affect the direction and strength of some
external stimuli and thereby the chance that a certain firm will
be exposed to these stimuli.

The two product characteristics - technical complexity and the
hardware-software relationship together form the concept of technology intensiveness[20]. The more technically complicated a product is, the smaller the possible number of producers and therefore
the higher the possibility of being exposed to external stimuli.
The higher the hardware content - with a given degree of technical
complexity - the smaller the information flow needed between seller
and buyer, and therefore the greater the chance for a potential
seller of being exposed to external stimuli. Products which include a more comprehensive package of software demand more extensive flows of information and more intimate contact between seller
and buyer.

The domestic market of a firm will affect its chances of being
exposed to external stimuli in two respects - through its size,
and through the location of the firm in that market. We hypothesize that the larger the domestic market, the more a firm can sell
there, thereby realizing economies-of-scale without being forced
to become an exporter, and the less the chance that it will be
exposed to external export stimuli. An important question in
connection with market size is the optimal scale of production in
relation to the size of the domestic market. We therefore hypothesize that the smaller the domestic market relative to the optimal size of production, the greater the chance to perceive internal export stimuli.

The location of the firm in the domestic market is important in
the respect that a firm located nearer to "information-centres"[21]
in this market or nearer national frontiers, will have a greater
chance of being exposed to external stimuli than has a firm located farther away. Of course, an opposite causal direction is also
conceivable here : firms with export intention may locate in the
neighbourhood of information centres.

Finally, differences in the range of potential export markets can
affect the external export stimuli. It is obvious that the possibilities of exporting certain products to some markets are limited
or non-existent[22]. However, when the unrealistic foreign markets
have been sorted out, it is important to consider differences in
distances between the firm and its potential customers in the
remaining, potential export markets. By distance we do not only
mean the geographical distance, but also the above mentioned concept of psychic, or cultural distance.

We believe that the more distant a foreign market is, the smaller
the chance that a potential exporter will be exposed to stimuli
from that market. The disturbances causes by distance will be
larger for more technology intensive products, having a high
proportion of software.

The Decision-Maker's Cognitive Style

We have now discussed the factors in our model that create stimuli
for export operations (boxes 4 and 5), and factors that influence
the strength of the stimuli. From the way in which the stimuli
factors are identified and defined, it follows that many firms
will be exposed to one or several such factors. Exporting as
well as non-exporting firms have been and presently are exposed
to these kinds of stimuli. Still, only a part of them are exporters or will become exporters. Explanations to this observation
is, of course, essential to our problem.

One such explanation could be that those firms which are exporters
have been exposed to a very special combination of stimuli, and
that one or a few unique combinations are necessary and sufficient
conditions for a non-exporting firm to move into the group of
exporting firms. However, we do not find this explanation a very
plausible one, and we base our opinion upon several studies that
we have made. This does not imply that two or more stimuli appea-
ring at the same time could not have a stronger effect upon a
firm than just one, or that the impact of a certain combination
could not be greater than the impact of another combination. What
we mean is that differences in the stimuli mix that firms are
exposed to does not alone explain why some of them today are
exporters, while others are not.

Instead we suggest that differences in the characteristics of the decision-makers in different firms could also have a significant effect upon the firm's willingness to enter into exporting. In analyzing the decision-making of the firm, we usually consider the decision-maker as a black box, leaving aside all differences between individuals. This simplification is in many cases clearly motivated and the vindication for it is probably stronger the more repetitive are the decisions. Such decisions are to a great extent based upon routines or programs to ensure that different individuals shall be able to develop similar decisions. But this is not the case when more non-programmable decisions are concerned. In these cases the decision-maker's assessment of his environment is a most critical issue. His way of problem finding, problem recognition and problem definition will have a decisive impact upon his behaviour as we can observe it, in the form of decisions made and activities undertaken.

Differences between decision-makers in these dimensions are often attributed to differences in their cognitive functioning. Cognitive differences between individuals basically is a question that belongs to the discipline of psychology. Although the term "cognitive" is a very common one in the organizational literature, explicit considerations of differences in cognitive functioning between individuals as an explanatory factor of decision-making in organizations are rare. We base our presentation here mainly upon a few sources of this kind[23].

The cognitive aspects of an individual which affect his assessment of the environment will be called cognitive style. The cognitive style of a single individual is an extremely complex entity, whose structure we will not even be able to sketch out briefly in this paper. In view of our problem, we will concentrate upon two aspects of it, namely the modes of information gathering and information evaluation.

"Information gathering relates to the essentially perceptual processes by which the mind organizes the diffuse verbal and visual stimuli it encounters".

"Information evaluation refers to processes commonly classified under problem solving. Individuals differ not only in their method of gathering data but also in their sequence of analysis of that data".

McKenney & Keen (1974), pp80-81.

Differences between individuals in aspects like those mentioned above are often classified into dichotomies, although this is, of course, a very critical simplification. Several terms have been proposed for classifications of these dimensions of cognitive styles. As regards information gathering, we will make a distinc-

tion between preceptive and receptive individuals, where the
former refers to individuals who to a great extent have precepts
which act as cues for both gathering and classification of data
they find ; their expectations have a considerable impact upon
the focus of interest. Receptive individuals, on the other hand,
are more sensitive to the stimulus itself ; they are more eager to
take the essence out of information they find instead of analyzing
it in relation to their precepts.

In connection with information evaluation, we will make distinction between systematic and intuitively oriented individuals. The
former tends to concentrate upon the structure of a problem, i.e.
the relation between different elements in the cognitive representation of perceived information. The intuitive individual
concentrates upon the elements in his cognitive representation of
reality, i.e. the differentiation rather than the structure or
causal linking between these elements[24].

Both of these dichotomies can be combined into a four field chart,
illustrating combinations of cognitive styles with reference to
information gathering and information evaluation, and such a
chart is presented in figure 2 below.

What are then the implications for our problem of these classifications of cognitive styles ? Our assumption is that certain
tasks and problems more or less require a specific cognitive style
if the outcome shall become what is considered desirable and satisfactory. Otherwise expressed, we mean that the outcome of a certain problem will depend upon cognitive characteristics of the
individual who is to solve it[25].

Figure 2 : Differences in cognitive styles with reference to
information gathering and information evaluation.
Source : McKenney & Keen (1974), p. 81.

```
                    Information    |  Preceptive
                      gathering    |
 Information                       |
 evaluation                        |
                 ──────────────────┼──────────────────
 Systematic                        |               Intuitive
                                   |
                                   |  Receptive
```

McKenney & Keen have divided problems into four categories, depending upon first, the problem solver's assessment of his ability to recognize it (a perceptual process) and second, his ability to act on relevant information (conceptual process). High values in both these dimensions imply a situation where the problem mainly is a question of planning. Another extreme case is at hand when the decision-maker faces low values in both these dimensions, i.e. when both information and operations are unknown[26]. This situation is probably the one that best fits that of the non-exporting manager being exposed to export stimuli. He is not only lacking information about export operations, but also methods for manipulation of the data he collects.

A critical issue now is to find out which cognitive style or styles are most suitable for developing a non-exporting firm into an exporting one, assuming that there are export stimuli factors available to initiate the process. Unfortunately, the empirical research about behavioural consequences of different cognitive styles has not yet reached a state of knowledge which enables us to make firm conclusions about this. A tentative hypothesis would be that the decision-maker in this situation should be intuitive in his cognitive orientation rather than systematic[27]. But we want to point out that this is, at the present stage, only guesswork. As Nyström has pointed out, it is possible that different cognitive modes are required during different stages of the problem-solving process[28].

What we want to stress is the importance of this factor when we are trying to explain why some firms become exporters sooner than others, and some remain non-exporters for ever. We believe that it would be highly interesting and probably rewarding to go further and deeper into this aspect of the problem in future research. Probably such an approach would lead to much more significant and valid explanations of export-propensity than the hitherto used approach of searching for single relationships between export debut and stimulating factors.

Another factor which may influence the probability that a certain decision-maker shall perceive and act upon export stimuli, is his degree of international orientation. This is a measure of his international outlook, i.e. to what extent he perceives and considers what is happening outside his own country as interesting. As has been suggested by Simmonds & Smith, differences between individuals in this dimension may explain differences in pre-export behaviour. In their limited sample of British firms that had just commenced exporting, Simmonds & Smith found a significant overrepresentation of individuals with high degrees of international orientation, e.g. many persons born abroad or with experience from living abroad [29]. In relation to the different problem categories mentioned above[30], we could say that a high degree of

international orientation on the decision-maker's part probably
improves his ability both to recognize information about export
opportunities and to act upon that information. It is therefore
more likely that a decision-maker with a high rather than a low
degree of international orientation, shall bring his firm into
situations which lead to exporting. However, it seems plausible
to expect that a correlation exists between certain cognitive
styles and the degree of international orientation.

The Pre-export Behaviour of the Firm

It has been common to look upon the first export sale as the decisive factor in studies where attempts have been made to explain
why firms become exporters. But we believe that perhaps it would
be more interesting to consider the behaviour of the firm during
the preceding period. In most cases the first export order is
probably a consequence of the firm's pre-export behaviour. With
pre-export behaviour we mean, as Hyrenius & Sjögerås, the behaviour of the firm up to the time it realizes its first export
sale. We have also found their distinction between different
kinds of pre-export behaviour useful for our purpose[31]. We will
therefore make a distinction between the following classes :

Active - where the firm actively is preparing for an export debut
Passive - where the firm is passively waiting for an export debut
Domestic - where the firm is not in any way deliberately planning
for or expecting an export sale
Reactivating - where a firm with discontinuous export experience
is planning efforts to continue exporting.

When a decision-maker in a non-exporting firm perceives export
stimuli, his decision problem is not primarily whether he shall
begin exporting immediately, but rather what kind of behaviour he
shall choose to follow.

Active pre-export behaviour is chosen when the decision-maker has
the conscious aim of commencing export sales in the future. The
preparations for export that follow such a decision could be of
two kinds. Either they could be concentrated towards information
collection or around information giving. The first case could be
interpreted as an indication of a decision-maker, who believes
that he has not got enough adequate information to act upon, while
the latter case indicates a decision-maker, who already has made
his decision to start exporting and is only carrying out his sales
strategy. It seems probable that firms demonstrating an active
pre-export behaviour will become exporters sooner than firms in
any other group. Another hypothesis is that those firms actively
preparing for export before their debut , will show a higher and
more continuous growth rate of exports during the period after
the first export sale.

Decision-makers, who choose to follow a passive pre-export behaviour pattern are not willing to act upon information which is
available to them. But unlike the decision-maker in the first
case, who decided to collect further information, this type makes
no efforts to acquire more data. This could indicate that he is
more intuitive and receptive, while the decision-maker in the
first case was intuitive and preceptive. The passive pre-exporter
believes that if he perceives further stimuli, this could enable
him to act positively. A fortuitous order from abroad could, as
an example, convince him that he has a lot of potential customers
waiting abroad. This kind of pre-export behaviour could also be
caused by weak stimuli. We hypothesize that firms following this
pattern of pre-export behaviour will need a longer time to become
exporters than those in the active group. It is also possible
that their development as exporters after the debut will show
greater discontinuities than the active group.

The third class - domestic pre-export behaviour - indicates either
that the stimuli were not perceived by the decision-maker or that
he took no notice of it. This kind of behaviour is probably the
most usual one, taking into consideration that non-exporting firms
regularly are exposed to export stimuli. The explanations behind
this kind of behaviour are assumed to be very much the same as
those mentioned in connection with passive behaviour. The stimuli
could be very weak, and therefore not perceived or noticed by the
decision-maker. If he is considering other problem areas in the
firm's activities, he may be relatively unable to receive the
message concerning totally new markets in which the firm lacks
experience. Such behaviour is connected to the decision-maker's
cognitive style, and hence we conclude that decision-makers who
fall into this category should exhibit a more preceptive and systematic cognitive style than others.

Firms demonstrating a domestic pre-export behaviour will probably
need a considerably longer time-period to become exporters than
those in the earlier mentioned groups. In fact, the chance of
becoming an exporter, while demonstrating a domestic pre-export
behaviour is rather small. Probably a transition from a domestic
to a passive or active pre-export behaviour is normally preceding
the export debut.

A very special case of pre-export behaviour is the group of reactivating exporters. Since these firms have already made their export
debut, they should not belong to this model at all. On the other
hand, we can expect to find many similarities between these firms
and non-exporters. Having realized one or a few export sales some
time ago without continuing to export, these firms face a situation that is not very different from the pre-export stage. Firms
that are reactivating could therefore be looked upon merely as a
special case of non-exporting firms and subsequently divided into

the two main groups, active and passive, depending upon their degree of preparation for another export "debut". The hypotheses expressed in connection with active and passive pre-export behaviour should be expected to be valid also for the reactivators[32].

Policy Implications for Export Promoters

What, then, are the policy implications of the model which has been presented above, for those who want to promote exports among small and medium-sized firms ? Let us first remember that promoting non-exporting firms into exporting is no panacea to trade-balance problems of today - but perhaps of tomorrow.

Governmental export promotion has been considered as an export stimulus in our model, although we have not explicitly discussed differences between different promotional measures. However, some conclusions can be drawn from our model, considering the non-exporting decision-maker's cognitive style as an important factor, which explains his information-gathering and information-evaluation behaviour. We have assumed that difference in cognitive style is an important factor to explain why some firms become exporters sooner than others. Export promotion in the form of direct economic benefits offered in relation to export operations will probably affect positively those decision-makers, who already have or soon will have demonstrated an active pre-export or export behaviour. The economic advantages will make their export marketing strategy look even more attractive. But it seems less likely that such benefits would affect the behaviour of those decision-makers, who chose a domestic and perhaps to some extent also passive pre-export behaviour. Financial support will affect neither their capability of information-gathering in a positive way, nor their ability to act upon the information available. Instead it seems more fruitful to control them through offering services which may affect their judgment of the problem situation, i.e. improves their ability to gather and act upon relevant information about export opportunities. Means for such purposes could be export education, information, consultant and advisory services, collective export activities etc.

A question which we will not make any attempts to answer at this stage is, which strategy gives the largest pay-off - to support already active pre-exporters financially, or to offer passive and domestic pre-exporters a range of export services ?

Some Empirical Illustrations

Parallel to the work on the model presented above, data has been
collected for an exploratory study about export-propensity[33].
Although this data has not been designed in complete accordance
with our model, we will in this article attempt to use part of
the data to give some illustrations of our model. A more thorough
empirical analysis will be performed in a forthcoming study.

The firms investigated produced "Tools and implements, Tableware,
Miscellaneous non-precious metalware and Machinery and Apparatus,
Non-Electrical"[34]. We have investigated 69 firms, 55 of which
were exporters and 14 non-exporters. The majority of the exporting
firms had made their export debut in the 1960's. All firms were
small with an average size well below 10 Mill. Swedish Crowns.
In the sample design, the intention was to acquire two groups of
firms, of about equal size, exporters and non-exporters, but it
turned out to be rather difficult to find non-exporters matching
the exporters in these branches of industry[35].

In our model above we identified four types of pre-export behaviour-
active, passive, domestic, and reactivating. Beneath we use the
symbols A, P, D, and R for the respective groups. The R-group will
not be used in any computations, since only two observations were
available. We divided the firms into these groups by using a
simple criterion : amount of information given and/or collected
before the export debut (for exporting firms) or during 1973 (for
non-exporting firms). The "A"-group consisted of 24 firms - all
exporters, the "P"-group comprised 27 firms - 23 exporters, the
"D"-group comprised 16 firms - 8 exporters, and the "R"-group
only two firms. These numbers give a first indication that active
pre-exporters have a higher tendency of becoming exporters than
passive and, above all, domestic pre-exporters.

The dissimilarities between different kinds of pre-export behaviour
according to our model basically is a matter of activity on the
part of the firm which is related to future export operations. One
way to control the consistency of the classification is therefore
to compare it to the procedure behind the firm's export sale. For
such an analysis, we have classified the firm's first export
order in the three groups "outward", mixed "outward/inward", and
"inward". "Outward" means that the firm got the export order
through its own active efforts, "inward" that the firm got a fortuitous order. The "mixed" group contains cases where both types
of stimuli were present. The results are illustrated in table 1
below.

Table 1. Characteristics of first export order in relation to the firm's pre-export behaviour.

| Group | First Export Order | | | |
	Outward	Mixed	Inward	Σ
A	11	3	6	20
P	1	6	7	14
D	1	1	3	5
Σ	13	10	16	39

The results in table 1 above show rather clearly that firms in the A-group got their first export order in a more active way than firms in the other groups. They also make their export debuts faster than other firms. The average age of the firm at the time of the first export order was for the A-group 8,3 years, for the P-group 9,7 years, and for the D-group 11,4 years.

We have also tried to check the firm's pronounced export motives against our classification of them into different groups. Distinction was made between three kinds of export motives, i.e. active, miscellaneous, and passive. The results obtained are illustrated in table 2 below.

Table 2. Export motives stated by the firm in relation to the firm's pre-export behaviour.

| Group | Export motives stated by the firms | | | |
	Active	Miscella-neous	Passive	Σ
A	18	4	2	24
P	14	4	9	27
D	1	3	7	11
Σ	33	11	18	62

These results, in our opinion, support the view that firms in the A-group have more "active" export motives than have firms in the P-group and that the latter have more "active" export motives than firms in the D-group.

The empirical illustrations reported above should, according to our opinion, be considered as a first indication to the relevance of certain elements in our model. In spite of this, the model still remains in a very preliminary formulation, which probably successively has to be further adapted in accordance to new findings from empirical research. We believe that almost any relation between different elements in the model can be taken, and definitely would be very interesting, as objects for such research.

Bibliography

Bernhart, M.H. (1973), Information Channels for Colombian Exporters. Unpublished masters thesis, MIT.

Byström, B., Glader, M. (1973), Industriell service. University of Umeå.

Carlson, S. (1974a), International Transmission of Information and the Business Firm, Annals of the American Academy of Political and Social Science, Vol. 412, March, pp.55-63.

Carlson, S. (1974b), Market Information : Selling Intensity and the Dynamics of International Economic Integration. Working report, Dept. of Business Administration, Uppsala (forthcoming in De Economist).

Cooper, R.A., Hartley, K., Harvey, C.R.M. (1970), Export Performance and the Pressure of Demand. London.

Forsgren, M., Johanson, J. (1975), Internationell företagsekonomi (International Business). Stockholm (forthcoming).

Hyrenius, H., Sjögerås, I. (1974). De mindre industriföretagens export-beteende (Export Behaviour in Small Industrial Firms - An Exploratory Study) with a summary in English. Lund.

Hörnell, E., Vahlne, J.E. (1972), The Deciding Factors in the Choice of Subsidiary Sales Company as the Channel for Export. Uppsala.

Karlsson, K. (1973), Exportbenägenhet hos små och medelstore företag (Export-Propensity in Small and Medium-Sized Firms). Unpublished thesis ,Dept. of Business Administration.Uppsala.

Knickerbocker, F.T. (1973), Oligopolistic Reaction and Multinational Enterprise. Boston.

McKenney, J.L., Keen, P.G.W. (1974), How Managers' Mind Work. Harvard Business Review, May-June, pp.79-90.

Mintzberg, H. (1970), Managerial Work. Analysis from Observation. Working report, Faculty of Management, McGill University,Oct.

Moussouris, S.G. (1967), Export Horizons of Greek Industries. Unpublished DBA dissertation, Harvard Business School.

Meidel, L.A. (1965), Comparative Export Practices in Small Firms in Scandinavia and the United States. Boston.

Nyström, H (1974a), Uncertainty, Information and Organizational Decision-Making : A Cognitive Approach. Swedish Journal of Economics, Vol. 76, n° 1.

Nyström, H.(1974b), Företagskreativitet och innovationer (Firm-Creativity and Innovations). Stockholm.

Nyström, H. (1974c), Cognitive Styles in Management and Reaction to Organizational Stagnation. Working paper, Dept. of Business Administration. Uppsala.

Olson, H.C. (1974), Studies in Export Promotion - An Attempt to Evaluate Export Stimulation Measures. Working Report. Dept. of Business Administration. Uppsala.

Olson, H.C. (1975), Studies in Export Promotion. Attempts to Evaluate Export Stimulation Measures for the Swedish Textile and Clothing Industries. Acta Universitatis Upsaliensis, Studia Oeconomiae Negotiorum no. 10. Uppsala.

Penrose, E.T. (1959),The Theory of the Growth of the Firm.Oxford.

Pinney, J.K. (1968), The Process of Commitment to Foreign Trade : Selected Smaller Indiana Manufacturing Firms. Unpublished PhD dissertation, Indiana University.

Richardson, J.D. (1971), On "Going Abroad" : The Firm's Initial Foreign Investment Decision, Quarterly Review of Economics and Business, Vol. 11, Winter.

Simmonds, K., Smith, M. (1968), The First Export Order : A Marketing Innovation, British Journal of Marketing, Summer, pp. 93-100.

Simpson, C.L. (1973), The Export Decision : An Interview Study of the Decision Process in Tennessee Manufacturing Firms. Unpublished PhD dissertation, Georgia State University.

Simpson, C.L., Kujawa, D. (1974). The Export Decision Process : An Empirical Enquiry, Journal of International Business Studies, Spring, pp 107-117.

Swedish Export Directory 1964, 1972, Stockholm. The General Export Association of Sweden.

Sweeney, J.K. (1970). A Small Company Enters the European Market. Harvard Business Review, September-October.

Weiner, P. (1967), A Study of the Attempts and Results of Directly
    Stimulating Exporting. Research Report to the Federal Reserve
    Bank of Boston, no 38, March.

Wiedersheim-Paul, F. (1972). Uncertainty and Economic Distance –
    Studies in International Business. Uppsala.

References

1. It is not a priori true that governmental export promotion
    efforts are most effective when allocated to firms that alrea-
    dy are successful exporters. On the other hand, this may be
    the case, but we cannot know until we have a more comprehen-
    sive knowledge about the export-propensity of smaller, less
    export-experienced firms.

2. See e.g. Neidel (1965), Weiner (1967), Moussouris (1967),
    Simmonds & Smith (1968), Pinney (1968), Sweeney (1970),
    Richardson (1971), Bernhart (1973), Simpson (1973), Hyrenius
    & Sjögerås (1974), Simpson & Kujawa (1974).

3. Exceptions are e.g. Simpson (1973), and Simpson & Kujawa
    (1974).

4. Of course, some exceptions can be found to this assumption,
    e.g. firms in extractive industries, international sourcing
    (e.g. electronics industries in Taiwan), some sub-contractors.

5. For a discussion of explanations to the export debut of indi-
    vidual firms, see Forsgren & Johanson (1975).

6. The concept of pre-export behaviour has been proposed by
    Hyrenius & Sjögerås (1974), p. 91. A similar distinction
    between different kinds of behaviour preceding the first
    export sale has been suggested by Bernhart (1973).

7. Hyrenius & Sjögerås (1974), pp 32-36.

8. Hyrenius & Sjögerås (1974) consider this deficient goal-
    fulfilment to be one of the most important explaining factors
    behind the export debut. See also Cooper, Hartley & Harvey
    (1970).

9. Penrose (1959) stresses this explanation.

10. See e.g. Simpson & Kujawa (1974), p 108, who do not explicitly
    mention the role of expectations as export stimuli.

11. Mentioned as explanation by the marketing director of a large
    Swedish international firm (in private communication with the
    authors).

12. See e.g. Simpson & Kujawa, op.cit. p. 108, Bernhart (1973),
    p. 3:4, Simmonds & Smith (1968), p 95.

13. This "follow-the-leader" behaviour has been thoroughly examined
    by Knickerbocker (1973).

14. For an investigation of a decreasing domestic market as an explanation of export, see Cooper, Hartley & Hafvey (1970).

15. Very roughly we can describe this measure as factors disturbing or preventing the flows of information in both directions between firm and customer. For more thorough discussions of the concept of psychic or cultural distance, see e.g. Wiedersheim-Paul (1972), and Calrson (1974a).

16. For a study of the effects of economic integration upon international trade, see Carlson (1974b).

17. Results from an evaluation of an export promotion program, whose effects did not appear as very dramatic, have been presented by one of the authors. See e.g. Olson (1975).

18. This ignorance of expectations can explain Simpson & Kujawa's conflicting results regarding free capacity as an export stimulus. See ibid., p 110.

19. Hardware refers to the proportion of the sales value made up of physical goods, while software refers to the proportion of the value made up of services rendered to the buyer or user before, during and after the delivery. Examples of software are programming of machine equipment for the specific needs of the buyer and education and instructing of the buyer's personnel in the use of the machines.

20. For a discussion of technology intensiveness, see Hörnell & Vahlne (1973), p 10.

21. By information centre we mean a concentration of industrial and commercial activity and corresponding services offered to firms in big cities, harbours etc. See e.g. Byström & Glader (1973).

22. E.g. Swedish-made equipment for central-heating of private houses may not be exported to tropical countries.

23. McKenney & Keen (1974), Nyström (1974a), (1974b), (1974c).

24. McKenney & Keen, op. cit. p 81, Nyström (1974a), pp 134-135.

25. This proposition has been supported by empirical studies carried out by McKenney & Keen, op.cit., pp 83-85.

26. Ibid, op.cit., p 86.

27. An important and interesting consequence of this reasoning
    is that the ability to perceive and act upon export stimuli
    requires the same kind of conditions as other kinds of crea-
    tive thinking, i.e. intuitive cognitive style. Consequently,
    it should be possible to find a correlation between exporting
    firms and other results of creative thinking, such as develop-
    ment of the firm's products, consumers, technology, etc.
    This conclusion corresponds to the findings of Simmonds &
    Smith (1968).

28. Nyström (1974c), pp 6)7

29. Simmonds & Smith (1968), p 95

30 Cf. P 12.

31. Hyrenius & Sjögerås (1974), p 91

32. The combination of a reactivating exporter demonstrating
    domestic pre-export behaviour could, on the other hand,hardly
    be considered as realistic.

33. See Karlsson (1973), thesis supervised by one of the authors.

34. Product groups listed in Swedish Export Directory.

35. This difficulty illustrates the effect of a limited domestic
    market. Simmonds & Smith (1968), in their investigation of
    new British exporters, faced the opposite problem : "Some
    difficulty was experienced in locating firms that had recently
    begun to export" (p 94).

ALIENATION AT THE TOP

Geert Hofstede

European Institute for Advanced Studies in Management, Brussels

A large European corporation suffered the resignation of three key executives within two months. Distressed by these losses, which were totally unexpected, the president asked a consulting psychologist to conduct postexit interviews with the three men. Were the three resignations in any way related ? Did they signal a serious crisis of which the president was unaware ?

The three men all received the psychologist very willingly. In fact, they appeared eager to supply this kind of feedback-from-a-distance to their former employer. The interviews revealed that on a direct cause-and-effect level, their almost simultaneous resignations were a coincidence. They had not been influenced by each other, and their new jobs were with different companies.

However, in many ways their three cases were strikingly similar. All three men were in their early forties - an age that normally is the peak of a man's working life, when he has both a past to build upon and a future to look forward to. All three so far had spent virtually their entire careers with the same large employer, had liked their jobs, and had been highly successful. All three had been very well paid, and prospects of improved earnings in their new jobs were minor or nonexistent ; job security was less in the new job than in the old. All three were quite positive about their former employer : "It is a great company. What I am now, I owe to them". However, all three complained about being increasingly frustrated by company bureaucracy as they had moved up, and all three moved to new positions that involved a bigger job in a smaller company.

No specific organizational crisis, then, caused these executives to resign ; instead, the cause was a midcareer crisis in their personal orientations toward their work - a common feeling of frustration, meaninglessness, and powerlessness that seemed to have grown parallel to the increase in their formal power as

This study was supported by a grant from executive search consultants Berndtson International S.A., Brussels.

measured by their hierarchical positions. They felt less and
less able to make the impact on the company that they wanted to
make, and for this they blamed not particular individuals but
a conglomerate of impersonal forces generated by "company bureaucracy".

The alienation phenomenon

The ambition to make a meaningful impact, however modest, in one's
life environment is common to most men. Many people worry nowa-
days about the state of mind of industrial and office workers who
have to do simple, repetitive tasks devoid of any meaning to them.
The word "alienation" is used to describe the effect of these
jobs on people.

Alienation is a term borrowed from sociology and used by different
authors to include different attributes, but it always centers on
an individual's feeling of powerlessness and meaninglessness, his
inability to influence or even understand the forces upon which
his life and happiness depend. This feeling is by no means limited to industrial workers. Over the past five or ten years, the
term has also been used to describe the state of mind of students
at American universities. Feelings of alienation may be found,
though to different extents, at all levels within bureaucratic
organizations.

The word "bureaucracy", in popular parlance, has acquired a strong
negative connotation - but in its original sociological context,
it refers to any formal system for simplifying the management of
large and complex activities. As such, it applies to public as
well as private organizations, the shop floor as well as the executive suite. Bureaucracies are born of necessity ; without them,
large-scale human activities would be unmanageable. The paradox is
that, by their very existence, they call forth forces that defeat
their own ends. The main problem appears to be that the models
of people on which bureaucratic structures are built are too different from real people.

Bureaucracies ask people to behave in standardized ways, whereas
real people are never standard. If we force them to behave as if
they were, the consequence is alienation. The three executives
who blamed their move on bureaucracy in the large corporation moved to escape the alienation they had begun more and more to feel.

Attitude survey

I would now like to describe an example of employee alienation in
a large multinational corporation that operates in many European

countries. This corporation markets its products through a subsidiary in each country. It operates sales offices in the major
cities, which are coordinated by a head office in each country.
All country head offices report directly to an international headquarters located in Europe.

In 1968 and 1969, this corporation conducted a series of attitude
surveys of all its employees and managers. These surveys seemed
to show an alienation problem at a surprising place - within the
corporation's international headquarters. Moreover, this alienation problem not only affected the headquarters' rank and file
employees but also its managers. In fact, there were reasons to
consider the problem more serious for managers at the international headquarters than for other categories of employees.

Attitude-survey results, far from being dull statistics, can reveal fascinating secrets about the functioning of organizations.
I shall present some of the main corporate findings on the alienation phenomenon, so that the reader can judge for himself.

In composing the survey questionnaire, we believed that one yard-
stick for determining the meaningfulness of a job would be a
person's feeling able to make some contribution to the overall
company result. We therefore asked (among other things), "How
satisfied are you with your opportunity to make a real contribution to the success of the company?". In Figure 1 the distribution of answers to this question is shown for three groups of
employees : managers (anyone responsible for coordinating the
work of others), professional employees (college-level, specialized personnel such as salesmen, engineers, and accountants),and
clerical employees (noncollege-level, administrative personnel).
Results are also divided according to three kinds of work locations: sales offices (within countries), country head offices,
and the international headquarters.

Figure 1 reveals that for all three categories of employees -
managers, professionals, and clerks - there is a consistent decrease of satisfaction from the sales offices to the international
headquarters. Also, managers are more satisfied than professionals, and professionals more than clerks, except in international
headquarters, where clerks are more satisfied than professionals.
In fact, the satisfaction level of managers in the international
headquarters (47 percent satisfied) is almost exactly the same as
for professionals in the country headquarters (48 percent) and
for clerks in the sales offices (46 percent).

That managers are more satisfied with their opportunity to contribute to the company's success than clerks was to be expected because, by definition, they have a more central role in the organization. But although the international headquarters also has a

Figure 1.   Satisfaction with Opportunity to Contribute to Company
Success

	Percent Scoring		
	Dissatisfied or very dissatisfied	Neither satisfied nor dissatisfied	Satisfied or very satisfied
Managers in :			
Sales offices	5	18	77
Country head offices	9	31	60
International headquarters	14	39	47
Professional employees in :			
Sales offices	6	32	62
Country head offices	16	36	48
International headquarters	24	50	26
Clerical employees in :			
Sales offices	14	40	46
Country head offices	17	42	41
International headquarters	21	46	33

central role, its satisfaction level is lowest. This level increases as we go to the country head offices, and from there to
the sales offices. Dissatisfaction indicating alienation, therefore, is least present at the sales offices and reaches a peak
at the international headquarters.

Other survey results

The attitude surveys also showed that satisfaction with opportunity to make a real contribution to the success of this company
tended to go hand in hand with satisfaction on other aspects of
job content. In a statistical analysis of the survey scores for
each of the various categories of employees, a close correlation
was found between satisfaction with opportunity to contribute and
the answers to two other questions, "How satisfied are you with
the challenge of the work you do - the extent to which you can
get a personal sense of accomplishment out of it?" and "How satisfied are you with the extent to which you use your skills and abilities on your job?". The three questions together form a statistical "cluster" that indicates, in general, satisfaction with
the intrinsic nature or content of the job. The close relationship between these three questions implies that the two other
questions should show differences between managers and others and
between sales offices and headquarters similar to those shown by
satisfaction with opportunity to contribute. Figure 2 allows us
to verify this (for simplicity's sake only percent satisfied answers are shown).

Figure 2 reveals the same kind of differences between managers,
professionals, and clerks and between sales offices, country head
offices, and international headquarters that Figure 1 showed.
However, the differences in Figure 2 tend to be smaller than in
Figure 1. Especially for managers, there are greater differences
between sales offices and headquarters on satisfaction with opportunity to contribute than on challenge or use of skills. This
suggests that the differences in managers' feelings of challenge
and use of skills may be the consequences of their different
satisfaction with opportunity to contribute.

The subjective importance of contributing to company success.

Satisfaction with opportunity to contribute is subjectively more
important to managers than it is to other organization members.
This was disclosed in the above-mentioned attitude surveys by a
parallel set of questions to the satisfaction questions ; these
parallel questions tried to elicit the importance of various work
aspects to the employee. Instead of "How satisfied are you with
...?" the questions began with "How important is it to you to..?"

Figure 2. Intrinsic Job Interest

| | Percent Scoring "Satisfied" or "Very Satisfied" | |
	Challenge of the Work	Use of Skills and Abilities
Managers in:		
Sales offices	77	65
Country head offices	66	61
International headquarters	56	55
Professional employees in:		
Sales offices	71	57
Country head offices	53	48
International headquarters	39	37
Clerical employees in:		
Sales offices	53	46
Country head offices	46	42
International headquarters	34	36

(for example, have a job that allows you to make a real contribution to the success of your company).

All in all, there were 22 importance and 22 satisfaction questions;
the 22 items covered the entire field of the relationship of a
person with his job - such as earnings, impact on personal life,
learning, security, interpersonal relationships, and advancement
opportunities. The importance questions allowed us to rank these
22 items in order of the importance attached to them by a certain
category of employees. Rank 1 would be given to the item that,
on the average, received the highest importance score ; rank 22,
the lowest. The relative importance attached to contribution to
company success by our various categories of employees is shown
in Figure 3.

Figure 3 proves what was stated above : Managers distinguish themselves from others by attaching much higher importance to contributing to company success. Whereas for professionals and clerks
this issue ranks from 12 to 18 out of 22, for managers it ranks
fifth in the sales offices, third in the country head offices,
and second in the international headquarters. In the international headquarters, the only work aspect managers rate more important
than contributing to company success is challenging work. In the
country head offices, managers view challenging work and a good
working relationship with your manager as being more important
than contributing to company success. In the sales offices, the
four items rated more important by managers are, in order of importance, challenging work, considerable freedom to adopt your own
approach to the job, an opportunity for advancement, and training
opportunities.

If we compare the satisfaction percentages (Figure 1) and the
importance rankings (Figure 3), we can see that the problem of
alienation - not making a real contribution to the success of the
company - is particularly acute for the international headquarters
managers by a combination of high attached importance (ranked second) and low satisfaction (47 percent satisfied). It is much
less pressing, for example, with clerical employees who, while not
very satisfied, indicate by their low importance scores that to
them many other aspects of the job can compensate for the lack of
satisfaction with opportunity to contribute to company success.
This way out is not open to most managers.

Images of the organization as such

Alienation does affect one's self-image but not necessarily one's
image of the organization one works for. In fact, the two may be
negatively related. The surveys also contained a question about
the image of company as such (not in terms of one's personal

Figure 3 : Importance of Contributing to Company Success.

	Average Rank Order
Managers in :	
Sales offices	5^{+}
Country head offices	3
International headquarters	2
Professional employees in :	
Sales offices	14
Country head offices	15
International headquarters	12
Clerical employees in :	
Sales offices	16
Country head offices	18
International headquarters	18

+ Rankings : 1 most important, 22 least important.

contribution to it) : "How satisfied are you with the extent to which this company is regarded as successful?".

The results for managers are shown in Figure 4. As the overall level of answering was very favorable, we have taken the cutoff point between very satisfied and satisfied. It is clear that in this case the highest success ratings come from international headquarters and the least high from the sales offices. This is the opposite to the trend for the question about the managers' personal contribution to the company's success. It seems that the lack of satisfaction of the international headquarters managers with their personal contribution is partly compensated by a sense of pride in the company - "Never mind my job, but it is a great company to be in".

Motivational consequences of "red tape".

When they were presented with the survey data, some people were surprised : they had expected that respondents in the subsidiaries would be the least satisfied because they would be frustrated by the headquarters interventions. This expectation was based on the implicit assumption that bureaucratic systems ("red tape") were invented by people in headquarters who obviously should like what they were doing. Our data show this assumption to be wrong. In fact, it is a gross over-simplification of the origins of bureau-cracy. The surveys did address the issues of the relationships between subsidiaries and headquarters, however. Managers and pro-fessionals in the country head offices were asked how frequently (if at all) the following problems occurred :

. International headquarters doesn't give people in our country
  head offices enough support.

. International headquarters interferes too much.

People in the sales offices were asked the same questions with regard to both international headquarters and the country head offices.

The answers are summarized in Figure 5 :

1. Those answering"very frequently or frequently" never exceed one-
   third of the managers or professionals questioned.

2. Sales offices had few problems with international headquarters
   (these were dealt with at country-head-office level), but they
   had about the same level of problems with their country head
   office as country head offices had with international headquarters.

Figure 4 : Success of the Company as such.

	Percent Scoring		
	No Feeling or Dissa- tisfied	Satisfied	Very Satisfied
Managers in :			
Sales offices	18	53	29
Country head offices	15	52	33
International head- quarters	11	45	44

Figure 5 : Distribution of Responses to the "Support" and "Interference" Questions

	From Country Head Office				From International Headquarters			
	Not enough Support		Too much Interference		Not enough Support		Too much Interference	
	Very frequently or frequently	Seldom or never	Very frequently or frequently	Seldom or never	Very frequently or frequently	Seldom or never	Very frequently or frequently	Seldom or never
Managers in :								
Sales offices	32	24	27	27	13	59	7	72
Country head offices	—	—	—	—	31	29	26	42
Professional employees in :								
Sales offices	30	27	23	34	5	75	3	83
Country head offices	—	—	—	—	25	34	21	47

(Expressed in percentages. The percentage of those answering "sometimes" are not shown).

3. In all cases, problems were somewhat more frequently seen as
   not enough support rather than as too much interference.

4. In all cases, problems were somewhat more frequently felt by
   managers than by non-managers.

However, a more important finding (not visible in Figure 5) was
that the answers to the questions on support and interference
were statistically only weakly related to those about other aspects of the managers' or professionals' job satisfaction. Feeling
a lack of support or too much interference, although frustrating,
did not seem to affect too much the way people felt about their
work. In the total picture of the attitude of people toward their
jobs it stayed at the level of a minor irritation. The feeling of
alienation that we related to not feeling able to make a real
contribution to the company's success goes much deeper. There is
no real adversary to blame ; the system in which one is absorbed
is unclear and the individual feels he is wasting his time, although working very hard.

The price of alienation

The price an organization pays for the alienation of its employees
will vary from company to company, job to job, and individual employee to individual employee. In general, alienated employees
will lower their aspirations to perform because they see their
performance as meaningless anyway. They are less likely to exert
an extra effort. An illustration of this : Surveyed managers in
country sales offices reported spending considerably more volunta-
ry overtime on their jobs than did managers in country and international head offices (observation of managers in action confirms
that sales office managers do spend longer hours working). In
spite of this, sales office managers did not claim to be overloaded any more frequently than did head office managers : a considerably greater fraction of sales office managers would accept these
long hours without feeling overloaded.

Other things being equal, employees with higher skill and education levels will expect more intrinsic satisfaction from their
jobs and will want to use their skills as fully as possible. They
are, therefore, more likely to quit if they feel alienated and if
alternative jobs are available. People who have experienced success in the past are more frustrated by alienation than are less
successful people.

This fact was demonstrated in a study within the same company in
which 326 participants of an in-company executive training program
were followed through their careers after training. The average
time span between training and follow-up was four years. During

this period, 20 participants had left the company (a very low turnover figure). However, out of these 20, 16 had been rated by their
trainers as being among the top third of their class. This means
that the one-third of most successful trainees were eight times
as likely to quit as the two-thirds of less successful ones.

Even if we discount the fact that trainers are not infallible in
their judgment, it is still a reasonable assumption that these
more successful trainees would also tend to be the better performers in their day-to-day jobs. This study therefore shows how
alienation may lead to selective employee turnover : The more
successful people tend to leave. The departure of the three
executives mentioned in the introduction to this article upset
their president because they, too, were star performers. There is
a real danger that a company headquarters by this process may become stuck with a residue of disillusioned low achievers, who in
turn expand the bureaucracy of which they themselves are the vic-
tims.

In the previous paragraphs we have assumed a potential need to
achieve and to make a contribution to the company's success in all
people ; we have blamed the situation rather than the employees
when this contribution was missing. We also recognize, however,
that persons and even entire cultures differ in their need for
achievement and their need to contribute. Jobs with a low potential to contribute to the company's success will, by a process of
natural selection, attract persons for whom the need to contribute
is low. Our data suggest that such people are more likely to stay
in headquarters jobs than are strong achievers.

Job enrichment for headquarters executives

On the shop and office floor, the danger of alienation has been
recognized and efforts are being made to restore humanity to jobs
that the bureaucratic process dehumanized. These efforts generally are called "job enrichment", to use Frederick Herzberg's terminology. Some approaches to job enrichment focus mainly on the
structure of individual jobs, the dominant trend in the United
States. In Europe, especially in Sweden and Norway, job enrichment has concentrated on changing group tasks rather than individual jobs.

Is job enrichment possible in the headquarters of large corporations ? It is unlikely in this case that restructuring individual
jobs will be sufficient because in the forces that lead to alienation, the entire bureaucratic system of the organization is
involved. Job enrichment approaches here should include not only
individuals but also groups and the role of entire departments.

Let us first look at the kind of jobs we usually find in headquarters. There is a great variety : top executives with their
personal staffs ; those who deal with the outside on behalf of the
corporation ; those who plan ahead for the short and for the long
term and those who look after the execution of these plans by the
various subsidiaries ; those who write policies for the corporation and those who check whether these policies are followed ;
those who coordinate the flow of funds, materials, people, orders,
and ideas between the various subsidiaries ; and those who possess
unique expertise or perform unique services that the subsidiaries
are not in a position to do by themselves. The bigger the headquarters becomes, the greater the number of those necessary to keep
the headquarters itself running.

Why, then, in our multinational corporation would alienation be so
much lower in the sales offices than in such a headquarters ? What
is different about jobs in sales offices ? At least two differences
are noteworthy :

. Sales office jobs compared with headquarters jobs contain a
   much more direct feedback about results - one knows whether
   one has worked successfully or not.

. Sales office jobs more than headquarters jobs involve a direct
   client or customer relationship - there is a visible person,
   the customer, who is either satisfied or not.

Now both direct feedback and a client relationship are recognized
by job enrichment experts to be among the key requirements for an
"enriched" job. Headquarters jobs, on the other hand, usually
receive little or no feedback on their success, and it is generally less clear who their client it - the subsidiary offices, higher
management ... or do they have clients at all ?

It is evident that, with headquarters containing such a mixed bag
of roles, the alienation phenomenon will not be the same among all
headquarters activities. In fact, the employee attitude survey
recorded that among these activities, the satisfaction with "contribution to company success" varied from 70 percent to only 20
percent of personnel scoring "very satisfied" or "satisfied"(taking managers, professionals, and clerical employees together).
We should, therefore, further investigate who in headquarters felt
alienated and who not, and why. For this purpose, I shall first
describe another study, the headquarters effectiveness study.

The headquarters effectiveness study

In the same multinational corporation that supplied the alienation
data, the chief headquarters executive, after the employee atti-

tude survey, decided he wanted feedback on the effectiveness of
his international headquarters operation. He asked the corporate
personnel research department to carry out a study of how people
in country head offices looked at the job done by their international headquarters counterparts. This survey, carried out half
a year after the employee attitude survey, became known as the
"Headquarters Effectiveness Study". In this study, the departments of the international headquarters were divided into seven
main functions (such as market research, finance, and personnel)
and then subdivided into 49 departments or activities. For each
activity, the person acting as the main "customer" in each country
head office was presented with a written questionnaire to be returned to the corporate personnel research department. Anonymity
of answers was guaranteed unless customers expressly wanted their
identity to be known. Of the more than 1100 questionnaires mail-
ed out, more than 800 (73 percent) were returned. The questionnaire contained some forced-choice questions along with a number
of write-in questions. The responses to the latter were assembled
for each of the 49 international headquarters activities and
sent to the person responsible for that activity.

Among other things, the forced-choice questions tried to have the
customers rate the headquarters activities on the two dimensions
of support and control. Support was defined as "advice and
counsel, help with specific problems, expert answers, and information that helps you to do a better job". Support given by the
international headquarters activity in the past 12 months was
evaluated by the country head office customers from the points of
view of quantity and of quality. Control was defined as "staff
supervision : monitoring country practices, policies, and procedures ; international coordination ; auditing ; and so on - all
aimed at ensuring a high level of overall performance". The customers were asked how they felt about the amount of control received from their international headquarters counterpart over the
past 12 months.

The results revealed that quantity and quality of support generally went hand in hand, making it possible to compute a support
index for each activity of the international headquarters, including both quantity and quality. Control and support were less
strongly related (if at all, control was related to quantity of
support but not to quality). Some headquarters activities were
seen as high in both support and control and some as low in both
support and control, but others were high in support and low in
control or low in support and high in control.

Relationships between perceived support and control and head-quarters alienation.

I have already mentioned that this headquarters effectiveness stu-dy (in which people in the country head offices rated the inter-national headquarters) followed closely after the employee attitu-de survey (in which people both in the country head offices and in international headquarters rated their own jobs). The resear-chers wondered whether any relationship would show up between the outcome of the two surveys. In the employee attitude survey, the seven main functional groups within the international headquarters varied considerably in their satisfaction with their opportunity to make a real contribution to the success of the company. Could the satisfaction or dissatisfaction of international headquarters employees with the meaningfulness of their jobs be in any way related to the way in which their function was perceived by their customers at country headquarters ?

Figure 6 shows the results of a comparison of both surveys. The seven main functional areas in international headquarters have been coded A through G according to the rank order of their em-ployees' scores on "satisfaction with the opportunity to contribu-te to the company's success". Thus A is the function with the highest average satisfaction (low alienation) and G with the lowest average satisfaction (high alienation). The same functional areas have been ranked according to their ratings received on support and control in the headquarters effectiveness study - that is, in the way they are perceived by their customers.

The results in Figure 6 are remarkable. Self-ratings of headquar-ters employees on satisfaction with opportunity to contribute run almost perfectly parallel to the ratings received on support as perceived by their customers in the country head offices. Such a similarity in ranking is extremely unlikely to occur by chance. On the other hand, no consistent relationship is visible between satisfaction with opportunity to contribute and ratings received on control.

This gives us a clue as to why not all parts of headquarters show equal alienation : Where the function is able to establish an effective support relation with its customers in the country head-quarters, alienation is less. Whether the function exercises con-trol (that is, formal power) does not appear to be related to feelings of alienation.

Let us look at the extremes in Figure 6 more closely. Function A, which has the highest scores on satisfaction with opportunity to contribute and support but also a high score on control, is a rela-tively small office (13 people) in charge of customer service. It is manned by ex-customer-service engineers who are well aware of

Figure 6 : Comparisons of Outcomes of Two Surveys.

Headquarters Main Functions	Employee Attitudes Survey[1]	Headquarters Effectiveness Study[2]	
		Support Index[3]	Control Score
A	1[4]	1	2
B	2	2	6
C	3	3	4
D	4	4	3
E	5	6	5
F	6	5	1
G	7	7	7

[1] Ranking of satisfaction with opportunity to contribute to company's success.

[2] Rankings of ratings by country head office counterparts.

[3] Quantity plus quality.

[4] Rankings : 1. high

the problems in the various countries. It maintains a tight control on the productivity of the customer-service activities in the
countries because it has a say in their budgets. However, the
headquarters staff has maintained the same service attitude toward
the engineers in the countries that these engineers are supposed
to show toward their customers : Calls for help are always hono-
red. Most people in the countries feel that the headquarters'
targets for productivity are tough but realistic.

Function G, scoring low on satisfaction with opportunity to contribute, support, and control, is the largest single functional
group : it comprises 75 people. This suggests that the size of
the headquarters group has something to do with both alienation
and effective functioning. I will come back to the issue of size
later on : size, however, does not explain all the differences
between functions. For example, functions E and F in Figure 6
with relatively unfavorable alienation socres, are at the same
time fairly small groups. Function G supplies support and control
in the marketing area basically in the same way that Function A
does to customer service. However, the marketing area is much
more complex than the customer service area. Therefore, more
people are needed at headquarters to deal with marketing problems;
most of them are experts in their own area, but as experts they
often have trouble communicating with subsidiaries. Also, the
rapid growth and frequent reorganizations of this part of the
headquarters staff has led to a lack of clarity as to responsibilities both in the subsidiaries and among the headquarters staff
themselves. A relatively large part of the staff is new at headquarters and inexperienced at this kind of work. People in the
subsidiaries, who do not think that headquarters can really help
them, will not so easily take their problems to headquarters ;
consequently, the headquarters staff feels isolated and is unin-
formed about what goes on in the subsidiaries. Because of this
lack of information, policies issued by the headquarters staff
may not sufficiently take the reality of the subsidiaries into
account ; this, in turn, diminishes the subsidiaries' confidence
in headquarters even more. It was remarkable that one small group
within Function G, which had been unaffected by most reorganizations and whose role was clear, was not dissatisfied but, on the
contrary, highly satisfied with its opportunity to contribute to
company success.

In general, we may conclude that the international headquarters
functions that have received favorable scores on support are comparable to the sales offices in which, as we have also seen, alienation is low. In both cases, there is a supportive relationship
with the customer that, to the members of the selling department,
involves a constant and natural feedback on the meaningfulness
of what they are doing. If the customer really feels helped, the
salesman feels rewarded. We have already seen (Figure 5) that

people in the sales offices and in the country head offices have
more problems with not enough support from headquarters than with
too much interference – that is, an excess of control.

Support, control and power

Our analysis leads to a very important conclusion for the battle
against headquarters alienation. If headquarters departments get
a role in which they are able to give true support (as defined by
its receivers), their members are not likely to feel alienated.
It is immaterial whether they simultaneously exert control. It
is perfectly possible to combine control and support. Control
roles without support are also possible, but they are likely to
be alienating to the role incumbents.

Traditional thinking about organizations has stressed control
rather than support relationships. The organization chart, for
example, is a diagram of the distribution of formal control in an
organization ; it does not show support relationships. It is much
easier to formalize control than support. However, in actual practice in organizations, this kind of control is often imaginary.
It is common knowledge that the importance of a job is not always
reflected in the organization chart. Control, as previously defined in the headquarters effectiveness study, aims at "ensuring
a high level of overall performance". It can do this only if it
has an influence on how things are done. But control without
support is an extremely blunt weapon. It can do things like sup-
pressing an expenditure or replacing a person. However, this in
itself does not ensure high performance or solve a problem. In
particular, the replacing of people – a popular solution in the
case of business problems – is often no solution at all. The
people may change, but the problems survive. (The case of Function G as described above shows even that the very act of shifting
people around too frequently breeds new problems). A real influence on how things are done is obtained through a process of support rather than control : supplying new know-how or tools and
becoming aware of the problems at the same time.

This analysis would not be complete if we did not look at something that underlies both control and support – power. Control, as
we described it, can be equated with formal power, but this is
only one side of the coin. We owe to the French sociologist
Michel Crozier a study of the phenomenon of power in bureaucratic
organizations. Crozier relates power – quite independently of the
formal organization chart – to uncertainty. Whenever events have
become completely certain or predictable in an organization, a
well-planned production process, or a perfect bureaucracy, no one
has much power however high his position. Real power rests with
those who command the sources of uncertainty. In the well-planned

production process, this may be the union leader who can authorize
a strike or the personnel officer who negotiates with the union
leader. In our case of international headquarters Function A
(customer service), the main source of uncertainty is problems
with customers. These are dealt with at the local office level.
However, by virtue of its support relationship with the countries,
the headquarters staff is called in whenever a problem becomes
really serious - a procedure that keeps them in direct contact
with the source of uncertainty : this is the real source of their
power. In the case of Function G (marketing), again the uncertainties arise mainly at the sales office level. In this case,
however, the lack of a support relationship - in the eyes of the
people in the countries - cuts the international headquarters
staff off from the sources of uncertainty, which means they have
no real power.

Power, in the above sense, is the opposite of alienation. This
kind of power means the ability to make a meaningful contribution
to what is going on. What our study has shown is that such power
is scarcely related to control (formal power) at all, but that it
depends on the existence of a support relationship.

Strategies for reducing headquarters alienation

Effective strategies for reducing headquarters alienation will,
as shown by the previous data, at the same time make the headquarters - and through it, the entire organization - more effective. The challenge is formidable, conflicting as it does with the
essence of the bureaucratic tradition. I can think of four strategies, four "R's", in increasing order of difficulty, as techniques for enriching headquarters management jobs : reflecting,
recruiting, rewarding, and restructuring.

Reflecting means presenting headquarters with a periodic mirror
to reflect its image with the subsidiaries it coordinates. The
headquarters effectiveness study described earlier in this article was such a mirror. That the company's top management conducted it at all represented a recognition that the opinion of
the people in the subsidiaries about headquarters did matter.
A reflecting study of this kind is to the headquarters what a
study of customer satisfaction is to a sales office. The headquarters effectiveness study generated an enormous amount of
qualitative feedback, which was further handled at the level
of each separate headquarters activity. Unfortunately, I do
not possess data on the amount of change brought about by this
feedback. However, an analogy with the process of change after
regular employee attitude surveys (something that has been
researched rather extensively) makes me suppose that the crucial
factor in determining further change is the setting of priorities

by higher management. This relates the strategy of reflecting
to recruiting and rewarding.

Recruiting of personnel for headquarters management jobs is
obviously of key importance for the role that headquarters will
fulfill in the organization. We have noted previously that, by
a process of natural selection, low achievers may be the ones
to stay whereas the most successful people may leave. We have
also seen the importance of the recruiting policy in the headquarters Function A case, where all managerial and professional
jobs were filled by expractitioners from the service field, a
practice that led to an effective support role for headquarters.
If headquarters has to give support, it is essential that only
people knowledgeable and experienced enough to be accepted as
supporters are recruited to headquarters. However, this presents a conflict with two other reasons for recruiting in headquarters ; training and shelving. In many companies, serving
a term at headquarters is an essential part of a person's training. Such a trainee is usually not the ideal supporter for the
subsidiaries : it is often by the blunders he makes in his
dealings with these subsidiaries that he really learns. The
other reason for recruiting to headquarters is shelving : Managers, especially higher managers,who have become redundant elsewhere in the organization and for whom at the time no equivalent
employment is available, are conveniently stored in a headquarters position, with a job title whose length generally is inversely related to its real content.

Recruiting for a support role at headquarters means that training assignments should be well distinguished and limited to
those positions where expertise is less necessary and that attempts at shelving should be vigorously resisted. Last, the
length of the headquarters assignment is very important. It
probably takes an average of two years for a headquarters mana-
ʒer to establish the necessary personal contact with his clients;
thus he only starts to be fully effective after that point. The
ideal duration for a headquarters assignment, therefore, is not
less than four years. An upper limit is less easy to mandate ;
six to eight years may be the period after which the headquarters manager's experience gets stale and he/she needs to have
more direct on line exposure to problems.

Rewarding is a crucial aspect of the headquarters' role dilemma.
The formal reward structure of headquarters operations often
prevents the building up of a support relationship. Headquarters people typically face upward - they are magnetically drawn
toward the power center of the organization, which is physically
close to them and from which they expect their rewards in the
form of decisions on their careers. It is important to be
visible to one's headquarters boss and to the higher bosses,up
to the president.

A support relationship with the subsidiaries, however, means a
facing outward and mostly downward in the hierarchy. Many headquarters people believe – with ample justification – they are
not rewarded for that. They are not against support but, because their rewards lie elsewhere, they accord it low priority. Top
management in headquarters communicates through its reward policy the kind of behavior it considers desirable. If the way to
be promoted is to serve your boss ("He needs this report before
Monday") rather than serve your clients in the subsidiaries,
this will be the headquarters' priority ; but the price to be
paid is alienation.

In a study I did of budget control systems in five Dutch companies, I compared the attitudes of lower line managers about cooperation with the budget department to the budget department's
criteria for performance appraisal. The latter were determined
by asking the budget people to rank ten possible criteria in the
order in which they thought their boss used them when appraising
their performance. It appeared that what line managers thought
about the budget deparment was related to where the budget people placed "tactfulness" as a performance criterion. In the
company where the cooperation was best, the budget people thought
that their tactfulness (in dealing with the line managers) was
their boss' first criterion in appraising their performance. In
the company with the worst cooperation, tactfulness placed
fourth.

The company that placed tactfulness first had an interesting
policy that I would recommend for any organization that wants
its personnel to give high priority to support. For staff or
headquarters jobs, this company determined who the clients were
whom the staff man was supposed to serve. When it was time for
the yearly performance evaluation, the staff man's boss was
requested to call these clients and ask their opinions about
the staff man's performance. Staff-line communications in this
company were the best of the five companies studied.

Restructuring is the hardest way to reduce headquarters alienation : it may also be the most effective one. It means that in
any case where a headquarters role leads to alienation, it
should be determined whether or not this role can be eliminated
completely. If a manager thinks he does not make a meaningful
contribution to the success of the company, maybe his job should
not be done at all. In the cases of the headquarters functions
A and G, we saw that size has something to do with alienation;
not so much the size of the entire organization, as of the units
in which people work. Making a meaningful contribution is easier
in a small group with face-to-face contact than in a large one;
the needs for coordination, which detract from the contribution
itself, increase disproportionally with the number of people.It

is therefore important to keep headquarters groups small and
to reduce their coordination with other groups to the minimum
necessary. From a study of organizational stress in the early
sixties, Robert L. Kahn of the University of Michigan and four
others drew a number of conclusions on how to limit the need
for coordination in organizations :

".... treat every coordinative requirement as a cost, which it
is. For each functional unit in the organization, ask how independent it can be of others and of top management. For each
position, ask how autonomous it can be made, what is the minimum number of other positions with which it must be connected,
and for what activities and purposes the connections are essential... The advocacy of minimal coordination contrasts sharply
with the notions of centralized leadership, with the idea that
ultimate and maximum control must originate from a central
source. Coordination only when justified by functional requirements or systemic risk also points up a common fault of management, a preoccupation with organizational symmetry and aesthe-
tics, and an emphasis on the regularities and beauties of the
organization chart. The organization which follows this principle of coordinative economy would not necessarily be small,
but it would not have grown haphazardly and it would not regard
size as an unmixed blessing. It would be decentralized, flat
and lean, a federated rather than a lofty hierarchical structure."

In such an organization, the risk of headquarters alienation
would be greatly reduced.

Conclusion

This article has been based on data collected in private business
enterprises. The increase in alienation when we move from the
periphery to the center of such organizations makes us recognize
that business and public organizations, after all, are not so
different. The stereotypes of the civil servant do apply to many
a headquarters executive in business. Large organizations have
problems in common, regardless of who owns them. However, business organizations have a tradition of greater flexibility. It
is easier to experiment with new forms of organization in business
than in government.

If we do not want to adopt the pessimistic view that our entire
society is doomed to increasing bureaucratization with a consequent alienation, such experimentation with less bureaucratic
organization forms is essential. We cannot stop with enriching
the jobs of manual and office workers ; in fact, some of the
failures of job enrichment projects at those levels may stem from

an absence of a job enrichment philosophy in the entire organization - including its headquarters management.

THE IMPACT OF MANAGERIAL TRANSFERS ON HEADQUARTERS-SUBSIDIARY
RELATIONSHIPS IN A MULTINATIONAL CORPORATION

ANDERS EDSTRÖM

European Institute for Advanced Studies
in Management, Brussels
and the Stockholm School of Economics

JAY GALBRAITH

The Wharton School
University of Pennsylvania

Coordination and control strategies in multinational corporations

Coordination and control strategies have been of central concern
to organizational theory and practice for some time (March and
Simon, 1958 ; Thompson, 1967 ; Pugh et al. 1969 ; Child, 1972
and 1973). A basic and reoccuring problem in the design of coordination and control strategies is to strike a balance between
local discretion to adapt behavior to local requirements and control from the center to avoid dysfunctional behavior in the face
of interdependencies and work flow integration. It is particularly acute for multinational corporations (MNC's) which operate
in a great variety of environments.

The strategies which organizations have employed to achieve coordination and control in an interdependent organizational system
vary. Child (1972;1973) discusses two main alternatives. First,
coordination and control can be achieved by confining decisions
to the top levels in the organizational hierarchy. By locating
important decisions at a level where an overview of interdependencies is possible, one can avoid dysfunctional local behavior.
This centralizing strategy of control is personal and direct. As
the organization grows, however, the centralized strategy of control tends to break down. The decision and information processing capacity of the top levels become insufficient and long
delays in decision-making reduce the responsiveness of local sub-
units since MNC's are large the centralized strategy cannot be
taken very far.

An alternative is then to shift to impersonal and indirect bureaucratic methods of budgeting, recording and reporting on an exception basis. Especially in multinational organizations there is a limit to the use of a bureaucratic strategy of control. With operations in many countries the MNC must deal with different markets, legal systems, institutional conditions and cultural norms. The variety in local conditions makes it difficult to design systems and procedures which are applicable in all countries.

A way to preserve bureaucratic control and still reduce the overload on headquarters is through the expatriate manager. A manager from the nationality of ownership assumes a key position on the management team of the subsidiary. This move will facilitate communication between subsidiary and headquarters and at the same time make sure that company policy will be applied. Company systems and procedures can also be adapted better to local conditions by the expatriate in cooperation with local managers. Control continues to be largely impersonal and bureaucratic. The expatriate will stay for a limited period and then move on.

A further step toward decentralization while maintaining overall integration is to employ a third strategy of coordination and control which can be called control by socialization (Edström and Galbraith, 1977). The fundamental idea is expressed well by Kuin (1972).

"A large and widespread organization must function with a high degree of delegation if it is to avoid the rigidity of bureaucratic rules. This means a manager should possess a deep-rooted sense of what the company's policy would be in the case of a particular issue he has to decide. Such a sense can only be instilled by experience, instruction, and personal contact at headquarters or in parts of the organization thoroughly familiar with the policies and style of the corporation" (Kuin, p. 91).

The use of socialization as a control strategy has been articulated several times in different forms (Stinchcombe, 1959 ; Kaufman, 1960; Hall, 1968). However, what makes the present situation different from those mentioned above is that organizational identification alone is not sufficient to maintain control. Even if individuals are willing to choose and execute behaviors which are functional for the whole organization, they are not able to do so when their positions are embedded in an interdependent network. They do not have sufficient information to determine impacts on other positions of the network which may be affected by their choices. It is here that extensive transfers are hypothesized to fill the gap. That is, transfer can increase knowledge of the network, develop multiple contacts within it and increase the likelihood that these contacts will be used in collecting

information to support local discretion. It is this contact development, informal organization development, generation of linking
pins (Likert, 1961), creation of integrators (Lawrence and Lorsch,
1967; Galbraith, 1973) and information collection behavior that
make transfer distinctive in this case. These intersubsidiary,
subsidiary-center contacts generate sufficient information which
along with socialization permit local discretion in situations of
interdependence (Hage, Aiken and Marrett, 1971).

We hypothesize that managerial transfer is a means for designing
the information system, the key information system, of large multinational organizations. The reason it is the key information
is that it is verbal information. For example, recent research
shows that top managers prefer verbal media transmitting current,
largely external data as opposed to written, detailed, but historical internal information systems (Mintzberg, 1973). However,
in multinational organizations external data enter by means of a
two-step communication process (Keegan, 1974). The new, strategic, ambiguous and consequential events that face the organization are perceived in subsidiaries and then communicated verbally
to the center. But it is still a verbal channel. It is access
to this verbal information that influences the distribution of
power in organizations (McCleary, 1960; Pettigrew, 1972; March
and Simon, 1958). For those interested in decentralizing power
in organizations, the transfer of top management between interdependent units may generate the contacts and communication to
bring about the power shift.

Transfer strategies

From talking to managers it became clear to us that there are
several different motives for transferring managers. The most
obvious motive for a transfer is to fill a vacancy which cannot
be filled locally because of lack of manpower with the required
skills. Company operations in developing countries have for a
number of years required a large number of expatriates since the
availability of skilled engineers and managers has been too restricted. This situation is gradually changing as the level of
education and industrialization is rising in many of these countries.

A second major motive for transfers is to provide international
experience to managers as an integral part in their development.
The justifications for international experience range from the
advocation of "a broadening experience" to learning more well
defined job related skills.

A third motive for transfers was never explicitly articulated but has emerged from our comparative analysis of data on transfers in four MNC's (Galbraith and Edström, 1977). We hypothesized that one of the organizations used transfers of managers to change or maintain its structure and decision processes, i.e. for organizational development. Some key elements of a transfer strategy for management development were identified. These are a high volume of transfers, transfers at all levels of the hierarchy, transfers of several nationalities and transfers between subsidiaries as well as between subsidiaries and headquarters.

A high volume of transfers is needed in order to create a critical mass of managers with international experience. By transferring a large number of managers one increases the probability that a newcomer will find himself working with others who have already had substantial international experience which in turn will facilitate his integration into the new environment.The expatriate will find himself in a pocket of internationalized, company-socialized locals.

Transfers at all levels of the hierarchy will make it possible for a selection and self-selection process to operate by which managers who have international skills and a strong commitment to organizational policies will be offered jobs as expatriates and will seek such opportunities. Transfers made at high levels thus involve managers who are thoroughly socialized and committed to the organization. Transfers at the top are particularly important since they involve access to and opportunity to participate in the informal system of strategic communication.

Transfer of managers of different nationalities are necessary for two reasons. One reason is practicality. In order to transfer someone to a subsidiary, it may be necessary that someone else transfers from that same company. The other reason is to assure that local managers contribute to company policy as well as learn about the overall system.

Multiple directions will be necessary if one is going to transfer a large number of managers. The particular pattern will depend on the philosophy of the MNC.If it is global, it will involve the transfer of all nationalities.

In an actual decision situation, a company may find it possible to combine several motives. When a subsidiary cannot fill a vacancy headquarters can select a person on the basis of his training needs. One can thus combine the need to fill a position with the need to provide managers with international experience. Similarly if one is conscious of the possibility of using transfers in order to maintain or develop a particular organizational structure one can let the selection of expatriates be guided by this

particular criteria. From the researcher's point of view, it makes it difficult to distinguish motives since they are confounded.
The motives also tend to be cumulative in the sense that a policy
maker who agrees with the organizational development motive tends
to be in agreement with the first two as well.

Hypotheses

We would hypothesize that the transfer of managers if intentionally persued for organizational development purposes will have two
main effects. The first is that the socialization process will
create organizational commitment. A more detailed analysis of
the mechanisms involved is provided in Edström and Galbraith
(1977).

The second major effect is on the network of verbal communication.
We would assume, for instance, that managers who have been transferred communicate with other organizational units more often
and/or more effectively, and that they have larger communication
networks than those who have not been transferred. Frequent
transfers of managers will give the individual an updated knowledge of the corporate system and a chance to create or renew
personal contacts.

As the socialized manager assumes a strategic role in the company, for instance, as a member of the management team of a subsidiary, he will have the possibility to influence strategic decision-making. It is through changes in the strategic nodes of the
corporate network that transfers will have an impact on the structure and decision-making processes of the MNC.

In the following we will be particularly concerned with the relationship between headquarters and subsidiaries within multinational corporations and in particular how the composition of the
management teams of the subsidiaries relate to communication and
decision-making patterns on the strategic level of the company.

Based on our previous argument in this paper and which is developed in more detail elsewhere (Edström and Galbraith, 1977) we
would expect that the influence of the management team on strategic decisions concerning their own subsidiary will vary systematically depending on the composition of the team. This may in
fact be more noticable in corporations which don't transfer for
organizational development reasons than in those which do. In
the latter type of organization we would expect little variation
in the composition of subsidiary management teams. They would,
except in unusual circumstances,consist of a mixture of local
nationals with international experience, expatriates and third

country nationals. In addition the frequent moves involved in a
transfer strategy for organizational development will make any top
manager less likely to be strongly committed to a subpart of the
organization. Since our empirical study is done in a corporation
which transfers mainly for management development reasons, the
hypotheses reflects this fact.

Hypothesis 1. The greater the international experience of local
managers on a subsidiary management team the greater will be its
influence on strategic decisions.

This hypothesis is based on our assumption that a successful
international experience particularly at headquarters will develop mutual trust between top management and the expatriate from
a local subsidiary. We have also argued that it will increase
the knowledge of the local manager of the overall corporate system and his communication net particularly at headquarters.

The effect of expatriates from the country of ownership on the
management team of a subsidiary, we would expect, will depend on
the extent of the expatriate's own previous international experience and that of the rest of the team. In a corporation where
the managers are not transferred repeatedly we expect that :

Hypothesis 2. The presence of expatriate managers from the nationality of ownership will increase the influence of corporate
headquarters.

This hypothesis is based on the assumption that expatriate managers will primarily identify with the MNC headquarter and have
its orientation.

In the case where a subsidiary management team consist of both
local nationals and expatriates and in addition the local nationals have international experience we would expect high influence
from both headquarters and from the subsidiary. This follows from
hypotheses one and two.

Regarding communication we have argued that transfers are a means
to build an effective informal communication network. We would
therefore expect that :

Hypothesis 3. The more international experience which is represented on a management team, the more frequent its contacts and
the larger its communication net with other units of the MNC.

Data collection

The data for our study have been collected from the headquarters

and European subsidiaries of one European based multinational organization. The company has a mixed functional and area organization. The role of the functional specialists is to give support
and advice to the operating companies within their respective
areas of competence.

The regional center is designed to coordinate and control the
operating companies within the region. It also serves as an intermediary between operating companies and the functional departments. There is essentially one operating company per country in
Europe. The regional centers and the functional departments are
in the same geographic location within the country of ownership.
The dominating transfer pattern is back and forth between headquarters and the operating companies. The company had about 300
expatriates in Europe in 1972 and the level has stayed approximately the same since then.

Data have been collected on the perceived influence of different
organizational levels on key decisions, the frequency of communication between levels for individual managers, the communication
media used and the size of the individual's communication net.
Data have been collected both at the European regional center and
from the different European subsidiaries (operating companies).

Personal interviews and questionnaires have been used for data
collection. Personal interviews were first held with fifteen
managers at the European regional center. A major part of the
interview was used to fill out the questionnaire and discussing
the different decision areas. After this first round of interviews a number of minor modifications of the questions were made.
A letter of introduction was then sent to twelve of the European
subsidiaries. Two subsidiaries were never approached. In one of
these, operations were being closed down and the other is a joint
venture where the MNC does not have a majority interest.

The second step in the data collection was a series of personal
interviews with the management teams of four of the European subsidiaries. The major part of the interviews were again devoted
to filling out and commenting the questionnaire. In addition we
posed questions on the use and impact of international transfers
of managers. After this second series of personal interviews
questionnaires were sent to the eight remaining subsidiaries. Complete answers were received from six of them. Two of the subsidiaries declined to participate even though both of them had
responded favourably to our letter of introduction. It may be an
indication of cultural differences that Austria and Switzerland
declined to participate while the only other refusal of an individual manager occured in the German subsidiary. Questions on influence and control are apparently very sensitive in the German
culture.

The questionnaire is divided into three parts. The first consists
of a number of questions on the influence of different levels of
the organizational hierarchy. The following is an example :

How much influence do you think each of the following persons or
departments has on the determination of the marketing strategy
of the associated company ?

	Very little	Little	Some	Quite a lot	A very great deal
Management team of the subsidiary (incl. managing director)	☐	☐	☐	☐	☐
Managing director of the subsidiary	☐	☐	☐	☐	☐
European regional directorate	☐	☐	☐	☐	☐
Central offices (excl. European regional directorate)	☐	☐	☐	☐	☐

A battery of eighteen similar questions has covered key decisions
in marketing, production, finance and personnel (Appendix). The
second part of the questionnaire includes questions on the use of
communication media, contact frequency and the size of the individual's communication net. The third part covers attitudes toward mobility.

In addition we have collected data on profit, size and organizational structure of the subsidiaries as well as the pattern of
reports which flow from the subsidiaries to the center. All data
have been returned directly to the researchers and no answer has
passed the central offices.

We would obviously have preferred to get more objective indicators
of influence and communication. The geographic dispersion of the
companies and the large amount of resources needed to obtain more
reliable objective indicators have forced us to resort to perceptual data.

Results

Each respondent has individually made a rating of the influence

of the different levels of the organizational hierarchy on key
decisions relating to each subsidiary. The ratings of the individuals in each subsidiary have been averaged to get one assessment
per subsidiary. Likewise the ratings of managers at the regional
center have been averaged according to what subsidiary they have
assessed. In the following analysis we will only use the regional
managers' and subsidiary managers' assessments of the influence of
the local and central levels of the hierarchy. Thus, instead of
using assessments of four levels we will aggregate and only use
two levels. Local influence is simply taken to be the sum of the
influence of the management team and the management director.
Central influence is the sum of the influence of the regional and
central offices.

The most natural rival hypothesis to our hypotheses 1 and 2 is
that influence is dependent on the size of the subsidiary. The
larger the subsidiary the larger is probably its strategic importance and hence naturally its influence. Table 1 shows the rank
correlation coefficients between size and local and central influence as judged by the subsidiary managers in different decision
areas. Size is measured by turnover. The influence in a decision area is calculated by adding the ranks of the different
questions which make up the decision area. The different subsidiaries are ranked according to the sum of these individual ranks.

Decision area Influence	Marketing	Finance	Personnel
Local influence	-.17	-.28	-.24
Central influence	-.40	+.08	-.79[xxx]

x   = 10% level of significance
xx = 5% level of significance
xxx = 1% level of significance

Table 1 : Rank correlation coefficients between size and influence

The results indicate no significant relationship between size and
influence except for decisions in the personnel area. For personnel decisions central influence declines with the size of the
subsidiary. For local influence even the sign of the correlation
coefficients are contrary to our expectations.

In order to investigate our primary hypotheses we have chosen to
distinguish between four groups of management teams. One consists of managers of local nationality without international

experience. The second consists of managers of local nationality but where one or more managers have had international experience. Almost without exception the experience has been at the central or regional offices located in the country of ownership. The third group consists of one or more expatriate managers from the country of ownership together with managers of local nationality. The fourth group is the same as the third except that the local managers have international experience. It appears that the expatriate managers from the country of ownership come in pairs typically one is managing director and the other finance manager.

In Table 2 we have illustrated the influence of each subsidiary. In each decision area we have divided the subsidiaries in two equal groups according to influence. "H" and "L" indicate whether a subsidiary falls in the high or low influence group. We have excluded production decisions from Table 2 since they are not comparable across subsidiaries.

Decision area / Subsidiary	Marketing		Finance		Personnel	
	Local	Central	Local	Central	Local	Central
1. LO	L	H	L	L	L	L
2. LO	L	L	H	L	H	H
3. LI	H	L	H	L	L	L
4. LI	H	L	H	L	H	L
5. LI	L	L	L	H	H	L
6. LI	H	H	L	H	L	L
7. E + LO	L	L	L	H	H	H
8. E + LO	L	H	L	H	L	H
9. E + LI	H	H	H	L	H	H
10. E + LI	H	H	H	H	L	H

LO = Local managers
LI = Local managers of which at least one has international experience
E = Expatriates

Table 2. Influence of subsidiaries with different composition of their management team on three strategic decision areas.

It seems that the subsidiaries with local managers and local managers with international experience are of two different types. Subsidiaries three and four have localties which do not seem to be overcome by the international experience of a few of the local managers. Subsidiary three was previously a national company but was bought by the MNC. The old managing director is still the

managing director of the subsidiary. He is still managing the
company with a strong hand. Subsidiary four has a 30% local
ownership interest which makes it necessary for it to pay attention to local interests. If we divide the group of "LI" into
two groups with two in each and then count the number of "Highs"
and "Lows" in the different decision areas of each group we can
get a more clear impression of the overall pattern (Table 3).

	Central influence	Local influence
LO	4L	4L
LI - 1	6L	5H
LI - 2	3H	4L
E + LO	5H	5L
E + LI	5H	5H

Table 3 : Central and local influence on three strategic decision
areas in subsidiaries with different composition of their management teams.

A subsidiary management team consisting of managers of the local
nationality without international experience seems to have both
low central and local influence. Hence the total control as
defined by Tannenbaum (1968) will be rather low. The subsidiaries
with a strong local anchorage but with some managers with international experience have consistently a high local influence and
a low central influence. Group three is really fairly close to
group one. The reason may be that the international experience
is confined to only one person out of four in these companies.

The results for group four show that expatriates from the country
of ownership on the management team of the subsidiary tend to be
associated with a high perceived central influence and a low perceived local influence. This is in line with what Perlmutter
(1969) has termed an ethnocentric orientation. Organizations
with an ethnocentric orientation characteristically recruit and
develop people of the home country for key positions everywhere
in the world. In our own terms we would expect this result according to our hypothesis 2. The results for group five indicate,
however, that when we have expatriates from the nation of ownership together with local managers with international experience
we have a situation of both high central and local influence. We
expect that this is due to the greater ease with which expatriates
can integrate into the local subsidiary in such cases. This we
conjecture will make them identify more strongly with the local
subsidiary and also get a better insight into the more specific
local needs and requirements.

We interpret the results as at least a weak support for our hypotheses 1 and 2. The most interesting result seems to us to be the interaction effect between the presence of expatriates and the international experience of the local managers. This lends support to the idea that a higher level of total control can be achieved in a highly dispersed organizational system. Whether it can be maintained because of identification or communication processes or both remains to be seen.

In Table 4 we have made an analysis of the frequency of communication and the size of the communication net as perceived by the managers in the different subsidiaries.

Characteristics of communication / Subsidiary	Frequency of communication with the		Size of communication net with the	
	Regional office	Central office	Regional office	Central office
1. LO	L	L	L	L
2. LO	H	H	H	H
3. LI	L	L	L	L
4. LI	L	L	H	H
5. LI	H	H	H	H
6. LI	H	L	H	H
7. E + LO	L	L	L	L
8. E + LO	L	L	H	H
9. E + LI	L	L	H	H
10. E + LI	L	H	L	L

Table 4: Characteristics of communication in subsidiaries with different composition of the management teams.

We would have expected a more frequent communication for subsidiaries seven to ten of Table 4. This is not confirmed by Table 4. A possible reason may be that communication is more concentrated to the expatriates and do not show up in an aggregate measure for the subsidiary. Another possible explanation is that the presence of expatriates to some extent reduces the need for communication. Questions do not need to be raised because the answer is already known at the local level. In Table 5 we illustrate measures of the frequency and size of communication nets of different subgroups of individual managers.

Characteristics of communication / Subgroup of managers	Frequency of contacts with			Size of communication net		
	Other subsidiaries	Regional office	Central office	Other subsidiaries	Regional office	Central office
Expatriates from the country of ownership	4.7	3.2	3.7	2.5	2.4	5.9
Managers of local nationality with international experience	4.7	3.2	3.2	2.0	2.3	3.1
Managers of local nationality without international experience	4.5	3.2	4.1	2.9	3.4	2.9

Table 5 : Characteristics of communication for different subgroups of managers

The only appreciable difference between the subgroups is that the
size of the contact net of expatriates with the central offices is
about twice the size of that for the other groups. To get to
know the central offices requires long experience of working at
headquarters which only the expatriate managers from the country
of ownership have. This indicates that expatriates are more effective as contact points with headquarters. To get further insight
into the influence processes it is necessary to uncover the contents of communication. We have not had the resources to do it
in this project.

The relationship between the size of the subsidiary and the frequency of contacts and the size of the contact nets is given in
Table 6.

Frequency of contacts with		Size of contact net with	
Regional office	Central office	Regional office	Central office
$.77^{xxx}$	$.62^{xx}$	.47	.09

Table 6 : Rank correlation coefficients between size of subsidiary and characteristics of communication.

It appears that size is strongly correlated with how subsidiary
managers assess their frequency of contacts with the European
regional office and the central offices of the MNC. The relation
is less pronounced between subsidiary size and the size of the
contact net. Given the results of Tables 5 and 6, we may conjecture that international experience is negatively related to the
frequency of contact and positively related to the size of communication net. We should also warn that the particular informal
and mainly verbal communication net for strategic information is
certainly difficult to reveal with the rather crude measurement
instruments which we have employed.

The influence of different levels of the organizational hierarchy
have also been assessed by managers who are working at the European regional center. Each manager has had to assess the influence with respect to one or in some cases two subsidiaries. We
have interviewed fifteen managers but since two subsidiaries
chose not to participate, some data had to be discarded. There
are two subsidiaries where we only have one assessment. For the
others we have at least two per subsidiary. The data of Table 7

should be interpreted with caution but do seem to indicate that
the assessment of influence by the regional managers seem to
correlate more closely with the size of the subsidiary than was
the case with the assessments of the managers working within subsidiaries (Compare Table 1).

Decision area Influence	Marketing	Finance	Personnel
Local influence	$+.82^{xxx}$	$+.36$	$+.53^{x}$
Central influence	$-.50^{x}$	$+.31$	$-.52^{x}$

Table 7 : Influence in different decision areas as assessed by
managers at the European regional center.

The perceptions of the managers at the European regional center
seem to be that local influence is higher the larger the subsidiary. Central influence shows a negative relation with size. The
exception is finance and capital budgeting decisions where the
direction of the relationship is positive in both cases.

The differences in results related to the level of the hierarchy
where the respondent is located underlines the difficulties in
using perceptional data. The frames of reference of the respondents are likely to be different. From the point of view of a
local subsidiary there is a relationship between the center and
one's own subsidiary.

At the regional center managers are constantly aware of the different relationships between the regional office and the different
subsidiaries. The regional manager is at the center of the wheel
regarding a network while the local manager views his own relationship with the center as a dyadic relation (the spoke). One
may ask whose perceptions best reflect the objective situation.
We have no possibility to determine that from our data. On the
other hand perceptions are not uninteresting. People tend to act
according to how they perceive their situation. If corporate
management is genuinely interested in decentralizing power it
makes a major difference on the impact of such change how the
management of the subsidiary perceives local and central influence.

Summary and conclusions

At the outset we formulated two hypotheses relating to the impact
of expatriates and international experience of local managers on
the perceived influence of different levels of the organizational
hierarchy. From the perceptions of managers working in the subsidiaries we got at least a weak support for our hypothesis 2.

For two out of four subsidiaries hypothesis 1 seemed to hold. In
both of these cases, however, there were other factors which
acted as strong local anchorages in support of local influence.
In the remaining two cases international experience was limited
to one person of a management team of either four or five which
may have been too little to make an impact. In neither of the
two cases did the managing director have international experience.

The results indicate also that management teams which are composed of both expatriates and local managers with international
experience perceive that both their own influence and that of
headquarters is high. It is conjectured that this represents a
situation where both local needs and overall system considerations are being met.

It was further shown that the communication patterns of locals,
locals with international experience and expatriates were essentially the same. The only difference was that expatriates had
more contact points within the central offices. We conjectured
that substantial experience at headquarters is negatively related
to the frequency of contacts, but positively related to the size
of the communication net. In other words knowledge and experience
of headquarters operations is a substitute for certain contacts
but when support and/or advice is needed, one has a more extensive and probably specialized net of people to rely on.

The perceptions of managers at the European regional center were
not consistant with those of the managers of the subsidiaries.
They indicated instead that local and central influence is related primarily to the size of the subsidiary.

It has also been apparent throughout the research how difficult it
is to empirically study the real life influence processes. This
requires an intimate familiarity with the workings of the organization and a kind of access which is very difficult to obtain for
an outsider. The results in themselves, even though limited, do
point, however, to the possibility of using transfer policy to
at least affect the subsidiary managers' perceptions of their own
influence as well as their perceptions of the influence of the
center.

Appendix

1. Questions on influence have covered the following key decisions
   for a subsidiary

   Marketing strategy
   Introduction of new products
   Determination of local product prices
   Sales promotion and advertising
   Investments in new retail outlets
   Setting of profit targets
   Production planning
   Production mix in the factories
   Commercial inventory levels
   Production capacity increases
   Capital budget
   Revenue budget
   Rate of return targets
   Employment levels
   Promotions
   Salary levels
   Training and development

2. The following questions were used to assess communication frequency and communication net.

   In a typical business month - how often do you have contacts
   (by telephone or meetings) with

	Every day	Every week	Once every two weeks	Once every month	More seldom
Other subsidiaries	☐	☐	☐	☐	☐
The European regional office	☐	☐	☐	☐	☐
Central departments	☐	☐	☐	☐	☐

   In a typical business month - how many people do you have contact with at

   Other associated companies   ....
   The European regional office   ....
   Central departments   ....

References

Child, J., 1972, Organization Structure and Strategies of Control:
A Replication of the Aston Study. Administrative Science
Quarterly, June , 163-177.

Child J., 1973, Strategies of Control and Organization Behavior.
Administrative Science Quarterly, March : 1-17.

Edström, A. and Galbraith, J., 1977, Managerial Transfer as a
Coordination and Control Strategy : The Multinational Case.
Forthcoming in Administrative Science Quarterly.

Galbraith, J. and Edström, A., 1977, Creating Decentralization
Through the Transfer of Managers. In Pondy, Kilman and Slevin
(Eds.), The Management of Organization Design, Vol. 2, Amster-
dam : North Holland.

Galbraith, J.R., 1973, Designing Complex Organizations. Addison
Wesley Publishing Co.: Reading, MA.

Hage, J., Aiken, M. and Marrett, C., 1971, Organization Structure
and Communication, American Sociological Review, October ,
860-871.

Hall, R., 1968. Professionalization and Bureaucratization,
American Sociological Review, Vol. 33, 92-104.

Kaufman, H., 1960, The Forest Ranger, The Johns Hopkins University Press.

Keegan, W.S., 1974, Multi-National Scanning : A Study of Information Sources Utilized by Headquarters Executives in Multi-
National Companies, Administrative Science Quarterly, September,
411-421.

Kuin, P., 1972, The Magic of Multinational Management, Harvard
Business Review, November-December, 89-97.

Lawrence, P.R. and Lorsch, J., 1967, Organization and Environment,
Division of Research, Harvard Business School, Boston, MA.

Likert, R., 1961, New Patterns of Management. New York : McGraw-
Hill.

March, J.G. and Simon, H.S., 1958, Organizations. New York:Wiley.

McCleary, R., 1960, Communication Patterns as Bases of Systems of
Authority and Power, Theoretical Studies in Social Organization
of the Prison, Social Science Research Council, Pamphlet 15,
March, Bobbs Merril Reprint 5-327.

Mintzberg, H., 1973, The Nature of Managerial Work. New York :
    Harper and Row.

Perlmutter, H., 1969, The Tortuous Evolution of the Multinational
    Corporation, Columbia Journal of World Business, January-
    February, 9-18.

Pettigrew, A.M., 1972, Information Control as a Power Resource,
    Sociology, May, 187-204.

Pugh, D., Hickson, D., Hinings, C. and Turner, C., 1969, The
    Context of Organizational Structures. Administrative Science
    Quarterly, Vol. 14, No 1, 91-114.

Stinchcombe, A.L., 1959, Bureaucratic and Craft Administration of
    Production : A Comparative Study, Administrative Science
    Quarterly, September, 168-187.

Tannenbaum, A., 1968, Control in Organizations. New York :
    McGraw-Hill.

Thompson, J.D., 1967, Organizations in Action. New York : McGraw-
    Hill.

A COMPARATIVE ANALYSIS OF ATTITUDES TOWARDS ORGANIZATIONAL LOYALTY AMONG AMERICAN AND EUROPEAN BUSINESSMEN

An Exploratory Study

Will Straver
Centre d'Education Permanente

Introduction

The literature on the concept of organizational loyalty indicates that real interest in the topic has developed in the Post World War II period. Earlier works do not question the validity of the concept of employee loyalty towards an organization, but rather discuss ways to achieve loyalty. Emerson and Helfeld (1948) question the value of government loyalty oaths. McCormick (1949) finds that management must earn employee loyalty. Bakke (1953) proposes that management must create the right environment for employees to be able to be loyal.

Most literature written during the 1950's attacks the concept of organizational loyalty because it hampers individuality. Kerr (1953) strongly advocates employee independence and individuality in order to create a healthy working relationship. Childs and Cater (1954) recommend that the employee avoid the threat of uniformity. Gouldner (1954) argues that too close identification limits the employee's horizon and ability to make decisions. Works discussing the importance of the individual culminated in Whyte's The Organization Man (1956).

In the late 50's and early 60's scholars writing about organizational loyalty turned their attention to two major subjects : factors that enhance loyalty or that form a barrier to loyalty on the one hand and conflicts between multiple loyalties on the other. For example, an employee may have strong loyalty to an organizational subgroup which takes priority over his loyalty to the organization as a whole. Also, an employee may have such feelings of loyalty to a certain religion that he will give priority to that cause over organization demands at crucial moments. Selznick (1957), Stewart (1961), Levinson (1966), Mayfield (1968), Thain (1968), Hirschman (1970) and Hanan (1971) describe ways in which organizational loyalty may be enhanced in a two-way

street relationship between employee and organization, i.e. his
management. Most of these writers also express awareness of barriers to organizational loyalty. Boulding (1958) realizes that
the limited number of top jobs available tends to reduce loyalty.
Schoonmaker (1968) emphasizes that the individual should act for
his own interest. This theme figures in writings about multiple
loyalties. Thompson (1961) proposes that organizational loyalty
is not the primary loyalty. Gawthrop (1969) and Patchen (1970)
discuss the multiple loyalty phenomenon in the setting of large
governmental branches. Toffler (1970) reiterates the problem of
transcience of loyalties.

Notwithstanding the abundance of literature on the concept of
organizational loyalty, relatively few scholars have conducted
research work on the topic. Those who have investigated the topic
have studied the relationships between professionals (nurses,
scientists and teachers) and their organizations (Bennis 1958 ;
Marshall 1964 ; Lewis 1967 ; Lee 1969 ; Shuster 1970 ; Sheldon
1971 ; Lee 1971 ; Herbiniak and Alutto 1973).

The present research tries to contribute to the investigation of
the concept of organizational loyalty in two ways. First of all,
its objective is to test and verify a number of statements concerning organizational loyalty that have been developed in the
literature or in research work in other organizational settings.
Secondly, its objective is to compare the attitudes of managers
in American organizations with those of managers in European
organizations. In view of the fact that few operational research
hypotheses have been developed so far, this research must be considered as exploratory work.

One major problem which arises when one wishes to investigate
organizational loyalty is that of a definition. Bakke (1953)
considers it "a by-product of the employee's organizationally
and personally effective participation in organizational activities". Stewart (1962) defines organizational loyalty as "a man's
strong personal commitment to give more than adequately of his
time, energy, talent, judgement, ideas and moral courage in the
best interest of the company with which he is affiliated". Gall
(1962), in referring to Chester Barnard, defines loyalty as
"domination by the organization personality".

It must be emphasized, however, that there is no one single definition that is used by all writers on the subject of organizational loyalty. All agree that it is related to a two-way relationship between individuals or their group and organizations. In
defining organizational loyalty, one or more of the following
concepts shown in Table I are used.

Table 1 : Concepts generally used to define organizational loyalty

. acceptance	. devotion	. obligation
. allegiance	. duty	. reliability
. attachment	. fidelity	. solidarity
. commitment	. identification	. support
. conformity	. obedience	. trustworthiness

Although most writers tend to emphasize concepts such as commitment, identification, support, solidarity, reliability and trustworthiness, it was felt that the use of these concepts needed
verification. Also, the method of permitting respondents to prepare a framework of definition of organizational loyalty before
proceeding with giving answers to specific statements on that
subject, could give more validity to those answers. Obviously,
the risk existed that too much variation in definitional content
would negatively affect the usefulness of the findings of the
survey.

Research methodology

The empirical research which is described in this paper was designed to investigate attitudes, perceptions and patterns of
organizational loyalty among selected samples of respondents from
the business world in the United States and in Europe. In the
United States, subjects were selected primarily on the basis of
access. All took advanced courses in Business Administration and
worked within a twenty-five mile radius of Washington D.C. The
total sample comprised forty-five businessmen. In Europe,
subjects were selected from among a universe of participants in
an executive development program at INSEAD in Fontainebleau. The
subjects represented fourteen European nationalities. The total
sample consisted of forty-one subjects.

Research limitations

This study is an exploratory research effort into the topic of
organizational loyalty. Its intention is to test and verify
statements on organizational loyalty developed by or derived from
works by writers and researchers on the subject. Its posture is
one of seeking to determine the state of development of the subject and to propose new areas of investigation.

Other survey limitations relate to sample size and sample composition, particularly where cross-cultural comparisons are made.
However, absence of significant differences in the study findings
would tend to lend support to universalists proposing general

applicability of management concepts and organizational, operational principles and relationships. Where findings would be
significantly different, research hypotheses could be developed
for testing under more controlled circumstances.

Questionnaire design

The questionnaire which was administered to the subjects was composed of three major sections. In the first section, the respondent was presented a list of fifteen concepts (see Table 1) from
which he was asked to select, in order of priority, the three
which defined best, in his opinion, the concept of organizational
loyalty. As was explained above, the purpose of this procedure
was (a) to see how operational were the definitions used by writers and researchers and (b) to permit the subject to establish
an appropriate frame of reference in responding to the following
sections of the questionnaire.

In the second section, subjects were asked to respond to thirty-
four statements on a five-point Likert scale. These statements
were developed from the literature and previous research studies.
The nature and origin of each statement is indicated in Table III.
Although all statements were developed and submitted to the respondents in a randomized fashion but in the same order for all
subjects, in order to avoid a pattern in their responses, these
statements may be classified in four major areas of concern to
scholars in investigating organizational loyalty :

(a) attitudes towards loyalty tests
(b) the meaning of loyalty in the organization
(c) implication of loyalty patterns
(d) strategic options to enhance organizational loyalty.

In the third section, respondents were asked to indicate which
three major factors would have to be present in the organization
so as to increase their loyalty to the organization.

Discussion of findings

1. Definition of organizational loyalty

The respondents' choices of concepts that, in their opinion,
define organizational loyalty are presented in Table 2. Two major
observations seem appropriate to these findings. First of all,
an important fact which is not indicated in the table is the
absence among the first five concepts of expressions such as obe-
dience and conformity. In both samples, these items ranked 14 and
15. These findings clearly indicate that the subjects subscribe

to the necessity to maintain an independent posture vis-à-vis the
organization.

Table 2 : Respondents' definition of organizational loyalty

American sample   European Sample

1. Commitment   1. Commitment
2. Identification   2. Identification
3. Support   3. Solidarity
4. Reliability   4. Reliability
5. Trustworthiness   5. Support

Secondly, whereas commitment, identification, support and reliability were selected in similar ranking order by both samples
(even trustworthiness was ranked sixth by the European respondents), a difference was observed on the choice of solidarity.
The Europeans ranked it third ; the Americans thirteenth.

These findings suggest that although substantial similarity and
agreement exist on the items explaining the context of organizational loyalty, the concept content may be interpreted in a
different fashion due to language or cultural differences.

Notwithstanding these possible differences, the basic similarity
in definition of organizational loyalty provides an adequate
framework for comparative analysis of the responses to the thirty-
four attitudinal statements.

*2. Responses to attitudinal statements - agreement between the
samples*

a) Factors affecting organizational loyalty. There were various
levels of agreement among the respondents in both samples that
the following factors may enhance loyalty : provision of information ; participation ; praise ; communication of organization
goals ; opportunity for further education ; communication; and
approval acceptance. Further, there was general agreement that
older people would be more likely to be loyal than younger ones.

The respondents were rather undecided about the usefulness of the
following factors as enhancers of loyalty : seniority and protec-
tion-security.

The respondents felt that adequate compensation is a necessary
condition for loyalty. They were further of the opinion that
loyalty oaths do not really test loyalty and might even detract
from loyalty.

b. Multiple loyalties. There were various levels of agreement
with the following concepts : multiple loyalties are not necessarily bad ; an employee may give priority to outside loyalties
without being disloyal to the organization ; and loyalties to
parts of the organization are not necessarily unacceptable.

c. Other statements. There were various levels of agreement with
the following concepts :

- loyalty is an essential ingredient for organization success ;
- one loyalty should not be all-consuming ;
- most people start out wanting to be loyal ;
- loyal employees are more co-operative and productive ;
- mobility somewhat measures levels of loyalty ;
- mobility does not imply absence of strong loyalty ;
- loyal employees sacrifice personal plans when necessary ;
- what is good for the organization may not be good for the
  individual ;
- the organization can be a place to develop roots ;
- ability is more to be desired than loyalty.

*3. Responses to attitudinal statements - significant disagreements
between the samples*

a. Factors affecting organizational loyalty. Significantly more
Europeans than Americans felt that pension plans and fringe benefits enhance loyalty. This finding may perhaps be partially
explained by the fact that these benefits have existed for a long
time in American corporations and start to be "transportable".
Hence, they are not considered particular benefits any more,where-
as in Europe these benefits are of more recent and less extensive
nature. Another possible explanation relates to the European
income tax structure. In view of high levels of imposition of
personal revenues, employees may prefer deferred payments and
fringe benefits in lieu of salary increases.

Offering the possibility to continue one's education was looked
upon as enhancing organizational loyalty by significantly more
Europeans than Americans. Although the answers to this concept
are biased due to the fact that all respondents participated in
educational programs, it is nevertheless interesting to develop
hypotheses to explain the difference in response between the
samples. First of all, there is much greater opportunity to
continue one's education in the United States (evening colleges)
than in Europe. Hence, Europeans are more desirous to be sent to
a program. Secondly, being permitted to participate in a company-
paid seminar may constitute an expression of potential future.
This expression may in turn enhance the employee's feeling of
loyalty.

Table 3 : Responses to Attitudinal Statements and χ^2 Values (based on a 5-point Likert scale)

Statements	Americans(45)			Europeans(41)			χ^2 Values
	Agree	Dis-agree	Unde-cided	Agree	Dis-agree	Unde-cided	
1. The longer an employee is with an organization today the more likely he is to be critical of it. (Brown, 1971)	14	10	21	14	9	18	0.01
2. The higher one's organizational rank or status, the greater his loyalty (Timbers, 1970)	19	6	20	16	5	20	0.16
3. Strongly loyal employees are usually more co-operative and productive than those less loyal (Peck, 1966)	31	7	7	27	8	6	0.23
4. Since employees are very mobile these days, their loyalty to their present organization can rarely be strong (Toffler, 1970)	7	5	33	7	6	28	0.32
5. Loyalty to an organization is usually more strongly felt by older than by younger people (Brown, 1971)	22	8	15	23	6	12	0.46
6. The employee gives the organization his loyalty in return for its providing him with protection-security (Gawthorp, 1969)	19	10	16	19	11	11	0.79
7. Organizational loyalty is a psychological necessity for the individual. In a fast changing world, in a world in which he must forever be on the move, the individual desperately needs roots and the organization is one of the most logical places to develop them (Whyte, 1956)	24	7	14	25	7	9	0.92

Table 3 (continued)

8. An organization has a right to expect high loyalty from its employees (Lee, 1968)	17	6	22	17	8	16	1.05
9. Multiple loyalties are bad from the organization's viewpoint because they lead to conflicts (Guetzow, 1955)	6	9	30	9	7	25	1.12
10. Employee disloyalty is strongly influenced by lack of communication (Peck, 1966)	37	3	5	36	3	2	1.12
11. In general, the more seniority an employee has in an organization, the stronger is his loyalty to it (Brown, 1971)	24	5	16	20	8	13	1.18
12. Praise is one of the most useful approaches by which a manager achieves employee loyalty (Peck, 1966)	26	5	14	19	7	15	1.27
13. The employee gives the organization his loyalty in return for its approval-acceptance of him as an individual (Gawthrop, 1969)	27	7	11	28	3	10	1.48
14. Loyalty to one object should never be so all-consuming that the individual has no further time or energy left to express loyalty to another object (Guetzkow, 1955)	40	5	-	37	4	-	1.70
15. High employee loyalty is an essential ingredient of organization success (Gall, 1962)	35	4	6	35	4	2	1.82
16. Once management has communicated the organization's reason for being, employee loyalty to it will more easily follow (Peck, 1966)	21	11	13	24	10	7	1.87

Table 3 (continued)

Item							Mean
17. Organizational loyalty means that the employee generally accepts that what is good for the organization is good for him (Whyte, 1956)	18	9	18	11	8	22	1.97
18. Employee loyalty cannot be bought (Peck, 1966)	23	9	13	27	5	9	2.01
19. High employee ability is more to be desired by the organization than high employee loyalty (Harbison & Burgess, 1954)	18	13	14	22	11	8	2.02
20. Multiple loyalties are quite acceptable provided they are compatible (Guetzkow, 1955)	41	3	1	33	6	2	2.02
21. Adequate compensation is a necessary condition for employee loyalty (Peck, 1966)	34	3	8	35	3	3	2.11
22. Loyalty to a division or department is frequently in conflict with loyalty to the organization as a whole and should therefore be discouraged (Guetzkow, 1955)	11	7	27	12	11	18	2.55
23. Employee participation in setting organization objectives is one of the most important ways to achieve employee loyalty (Peck, 1968)	33	5	7	34	5	2	2.61
24. The most loyal employees are usually those who are best informed (Peck, 1966)	29	4	12	26	8	7	2.63
25. Loyalty oaths or similar "test" of loyalty detract from real loyalty (Brown, 1971)	32	7	6	28	11	2	2.98

Table 3 (continued)

26. An important measure of employee loyalty is the number of people leaving the organization (Whyte, 1956)	23	7	15	28	6	7	3.30
27. Loyalty oaths or similar "tests" of loyalty do little to either indicate or test organizational loyalty (Emerson & Helfeld, 1948)	43	1	1	34	3	4	3.67
28. Cultivating loyalty should not be too difficult because most people start out wanting to be loyal (Peck, 1966)	24	16	15	30	4	7	3.80
29. If an employee frequently gives priority to outside loyalties over loyalty to his organization, he is in effect disloyal to that organization (Groazins, 1956)	9	4	32	13	9	19	5.79^x
30. Most employees express their loyalty to an organization by being loyal to a particular individual in that organization (Gall, 1962)	32	7	6	19	6	16	7.77^{xx}
31. Loyalty to an organization is frequently merery a habit pattern (Guetzkow, 1955)	24	8	13	10	14	17	7.77^{xx}
32. The most loyal employees are those most likely to sacrifice personal plans to satisfy job demands (Lee, 1968)	33	7	5	18	9	14	8.76^{xx}
33. If an organization provides its employees with the opportunity to continue their education, their loyalty to it is likely to increase (Thain, 1968)	23	11	11	33	7	1	10.85^{xx}

34.Pension plans and fringe benefits are increasingly
important factors enhancing employee loyalty
(Whyte, 1956)

18	3	24	27	7	7	12.56^{xx}

x   significant at 0.10

xx significant at 0.05

b. Multiple loyalties. It is interesting to observe that the American subjects feel that loyalty to an organization is expressed by being loyal to an individual to a much greater extent than the Europeans. One could develop the hypothesis that climbing up the ladder of hierarchy in large American organizations lends itself better to loyalty to a person at a superior level than in smaller European companies. In a similar way, loyalty to a division or a department appeared to be acceptable to relatively more American than European respondents.

The place which organizational loyalty occupies among multiple loyalties appears to vary significantly in the minds of the European and the American subjects : the latter respondents find giving priority to outside loyalties much more acceptable than do their European counterparts. Yet when it comes to sacrificing personal plans to meet job demands, the American subjects are significantly more positive in their response than the Europeans. So, the Americans seem to have a much more free and flexible attitude that permits to shift loyalty emphasis and expression to where the need is.

c. Other statements. Significantly more Americans than Europeans felt that loyalty to an organization is frequently merely a habit pattern. The implication of this finding can be found in relation to the differences in responses discussed above : the American subjects are more at ease in living with a multiple loyalty structure, giving priorities to where temporary demand is. The European subjects are perhaps more selective in giving their loyalties and less flexible in moving from one priority to another.

4. Factors which may enhance organizational loyalty.

This section was added to the questionnaire as a possible check on the responses of the thirty-four attitudinal statements. Are the significant differences in responses to these statements observed in the preceding text reflected in the factors which the subjects identify as loyalty enhancers ?

The factors identified by the two samples are shown in Table 4 in the order of frequency with which they were mentioned. The findings support the hypotheses developed before doing the analysis of significant response differences between samples.

(a) The European managers apparently are in a squeeze. The problem of personal income tax level was mentioned. However, another explanation may perhaps be found in the fact that the European survey was conducted in 1974 in a period of high inflation and economic crisis, whereas the U.S. survey was conducted in 1971 when economic conditions were more favorable.

(b) The European managers may possibly be faced with the problem of having relatively fewer options for growth inside their relatively smaller companies or perhaps even inside their countries than do Americans.

Possibly, advancement is one of the few means left to increase compensation levels. Even the extent to which fringe benefits can increase real salaries is limited as excessive benefits usually catch the eye of tax officials.

Table 4 : Factors Enhancing Organizational Loyalty

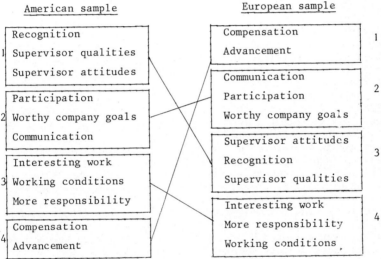

American sample

European sample

1
Recognition
Supervisor qualities
Supervisor attitudes

2
Participation
Worthy company goals
Communication

3
Interesting work
Working conditions
More responsibility

4
Compensation
Advancement

1
Compensation
Advancement

2
Communication
Participation
Worthy company goals

3
Supervisor attitudes
Recognition
Supervisor qualities

4
Interesting work
More responsibility
Working conditions

Yet, two additional important observations may be made :

(a) The first three factors mentioned by the American respondents indicate a very close identification with the hierarchical superior. This confirms the significant difference found before in the expression of organizational loyalty to an individual : the American respondents were significantly more favorably disposed towards the proposition than their European counterparts.

The first three factors selected by the European respondents reflect to a much greater extent individual desires and individual relationships with the organization as a whole.

(b) A closer look at the factors identified by the respondents as loyalty enhancers shows similarity between these factors and factors identified as motivator or maintenance factors. Furthermore, it may be essential to search for deeper explanations in the environment of the company and the employee if one is to fully explain the mix between motivators and maintenance factors. The hypothesis that loyalty enhancers selected by the European subjects, in particular compensation and advancement, are closely related to societal/environmental conditions rather than being an internal company dichotomy between motivators and maintenance factors operational in various socio-psychological individual or group situations.

Summary and conclusions

The present research which was designed to conduct an exploratory study of attitudes towards organizational loyalty among a sample of American and a sample of European businessmen, has uncovered limited differences in attitudes which have important implications when real factors underlying the attitudes are analyzed. Only when the respondent had made the step from attitudes towards statements indicating his own preferred loyalty enhancers was it possible to explain the differences in attitudes.

The analysis of differences in preferred loyalty enhancers suggests that one has to look beyond motivators and maintenance factors into the company's and individual's environments to seek deeper explanations. The meaning for organization management is clear : one cannot interact with employees on the sole basis of psychological and sociological models of analysis of intra-company behavior. Nor is it adequate to talk solely about the employee's outside group memberships and loyalties. Changes in the economic, educational, cultural, sociological, political and legal environments demand more in-depth analysis of the influence these changes may have on employees.

Implications for management

In view of the potential impact of environment factors on employee attitudes towards organizational loyalty, a new approach to achieving employee loyalty to the organization seems imperative.

Company loyalty is only one among the multiple loyalties which may call for the individual's attention. The process by which an organization tries to achieve employee loyalty may well be similar to the marketing system through which a company tries to achieve brand loyalty. In other words, can a company provide those products (motivating/maintenance factors) that its clients (employees)

want, at a profit in social/monetary terms (employee organizational loyalty and contribution to profitable operation)?

The life-styled marketing approach appears to be an appropriate
tool to further explain organizational loyalty. Such an approach
is defined by Hana (1972) as "a strategy for seizing the concept
of a market according to its most meaningful, recurrent patterns
of attitudes and activities, and then tailor-making products and
their promotional strategies to fit these patterns". To make this
definition operational for the proposed approach, "market" would
be paralleled by "employee(s)", "products" by motivating/mainte-
nance factors and "promotion" by communication.

In other words, company management will need to look beyond the
organization's boundaries and its internal framework of values.
It must look into the entire life-style of its employees as
affected by social, cultural, political, legal, economic, etc.
factors. This means placing the company within a total environment context and developing employee policies from an analysis
of outside factors rather than developing these policies from an
internal company viewpoint and merely adapting them occasionally
to changes in the environment.

References

Bakke, E. Wight. The Fusion Process. New Haven, Connecticut :
    Labor and Management Center, Yale University Presse, 1953.

Bennis, Warren G. ; Berkowitz, Norman ; Affinito, Mona ; and
    Malone, Mary. "Reference Groups and Loyalties in the Out-
    Patient Department". Administrative Science Quarterly, II
    (December, 1958), 481-500.

Boulding, Kenneth E. "The Jungle of Hugeness". The Saturday Review
    XXXI (March, 1958), 11-13 ; 50.

Brown, David S. Unpublished Notes, The George Washington Univer-
    sity, Washington D.C., 1971.

Childs, Marquis W. and Cater, Douglas. Ethics in a Business
    Society. New York : Harper & Row, 1954.

Commager, Henry S. "Who is loyal to America?". Harper's Magazine,
    XV (September, 1947), 195-196.

Emerson, Thomas I. and Helfeld, David H. "Loyalty among Government
    Employees". Yale Law Journal, LVIII (December, 1948), 1-143.

Gall, William R. "Not by Loyalty alone". Journal of the Academy
    of Management, XXVII (August, 1962), 117-123.

Gawthorp, Louis C. Bureaucratic Behavior in the Executive Branch:
    An Analysis of Organizational Change. New York : The Free
    Press, 1969.

Gouldner, Alvin W. "The Problem of Loyalty of Groups under
    Tension". Social Problems, II (October, 1954), 82-88.

Guetzkow, Harold S. Multiple Loyalties : Theoretical Approach to
    a Problem in International Organization. Princeton, N.J. :
    Princeton University Press, 1955.

Hanan, Mack. "Make Way for the New Organization Man". Harvard
    Business Review (July-August, 1971), 128-138.

Hanan, Mack. Life-styled Marketing. New York : American Manage-
    ment Association, 1972.

Harbison,Frederick H., and Burgess, Eugene W. "Modern Management
    in Western Europe". American Journal of Sociology, LX (July,
    1964)

Hirschman, Albert O. Exit, Voice and Loyalty : Responses to
    Decline in Firms, Organizations and States. Boston : Harvard
    University Press, 1970.

Hrebiniak, Lawrence C., and Alutto, Joseph A. "Personal and Role
    Related Factors in the Development of Organizational Commit-
    ment". Administrative Science Quarterly, 1973 : 18, p.555-572.

Kerr, Clark "What Became of the Independent Spirit ?".Fortune,
    LXVI (July, 1953), 110-111.

Lee, John W. "Organizational Loyalty : A Second Look". Personnel
    Journal, XLVII (July, 1968), 464-466 ; 510.

Levinson, Harry. "Employers Ask : Whatever Happened to Loyalty?"
    Public Management, XLVIII (July, 1966), 160-165.

Levinson, Harry. "What Happened to Loyalty?". Think, XXXII
    (January-February, 1966), 8-12.

Lewis, Lionel S. "On Prestige and Loyalty of University Faculty".
    Administrative Science Quarterly, XI (March, 1967), 629-642.

McCormick, Charles P. The Power of People. New York : Harper &
    Row, 1949.

Marshall, Howard D. The Mobility of College Faculties. New York:
    Pageant Press Inc., 1964.

Mayfield, H. "Loyalty is a Two-way Street". Supervisory Manage-
    ment, XIII(August, 1968), 21-22.

Oates, David. "Is Company Loyalty Dead?". International Manage-
    ment, (November, 1974), 12-16.

Patchen, Martin. Participation, Achievement and Involvement on
    the Job. New York : Prentice-Hall Inc., 1970.

Peck, Daniel. "Company Loyalty : Nine Executives Present Their
    Views". Administrative Management. XXVII (September,1966),
    26-28.

Schoonmaker, A.N. "Individualism in Management". California
    Management Review, XII (Winter, 1968), 9-22.

Selznick, Philip. Leadership in Administration. Evanston,III :
    Row & Peterson, 1957.

Sheldon, Mary E. "Investments and Involvements as Mechanisms
    Producing Commitment to the Organization".Administrative
    Science Quarterly, 1971, 16, p. 143-150.

Shuster, Louis J. "Mobility among Business Faculty". <u>Academy of Management Journal</u>, XIII (September, 1970), 325-336.

Stewart, Nathaniel. "A Realistic Look at Organizational Loyalty". <u>Management Review</u>, L (January, 1961), 19-24; 80-84.

Thain, Richard J. "Educational Opportunity as a Corporate Loyalty Lever". <u>Personnel Journal</u>, XLVII (April, 1968), 252-258.

Thompson, Victor A. <u>Modern Organization</u>. New York: Alfred A.Knopf, 1961, p. 185.

Toffler, Alvin. <u>Future Shock</u>. New York : Random House, 1970.

Whyte, William H. <u>The Organization Man</u>. New York : Simon & Shuster, 1956.